Photoshop® CS2

Before & After Makeovers™

WILEY

Wiley Publishing, Inc.

By
Taz Tally

Photoshop® CS2 Before & After Makeovers™

Published by
Wiley Publishing, Inc.
111 River Street
Hoboken, NJ 07030-5774
www.wiley.com

For general information on our other products and services, please contact our Customer Care Department within the U.S. at 800-762-2974, outside the U.S. at 317-572-3993, or fax 317-572-4002.

For technical support, please visit www.wiley.com/techsupport.

Wiley also publishes its books in a variety of electronic formats. Some content that appears in print may not be available in electronic books.

Library of Congress Control Number: 2005927618

ISBN-13: 978-0-471-74901-1

ISBN-10: 0-471-74901-X

Manufactured in the United States of America

10 9 8 7 6 5 4 3 2 1

1K/SY/RS/QV/IN

WILEY

Meet the Author

Dr. Taz Tally is President of Taz Tally Seminars, a computer publishing, consulting, and training company. He is the author of numerous books — including *Photoshop CS2 Before & After Makeovers*, *Acrobat and PDF Solutions*, *Avoiding the Output Blues*, *Avoiding the Scanning Blues* (a Doubleday Book Club featured selection), *The UMAX MagicScan Manual*, and *SilverFast: The Official Guide* — and he served as a contributing author to *The Photoshop World Dream Team Book*. He has produced numerous instructional videos, CDs, and DVDs on scanning images, prepress issues, Photoshop, color correction, font management, and keyboard shortcuts, and was the instructor for the video training series *DeskTop to Print*. A frequent presenter at seminars and trade shows throughout the U.S., Taz is also a member of the Photoshop Dream Team — mainstays at the biannual Photoshop World conventions. He is also a frequent contributor to *Photoshop User* magazine, for which he writes a regular prepress column.

When he is not touring the country presenting his seminars, Taz generally heads off to the outdoors. One of those outdoor places he especially enjoys is his home in glorious Homer, Alaska, where he revels in mountain biking, kayaking and hiking, Nordic skiing, and nature photography with his Cardigan-Welsh-Corgi Zip. Taz has also been sighted skiing the powder snows in Utah, diving with the whales in the waters off of Hawaii, and prowling the terrains of the desert Southwest and Mexico.

Author's Acknowledgments

A project like the *Photoshop CS2 Before & After Makeovers* book you hold in your hands is never accomplished by one person alone, so it's no surprise that I have many people to thank for their critical help. First, I'd like to thank my agent, Matt Wagner of Fresh-Books, who was the spark plug for this project — I have him to thank for bringing me together with the Wiley team. I have come to value Matt's insights and guidance very much. Matt . . . here's hoping for many more projects together! Next, I'd like to tell Paul Levesque, the very capable project editor for this title, what a joy he has been to work with. As we put this project together, Paul was not only pleasant and capable, but also a good partner who was willing to work together to meet the various challenges that inevitably arise when tackling any new, from-scratch project . . . thanks, Paul! If this book is easy to read and understand, we can all credit Barry Childs-Helton, the gifted copy editor, who took my often contorted text and reworked it into far more readable and enjoyable prose. I also want to highlight Dave Herman, the tech reviewer, for not only making sure that I was accurate and consistent, but for providing many good content suggestions as well . . . this book is greatly improved from Dave's additions. I also want to thank the Wiley design team for their initial design work and also their on-the-fly redesigns as this project evolved . . . armfuls of kudos to you! And of course credit for overall project management goes to Bob Woerner, Wiley's truly gifted acquisitions editor.

Dedication

For Sherri,
For your friendship and guidance.

Publisher's Acknowledgments

We're proud of this book; please send us your comments at www.wiley.com/.

Some of the people who helped bring this book to market include the following:

Acquisitions, Editorial, and Media Development

Senior Project Editor: **Paul Levesque**

Acquisitions Editor: **Bob Woerner**

Copy Editor: **Barry Childs-Helton**

Technical Editor: **David Herman**

Editorial Manager: **Leah P. Cameron**

Media Development Manager: **Laura VanWinkle**

Media Development Supervisor: **Richard Graves**

Editorial Assistant: **Amanda Foxworth**

Composition Services

Project Coordinator: **Adrienne Martinez**

Book Designer: **LeAndra Hosier**

Layout and Graphics: **Elizabeth Brooks, Lauren Goddard, LeAndra Hosier, Barbara Moore, Lynsey Osborn**

Special Art: **Neil Fraser**

Proofreaders: **Laura L. Bowman, Jessica Kramer, Joe Niesen, Dwight Ramsey**

Indexer: **Sherry Massey**

Cover Design: **Daniela Richardson**

Publishing and Editorial for Technology Dummies

Richard Swadley, Vice President and Executive Group Publisher

Andy Cummings, Vice President and Publisher

Mary Bednarek, Executive Acquisitions Director

Mary C. Corder, Editorial Director

Publishing for Consumer Dummies

Diane Graves Steele, Vice President and Publisher

Joyce Pepple, Acquisitions Director

Composition Services

Gerry Fahey, Vice President of Production Services

Debbie Stailey, Director of Composition Services

Table of Contents

Introduction

The rationale for this book can be found in the simple fact that you, Dear Reader — like most of us — are often presented with images that are less (and often far less) than perfect, and are then faced with the prospect of improving and/or altering such images so they can be used in one type of publishing project or another. In other words, many of your images need to be "made over" — and, sensible person that you are, you're inclined to tackle the job using Photoshop.

Before & After Makeover: The Concept

And so was born the *Photoshop CS2 Before & After Makeovers* concept — whose realization you now hold in your hands. In this book, you'll get a chance to work with images that mirror the kinds of challenges you are sure to encounter in your photographic career. These challenges include image dimension and resolution problems, poor cropping, exposure challenges (stuff like low brightness, poor contrasts, or backlit subjects), incorrect highlight and shadow points, unwanted color casts, composition challenges that require the removal (or addition) of image elements, damaged images in need of repair, and images that need to go from color to B&W or B&W to color (or even to duotone). Add to that the fact that most images could use *some* form of sharpening — and some could benefit from adding one effect or another — and you can see that the whole "makeover" thing can cover a pretty wide area. Approaches and skills that address all these challenges are included between the covers of *Photoshop CS2 Before & After Makeovers.*

Before

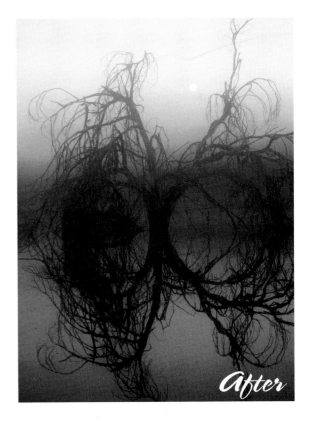

After

How to Get Around in This Book

I divide my Photoshop makeover world into 14 distinct areas, which just so happen to correspond to the 14 chapters you'll find in this book. Here's a chapter-by-chapter overview of what you can expect:

Chapter 1: Essential Makeover Tools

This chapter covers some of the most important concepts and tools you'll need to get a handle on, especially if you ever want to carry out the makeovers in the other parts of the book. Get ready to get your hands dirty, tackling issues like interpolation and how best to use key Photoshop tools such as levels, curves, layers, channels, and masks.

Chapter 2: Dimensional Makeovers

In this chapter, you find out how to adjust the dimensions and resolution of your images while minimizing damage to them. In addition, you get a look at combining views by using Photoshop's amazing Panorama tool.

Chapter 3: Exposure Makeovers

Here you get at crack at correcting brightness and contrast, setting highlight and shadow points, and dealing with the all-too-common problem of backlit images. Just as importantly, you get some practice at applying these corrections in the proper order.

Chapter 4: Color Makeovers

The good news first: Correcting color is not as tough as you think. Right off the bat you learn about the importance of color-correcting highlights. Other key topics include adjusting skin tones, color-correcting with (and without) neutrals, matching colors across images, boosting colors, applying quick-and-dirty color corrections, and (as a bonus) all you'll ever need to know about the key concepts of linearization and neutralization.

Chapter 5: Composition Makeovers

Here you focus on changing what kind of content stays in (or gets added to) your image. You learn how to extract image components and take them elsewhere, as well as how to crop to improve image composition, Straightening crooked images, removing distracting elements, removing and replacing backgrounds, vignetting images, and even changing the depth of field get added to the mix as well.

Chapter 6: Repair Makeovers

In this chapter, you find out how to repair a range of image problems that arise from various kinds of wear and tear. Repairs include reenergizing faded images, removing noise and compression damage, removing dust and scratches, zapping blemishes, and making *anyone* look years younger (in a Photoshop image, anyway).

Chapter 7: Color-Mode Makeovers

This chapter shows you some of the best techniques for reinventing your image by using a fundamentally different image mode — while maintaining (or even improving) image quality and impact. Mode conversions include color-to-grayscale, grayscale-to-color, desaturating images, creating duotones, and converting grayscale and color images into high-impact B&W images.

Chapter 8: Adding Elements as a Makeover

Your focus here is on adding components (borders, type, vector elements, whatever) to your images. You round things off by examining how to create montages by putting images together to create other images.

Chapter 9: Sharpening Makeovers

Honing your sharpening skills is so important that it gets its own chapter. You learn all about controlling such sharpening attributes as Amount, Radius and Threshold — and get the skinny on controlling where sharpening is applied in your images.

Chapter 10: Shadow Makeovers

Shadows are key components to many images. Here you explore a variety of shadow types — including object shadows, full-image shadows, cast shadows, motion shadows, and internal shadows.

Chapter 11: Effects Makeovers

Sometimes a special effect is all you need to create just the right look or impact. In this chapter, you have a chance to work with a wide range of image effects — including Painting, Motion, Glows, Metal, and Chrome — and pick up tips and tricks on how to deal with line art and create a presentation background by using effects.

Chapter 12: Extreme Makeovers

In this final chapter, you work through examples of really going overboard . . . and having a grand time while creating images that look . . . well . . . extreme, when compared with their starting states! Included here is an example from Neil Fraser, guest artist who won an award for his extreme efforts.

Special Features

What would a Photoshop book be without images to play around with? To that end, the folks at Wiley Publishing, Inc., have kindly agreed to host all the Before images you'll encounter here on one handy corner of their corporate Web site. If you want to follow along with a makeover, just fire up your Internet browser, surf on over to www.wiley.com/go/makeovers, and download the image directly from the site. There you'll also find two bonus chapters — Collection Makeovers and Repurposing Makeovers for your reading pleasure.

Your Invitation to Participate!

I hope you have as much fun working with this book as I did putting it together. I am sure (at least realistically hopeful) that you'll take the ideas, approaches, and skills presented in this book and apply them in all sorts of creative and effective ways that I cannot even imagine. If you're so inclined, and would like to share a makeover project or two of your own that you particularly enjoyed, please send your Before and After images on to me at ttallyphd@aol.com — and I might just place your projects (with your permission, of course) in the next version of *Photoshop CS2 Before & After Makeovers*. (Volume 2, anyone?)

Before

After

1 ESSENTIAL MAKEOVER TOOLS

Performing any kind of makeover, Photoshop or otherwise, requires the use of makeover tools. Some tools that you work with in Photoshop — such as the Image Size and Canvas Size dialog boxes — affect the entire image. Other tools — such as the Magic Wand and Crop tools — typically affect only a portion of an image. And still other tools (say, the Levels dialog box and the sharpening tools) can work either way. In this first chapter, I show you how to use the key tools that give you a head start for performing your makeovers.

For example, you'll want to adjust some key preferences in Photoshop and even change them from time to time as you proceed with your makeovers. Setting and adjusting preferences allows you to control how Photoshop works and responds — and often can dramatically speed up your work.

Getting comfortable with histograms is another good way to facilitate certain makeovers. A *histogram* is a graphical display of the distribution of image data. You use histogram data to help evaluate and correct images. The most useful histograms, such as those in the Levels dialog box in Photoshop, are those you can edit.

Also in this chapter, I help you weed through Photoshop's plethora of tools and offer expert advice on

> **Selection tools and techniques** for targeting specific areas of your images to make over

> **Layers** for isolating and positioning made-over sections of an image

> **Editing tools and filters** for refining selections and applying effects

Getting familiar with the tools presented in this chapter (and others like them) can boost your performance on a wide variety of Photoshop makeovers.

Regulate Image Quality and Working Speed

Photoshop's preferences are your access points for controlling operating traits and quality levels for your makeovers. Preferences are organized in a sequence of nine panels, which you can access through the keyboard shortcuts ⌘+1–9 (Mac) and Ctrl+1–9 (PC).

① Choose Photoshop⇨ Preferences⇨General (on a Macintosh) or Edit⇨Preferences⇨ (on a Windows machine).

The first preferences to appear when you activate the Photoshop Preferences dialog box are the General Preferences. You can change the settings displayed in the Preferences dialog box by selecting categories from the drop-down menu at the top left.

② Choose Bicubic from the Image Interpolation drop-down menu.

Bicubic is a good default selection for performing resizing or resolution makeovers on continuous-tone images such as photographs. This setting controls how new pixels are created when (for example) you use the Image Size dialog box to resize or resample an image.

Note: If you want to change your Image Interpolation setting on the fly, you can use the Image Size dialog box to do it.

③ Deselect Export Clipboard.

Unchecking this option speeds up application switching by preventing Photoshop from copying its clipboard contents to the clipboards of other applications during switching.

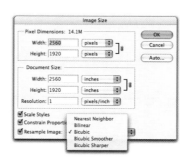

Other choices for Image Interpolation include

> **Bicubic Sharper:** for adjusting low bit-depth images such as screen grabs and `gif` files.

> **Bicubic Smoother:** for working with images that have important low contrast areas, such as skin tone areas in soft portraits.

> **Nearest Neighbor and Bilinear:** for dealing with simple line-art images.

Select this option only if you want to copy and paste from Photoshop into other programs. *Note:* I rarely do this, so I keep mine deselected.

❹ Select Zoom Resizes Windows.

Turn on this option so that when you zoom an image up or down, the image window zooms as well. That way you don't have to manually resize or scroll around the window to see as much of your image as possible.

❺ Select Save Palette Locations.

This option allows you to return routinely to the same placement or palettes whenever you work in Photoshop.

Photoshop Confidential

Interpolation

Any time you resample an image in Photoshop using one of its interpolation algorithms, you are asking Photoshop to create new pixels. And, if you are sampling up — creating more pixels, in other words — Photoshop has to add pixels where previously none existed. This sampling up interpolation nearly always results in some image softening and often leads to noticeable image degradation. Sampling down, while typically less damaging — the interpolation here involves the averaging of pixels that already exist — can still result in recognizable image softening. So this type of image interpolation should not be applied helter skelter — and of course should only be applied to a copy of the image, never to the original. And remember that each interpolation event leads to further image degradation, so get it right the first time! If you are frequently challenged with resampling images, and particularly if you must resample up by large amounts, such as sampling up 2"x3" 72ppi Web images to 5"x7" 300ppi print images, then you might consider using a Photoshop plug-in named Genuine Fractal (from onOne software, at www.ononesoftware.com), which is a much more sophisticated interpolation tool, designed specifically for performing these types of resampling chores.

⑥ Deselect Use Shift Key for Tool Switch.

With this option unchecked, you can change tools with simple alphanumeric-key shortcuts — without having to hold down the Shift key while you do so.

⑦ Select Automatically Launch Bridge.

The Bridge is such a powerful image-management tool, you'll want to use it all the time! Might as well have it handy.

Note: While very cool, the Bridge is a memory hog, so it works best on a fast computer with plenty of RAM. And if it is slowing you down, you can close it temporarily.

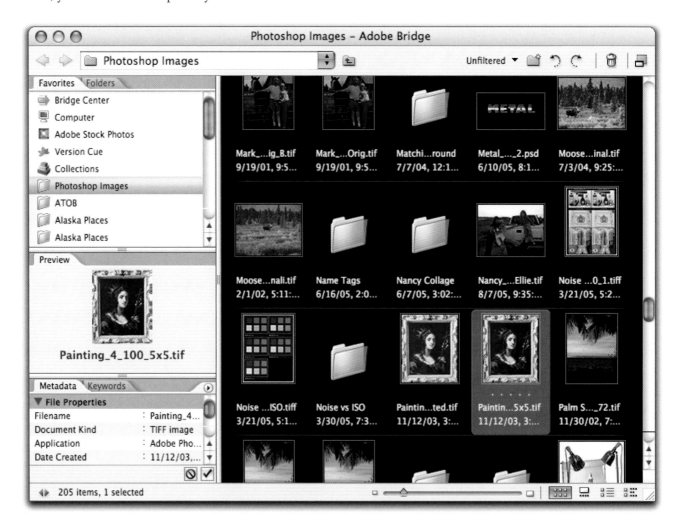

Streamline File Saving and Handling

1 Select File Handling from the Preferences drop-down menu.

Settings in this category allow you to control how Photoshop saves images.

2 Select Ask When Saving from the Image Previews drop-down menu.

Making this selection means you can choose which previews you want to include when you save an image.

3 Select Always from the Append File Extension menu.

Selecting Always forces Photoshop to add a three-character extension to every filename, making the file easier to recognize — for both humans and computers!

4 Check Use Lower Case.

Using lowercase characters for file extensions makes them more universally acceptable to a wider range of operating systems.

5 Check Ask Before Saving Layered TIFF Files.

This selection reminds you to flatten layered TIFF files to reduce their complexity — which (in turn) allows them to print more easily.

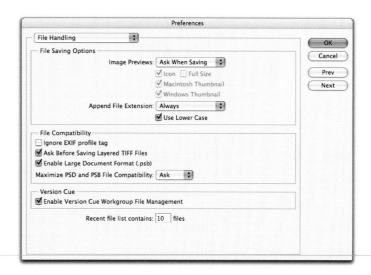

I recommend the following choices for previews:

> **For print-oriented images** (for example, those going to a page-layout program): Select the Icon, Macintosh Thumbnail, and Windows Thumbnail check boxes.

> **For Web-bound images:** Uncheck all check boxes. Web browsers don't use previews, so preview images are unwanted baggage that bloats file size and slows down the delivery of your Web images.

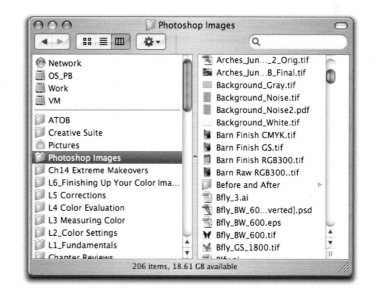

Control Appearance of Image Display and Workspace Elements

Settings in the Display & Cursors and the Guides, Grid & Slices dialog boxes help you control how your image channels display, how selections look when they move, and how cursors, grids, and other workspace elements appear.

① Select Display & Cursors from the Preferences drop-down menu.

The Preferences dialog box updates to reflect your selection.

② Deselect Color Channels in Color.

When you edit color images, you really just edit the grayscale values on various channels. For this reason, typically it's better to view the grayscale values instead of the false color.

③ Select Use Pixel Doubling.

This selection reduces the on-screen resolution of any moving selection by a factor of four and makes the moving process much faster.

④ Click the Full Size Brush Tip option in the Painting Cursors area.

With this option active, you see the actual size of a painting tool before you use it.

⑤ With the Guides, Grid & Slices preferences showing, click a color box in any Guides or Grid area to edit the color used.

Select colors that look different from each other — for example, red and green — so you can easily distinguish your workspace elements.

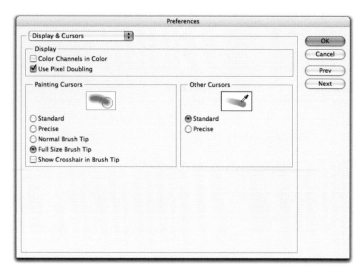

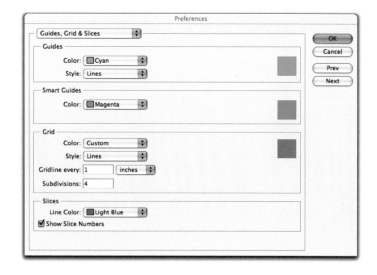

Speed Up File Swapping with Proper Scratch Disks

Use the Plug-ins & Scratch Disks preference dialog box to control which storage location Photoshop uses to swap files while it's working. To achieve the best possible program performance during your makeover projects, you want to supply Photoshop with a large, *contiguous* (not fragmented), virtual-memory swap-file space: a Scratch Disk.

① Select Plug-ins & Scratch Disks from the Preferences drop-down menu.

The Preferences dialog box updates to reflect your selection.

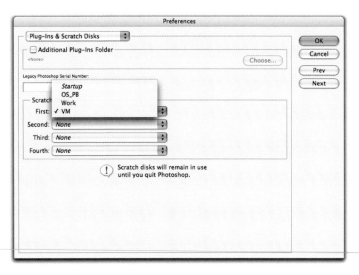

② Select VM from the list of available volumes in the first drop-down menu.

This choice assigns the VM volume (hard drive or partition) as the Scratch Disk for Photoshop.

③ Quit and relaunch Photoshop.

Resetting the Scratch Disk area is one of several preferences that require you to quit and relaunch Photoshop before the preference takes effect.

Photoshop Confidential

Creating Scratch Disks

The best way to supply Photoshop with file-swapping space (better known as a Scratch Disk) is either to install a separate internal hard drive and assign that whole drive as the Scratch Disk, or partition a large hard drive and assign one of those partitions as the Scratch Disk. A 5GB Scratch Disk should be able to handle all your makeover needs. I named my Scratch Disk *VM* (which stands for Virtual Memory).

Heed my voice of experience — I've tried all kinds of hardware as Scratch Disks, and can say with confidence:

When possible, use an internal hard drive for your Scratch Disk. (External hard drives tend to be connected to slower data busses. Result: Data transfer takes longer than it would on an internal bus, and that slows down your Photoshop processes.) And NEVER use removable media (such as Zip disks) or shared media (such as network drives or partitions) — not unless you want your data to transfer at glacial speed and your Photoshop project to take an eon.

Achieve Effective Memory Use

To control how much active memory (both RAM and cache) is available for Photoshop to use, you set preferences in the Memory & Image Cache category.

① Select Memory & Image Cache from the Preferences drop-down menu.

The Preferences dialog box updates to reflect your selection.

② For most makeover projects, set Cache Levels at 6–8.

Note: You will have to quit and relaunch Photoshop for this preference to be changed.

③ Set the Maximum Used by Photoshop percentage so that the amount of RAM available to Photoshop is at least five times the size of the files you'll be working on.

If you are opening 100MB files, then the RAM you allocate to Photoshop should be at least 500MB.

Note: Your Preferences dialog box shows the total Available RAM; always reserve at least 100MB of this amount for your operating system to use.

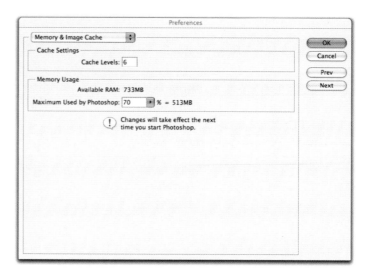

You may want to lower the Cache Levels to 3 or 4 for special situations (or combinations thereof). For example:

➤ When you're performing fine-tuning edits (say, blemish removal and other touchups) using editing tools like the healing brush

➤ If you're using a pressure-sensitive pen such as a Wacom pen and tablet

➤ When you notice your editing performance is lagging a bit

Photoshop Confidential

Copying Your Preference File

One really good habit to acquire is to make a copy of your current Preference file whenever you make a change. Keeping a copy of your existing preference settings allows you to replace a damaged or corrupted Preference file with your own settings rather than a default setting. I routinely make a copy of all my Preference files (for all applications, not just Photoshop) so that I have recent backups for them all. To make a backup copy of your Preference file, go to Boot Drive➪Users➪Home➪Library➪Preferences on a Mac and look in the Photoshop application folder on Windows to find your Preferences location. Rather than search out specific application preferences, I typically just copy the whole folder. You can then replace specific preferences from the copied folder when needed.

Alter Image Attributes with Histograms

The barn image on this page — with the variety of colors and light levels — represents a typical image you can work with in Photoshop. This image could use some enhancement to spiff up its brightness and contrast as well as its color saturation. The following steps show you how to view, evaluate, and perform edits by using available histogram data.

① Choose Image⇨Adjustments⇨ Levels.

The Levels dialog box makes an appearance.

② Evaluate the histogram.

The *histogram*, a graphic depiction of image data, appears in the center of the Levels dialog box. The right end depicts the highlight data, the left end depicts the shadow data, and the middle of the histogram shows the midtone data.

③ Move both the highlight and shadow markers in toward the data.

Make sure that the Preview check box at the lower right is selected, and then move the markers until they just touch the main body of the image data.

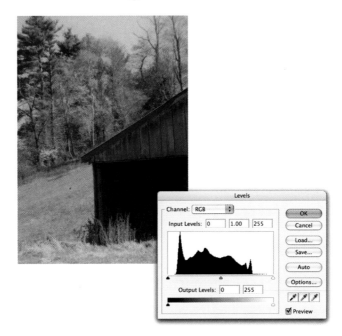

Note the following aspects of this particular histogram:

> ➤ The high peak of data near the shadow (left) end, representing the darkest portion of the image (the barn's interior).

> ➤ The placement of the highlight (white) and shadow (black) markers, just below the histogram.

> ➤ How these highlight and shadow markers fall well outside the image data. This placement occurs when an image is not well exposed with proper placement of the highlight and shadow points.

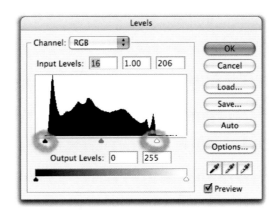

Alter Image Attributes with Histograms *(continued)*

④ View the change in the appearance of the image and click OK.

Notice that the barn image is brighter and has better contrast, and that the colors are more saturated.

⑤ Choose Image⇨Adjustments⇨ Levels to view the changed histogram.

Notice that now all the image data tucks in just between the highlight and shadow markers. You can also see missing data points — the vertical white lines — caused by the redistribution of image data. With the data spread out over a wider range of gray, there aren't enough original grayscale values to fill all data slots.

Before *After*

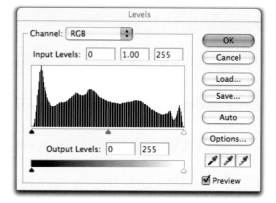

Adjust Brightness and Contrast with the Curves Dialog Box

The Curves dialog box, like the histogram, allows you to edit and redistribute image data. But unlike the histogram, the Curves dialog box offers no graphical display of the data. So using the dialog box takes a bit of imagination.

Because it is graphical, you'll tend to use the histogram to set highlights and shadows as in the preceding task. But with the Curves dialog box, you'll be more likely to make changes in the image data that exists between the highlight and shadow points.

One common use of the Curves dialog box is to adjust brightness and contrast, as demonstrated in the following steps. I start with the histogram-corrected barn image.

① Choose Image⇨Adjustments⇨ Curves.

In the activated Curves dialog box, notice that the *curve* is a straight line through a graph. The horizontal (x) axis is input; the vertical (y) axis is output.

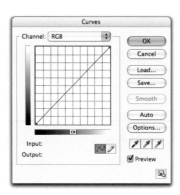

② Locate the highlight end.

Position the highlight (white) end of the horizontal gradient at its right end by clicking anywhere on the gradient until the highlight is on the right side.

③ Opt+Click (Mac) or Alt+Click (Windows) anywhere on the grid.

Doing this creates a finer mesh of grid lines and allows you to make finer adjustments.

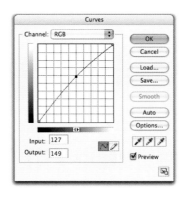

④ Brighten the image.

Point and click the middle of the curve and pull the curve line up one square on the grid.

See how the image brightens overall and the contrast remains unaffected? With this kind of adjustment, the slope of the curve is

Adjust Brightness and Contrast with the Curves Dialog Box *(continued)*

lowered (that is, flattened) in the midtone, and the contrast is lowered due to the concentration of image data in the midtone region.

⑤ Increase the image contrast.

Point and click midway between the midtone point and the highlight end of the curve (that is, at the ¼-tone point). Then drag this point up by half a grid square. Similarly, point and click midway between the midtone point and the shadow end of the curve, at the ¾-tone point, and then drag this point down by half a grid square.

The contrast of the image increases as a result of applying this S-shaped curve: The slope of the curve is flattened (lowered) in the ¼-tone and ¾-tone regions, and the image data is concentrated where curves are flattened.

⑥ Choose Image⇨Adjustments⇨ Levels.

Doing so calls up the Levels dialog box.

The resulting histogram has changed again and shows more missing data points (that is, more and wider vertical white lines) due to additional loss of image data from the Curves adjustments.

Because the Curves dialog box adjusts the image data gradually all along the path of the curve, you can create smooth transitions across your images. By contrast, the histogram has only three markers (highlight, midtone, and shadow markers). This is why the Curve tool is typically the superior of the two tools for adjusting all the image data between the highlight and shadow points.

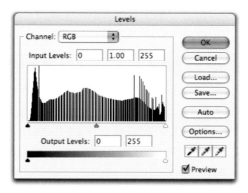

Make Simple Selections with the Magic Wand

Making proper selections is a fundamental skill in Photoshop. No wonder one of the most basic and commonly used selection tools is the Magic Wand. Learning the proper use of the Magic Wand helps you make higher-quality selections and prepares you for the proper use of other selection tools.

① With an image open in Photoshop, click the Magic Wand tool in the toolbox.

Notice the context-sensitive Options bar that appears at the top of the Photoshop screen area, just beneath the Photoshop menus. The content of this Options bar changes as you select various tools.

② Create an initial selection.

With the intention of selecting the sky, I click in the pink sky area near the upper-right corner of this image of Kachemak Bay, Alaska. (The default control settings, with a Tolerance of 32, allow the Magic Wand to select all the Contiguous pixels within a range of 32 grayscale values of the pixel I click.)

Often the first selection attempt doesn't yield the results you want. You can proceed to correct the situation by either starting again or modifying the initial selection.

With the Magic Wand tool selected, you have these options available:

> **Tolerance:** Controls the range of pixels selected by the threshold value entered.

> **Anti-Alias:** Controls whether the selected edge will have any partially selected pixels.

> **Contiguous:** Determines whether the selection includes all pixels falling within the Tolerance range across the entire image, or just those pixels touching the Magic Wand.

> **Sample All Layers:** Determines, in a multilayered document, whether the selection includes pixels within the currently active layer only.

Make Simple Selections with the Magic Wand *(continued)*

③ Redo the initial selection.

Using the Options bar, set the Magic Wand Tolerance to 50 and click the same spot you did in your initial selection. You can see that the selection area expands to match the increase in the range of selected pixels from 32 to 50.

Fine-tune Selections with Keys and Palette Controls

Photoshop gives you numerous ways to modify a selection you've already made. Here are a couple that I find most useful.

1 Shift+click with the Magic Wand tool to expand a selection.

Using the Shift key when you click outside an existing selection with the Magic Wand allows you to add to the area included in a selection. Likewise, using the Opt+click or Alt+click key combination allows you to subtract from a selection. The area added to the existing selection includes the pixels that fall within the range specified by the Magic Wand's Tolerance setting.

2 Adjust the Tolerance setting and choose Select⇨Grow to expand a selection.

The Grow tool works with the Magic Wand controls, for example, by using the threshold value in the Tolerance setting. Reset the Magic Wand Tolerance to 24, and the selection will grow by a range of 24 pixels.

Note: With any selection tool, you can adjust the range of pixels that will be selected before you use or reuse that range.

3 Adjust the Tolerance setting and Shift+click with the Magic Wand to incrementally expand the selection.

Adjust the Tolerance to 10 to reduce the range of pixels that the Magic Wand will select. Place the cursor between the current selection and a larger area you wish to include and Shift+click to expand the selection.

You may have to click in several locations — at progressively smaller Tolerances — to complete the selection process so it includes just the area you want. **Note:** If a selection move expands into an unwanted area, you can either undo the selection (with a ⌘+Z or Ctrl+Z) or reduce the selection (using Opt+click or Alt+click).

Complete Precision Selections Using Channels

Another useful technique that helps you make precise selections involves using channels to seek higher contrast edges at the boundaries of your sought after selection. If you know upfront that you need an intricate selection boundary, you can start out on the Red channel to make the whole selection process easier and faster.

① Choose Window⇨Channels.

Doing so activates the Channels palette.

② In the Channels palette, click on the Red channel.

The Red channel image appears on-screen.

The idea here is that, by activating the Red channel, I can use the relatively high contrast between sky and clouds to give me a precise edge to finish this selection process.

③ Continue your selection using the Magic Wand tool.

You may want to use a Tolerance setting around 10 to complete a selection like this.

④ Back in the Channels palette, select RGB to return to the composite image so that you can review the selection.

Other selection tools — such as the Color Range tool (choose Select⇨Color Range) — use similar, Tolerance-like techniques to adjust pixel range. The Color Range's similar adjustment is called Fuzziness.

High-Quality Selection Secrets

One secret to creating high-quality selections in Photoshop is making the edges of your selections gradual or gradational, not abrupt. Abrupt edges are very obvious and scream, "Here is an edit!" Making sure that the pixels along the edges of your selections are semitransparent creates gradual or *gradational* edges. The semitransparent nature of a selection allows that edited selection to blend in with the surrounding areas of the image that have not been edited.

You can create semitransparent edges in numerous ways, including these: 1) creating an anti-aliased edge, 2) feathering an edge, and 3) blurring the edge of a mask of the selection. The method you use depends upon the image, the selection area, and what you intend to do with the selection. Being familiar with several methods for controlling the width and transparency of your selections grants you greater control over your image. In my experience, when you want to exert the greatest control over your selections, you will convert your selections to masks (either as a QuickMask or as a saved alpha channel mask) and then adjust those masks using blurring — blurring offers 0.1 pixel adjustments, compared with feathering, which works in full pixel increments — or by editing the masks with a soft edge of one of the painting brushes.

Refine and Retain Selections with Masks and Channels

Masks are selections that you can use to isolate a portion of an image for the purpose of editing that portion, or alternatively, for protecting it from a specific edit. Masks are typically saved, either temporarily (as with a QuickMask) or more permanently (as an Alpha Channel). You can also edit and reload masks.

Get a Good View with QuickMasks

A QuickMask is a colored mask that shows you the true extent of the selected area.

Here is the dirty secret — the normal (or marching-ants) selection that you see on-screen may not show you your entire selection. The truth is that if you have a gradational (that is, anti-aliased, feathered, or blurred) edge on your selection, the normal selection shows you only those pixels that are *at least 50% selected*.

A QuickMask view of that selection doesn't stop there; it shows you the entire selection, including the semitransparent edge. Being able to view the entire selection — especially the crucial edge area — is a critical capability when you're attempting to create precise, high-quality selections, masks, and edits. Open an image, make a selection, and follow these steps:

1 Click the QuickMask button (the right Mode button) to invoke the QuickMask (Q) view.

You can find the mode buttons directly beneath the foreground and background color squares near the bottom of the Photoshop tool palette. The left button is the default Normal mode.

In the QuickMask view, the unselected area is painted in the selected QuickMask color. (The default QuickMask color is red,

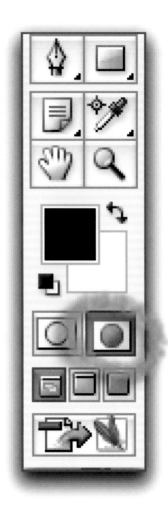

which you can change by double-clicking the QuickMask button.)

2 Using your Spacebar and ⌘/Ctrl keys, zoom in on the edge of the QuickMask selection.

When you view the anti-aliased edge, notice the semitransparent pixels along the edge of the selection.

3 Click the Normal mode button to return to Normal view.

You're back where you started from.

Widen the Selection Edge by Feathering

Often an anti-aliased edge is not wide enough to form a high-quality edge. When you need a wider semitransparent edge, feathering may be the next step.

1 Choose Select⇨Feather.

Doing so calls up the Feather Selection dialog box.

2 In the Feather Selection dialog box, set the Feather Radius to 1 pixel.

A 1-pixel feather provides a slightly more gradational edge, without going overboard. But you can adjust this to suit the needs of the selection.

3 Click the right Mode button (or press Q) to view the QuickMask.

Remember that you are still zoomed in on the image. Notice how the 1-pixel Feather Radius widens and smoothes out the edge transition.

4 Click the Normal mode button to return to Normal view.

Normal, yes, but now a feathered normal.

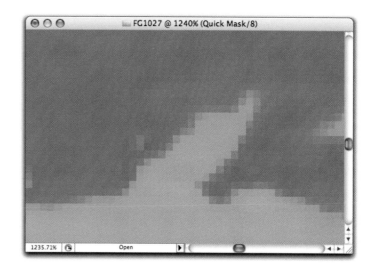

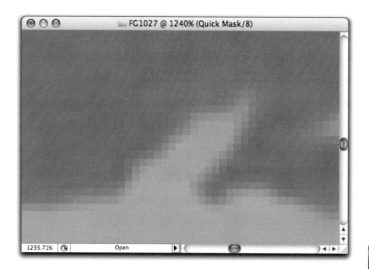

Refine and Retain Selections with Masks and Channels (continued)

Save a Mask as an Alpha Channel for Later Use

You may often find that saving a selection — for editing or other use later — is desirable. With an image that has an active selection open in Photoshop, follow these steps when saving:

① Choose Select⇨Save Selection.

The Save Selection dialog box makes an appearance.

② Select the New Channel option and type in a name.

Name your selection something that you'll recognize and understand later. For this image, I named the selection *Sky F1* because I created the *Sky* selection with a *Feather Radius* value of *1*.

③ Choose Window⇨Layers and click the Channels tab in the Layers palette.

The palette updates to show the Channels palette.

④ In the Channels palette, click the box to the left of the name you entered to view your new Alpha channel mask.

I clicked the box to the left of Sky F1 to look at the channel I created from the Feathered selection.

The white area of this mask represents the selected area; the black pixels are outside the selection.

⑤ Press Z to call up the Zoom tool and then zoom in on the mask edge.

The gray pixels along the edge of the mask represent the semitransparent pixels.

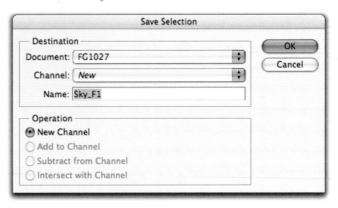

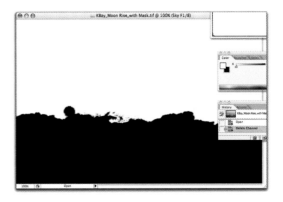

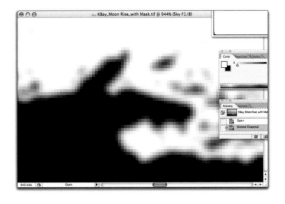

Blurring and Loading a Mask

The third — and in many ways the most powerful — selection edge-control technique involves blurring a selection mask. The power of this technique comes from the minute control you have when using a Blur tool. Open an image, make and save a selection, and follow these steps.

① Choose Filter⇨Blur⇨Gaussian Blur.

Doing so calls up the appropriately-named Gaussian Blur dialog box.

② In the Gaussian Blur dialog box, select the Preview check box and set the blur radius (in pixels) to 1.0.

The Preview window will give you a peek at what your changes will end up doing.

③ Click OK to apply the blur.

Zoom in on the selection mask and notice how the edge is now smoother than before.

④ Choose Select⇨Load Selection.

Doing so calls up the Load Selection dialog box.

⑤ In the Load Selection dialog box, navigate to the selection you want and then click OK.

In my example, the one available mask (Sky F1) is preselected in the Channel drop-down menu in the Load Selection dialog box.

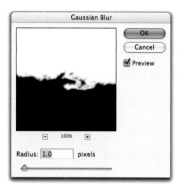

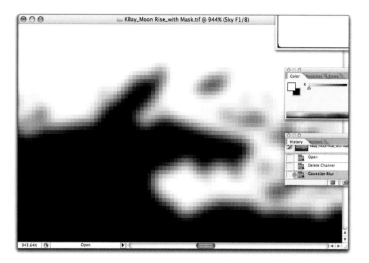

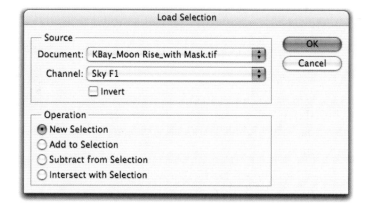

Refine and Retain Selections with Masks and Channels (continued)

⑥ Back in the Channels palette, click the box to the left of the composite RGB channel to return your view to the original image.

Notice how the new selection is loaded in the exact same location as before, but with a smoother path.

⑦ Click the right Mode button to view the QuickMask.

The high-quality, gradational selection edges you see in this QuickMask view compare favorably with the original anti-aliased edge shown in the earlier section, "Get a Good View with QuickMasks."

Now any edits that you might perform on this selection will be applied in a very gradual — therefore visually pleasing — manner, along the edge of the selection. This prevents any abrupt, obvious transitions.

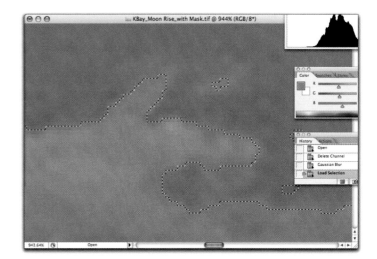

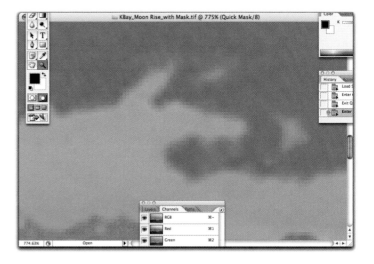

Working with Editing Tools: The Brush Tool

Photoshop provides a variety of editing tools, including the Paint Brush, the Healing Brush, and the Clone (Rubber Stamp) tool. Each of these tools has a variety of characteristics that can be set to control the application of the tool. The Brush tool is a convenient example.

The Brush tool can — and should — be used for many different purposes. You can, of course, simply paint pictures with the Brush tool (a skill I don't have, so I won't embarrass myself by attempting to do that here). The Brush tool can also be used as a powerful and flexible editing tool. For instance, the Brush tool can be used to edit selection masks. Here's how:

Editing a QuickMask

After you have created a QuickMask (or an Alpha Channel mask) using basic selection tools as you did above, the selection is often not quite the way you want it. You can edit the mask by using the Brush tool — in this case, you add some of the wispy edge clouds to the red portion of the QuickMask. The Brush tool's characteristics are almost infinitely configurable, allowing you to match the texture and opacity of the QuickMask in the surrounding clouds.

❶ Select the Brush tool.

You can either click the Brush tool in the toolbox or simply type the character **B** for *Brush*. If you toggle on the Brush tool (keep pressing the B key), you notice that several variations of the Brush tool include a Pencil version and a Color Replacement version. Handy. Keep it in mind.

❷ Configure the Brush tool's Options bar.

As soon as you select the Brush tool, the Options bar displays the various brush options available to you.

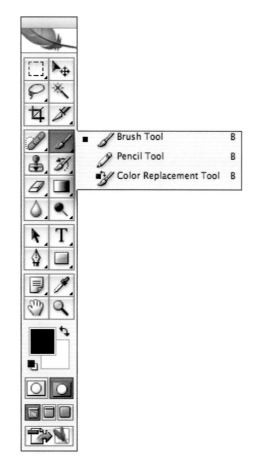

Working with Editing Tools: The Brush Tool *(continued)*

Since the clouds along the edge of the QuickMask selection are rather spotty (and therefore thin and only partially selected), set the opacity and the flow of the brush to 50%. Choosing 50-percent opacity creates a 50-percent selection, and choosing 50% Flow delivers a discontinuous (spotty) flow of pixels.

❸ Configure the Brushes Palette.

First choose Window⇨Brushes to activate the Brushes palette, click the Brushes tab and then drag the Brushes palette onto the desktop. Doing so allows the palette to remain active and be placed where you want it.

In the Brush Presets listing on the left, click the Shape Dynamics selection, then set the Size Jitter at 60%, select Fade from the Control drop-down menu, and set the control to 50. Feel free to adjust these values to view the impact. Note that you will have far more flexibility and sensitivity with these types of adjustments if you are using a pressure sensitive digitizing pen and tablet like those made by Wacom technologies.

In the same Brush Presets listing, click Scattering and set the following characteristics: Scatter both axes 300 percent; select Fade from the Control menu (and set Fade at 25); set the Count to 16.

Finally, returning to the same Brush Presets listing, click Texture and set the Scale to 400%.

Note that, with each change in your brush configuration, you see a change in the sample brushstroke at the bottom of the palette.

❹ Working on the edge of the clouds, click the Brush tool on various locations until you have covered the cloud area you want.

The idea here is that, instead of painting strokes, you simply point and click. Clicking

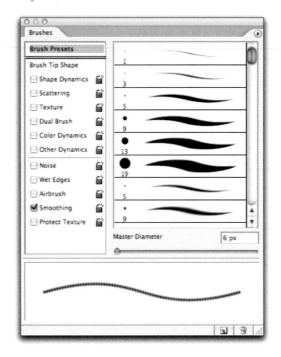

more than once on a location increases the density of the brush mark and therefore the selection.

Note: This edited QuickMask should now be saved as a new Alpha Channel to preserve the selection.

The other Photoshop tool palette editing brushes and tools, such as the Airbrush, Blur, Sharpen, Dodge, and Burn brushes, can be configured in a similar fashion. Experiment with the various settings to learn the various brush and tool settings.

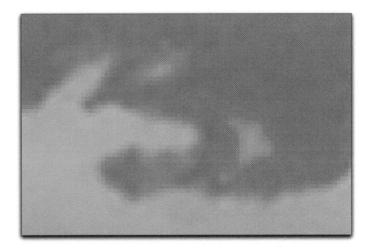

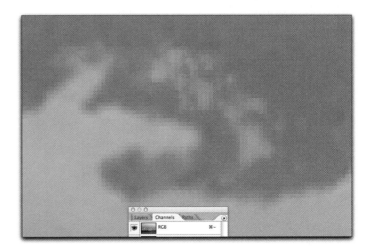

Sharpening and Blurring Filters

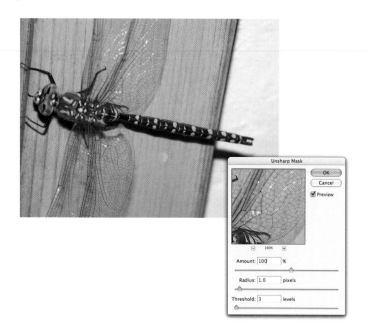

Whole images, selections of images, and masks can benefit from the use of sharpening and blurring filters. Starting with the Gaussian Blur filter — the one we used earlier in this chapter to edit a mask — here's how a sharpening filter typically works:

① Choose Filter⇨ Sharpen⇨ Unsharp Mask to call up the Unsharp Mask dialog box.

Position the Unsharp Mask dialog box and zoom in on the image so you can clearly see the details of the dragonfly wings.

② Configure the Unsharp Mask filter.

The Unsharp Mask filter has three settings: Amount, Radius, and Threshold. Understanding the impact of these three settings is important to creating the sharpening results you want.

The Amount setting controls how much *sharpening* (that is, increase in contrast between pixels) occurs. The Radius controls the width (in pixels) on both sides of a sharpened edge — and how it's affected by the sharpening. The Threshold determines where (that is, on which pixels in an image or selection) to apply the sharpening. This happens by setting a minimum (threshold) difference in grayscale value that must exist between two pixels before the Unsharp Mask can be applied to those pixels.

Here you should set the Amount to 100%, the Radius to 1 pixel, and the Threshold to 3 pixels. These values noticeably sharpen the wing pattern, but leave the spaces between the pattern lines smooth.

Note: Keep in mind that a little sharpening goes a long way! It's easy to oversharpen an image. Because sharpening increases contrast along high contrast pixels, it is easy to push the difference in luminance too far, which creates halos. For instance, if we apply an amount of 200% rather than 100% to the dragonfly wings, halos develop along the edges of the wing filaments. The accompanying figures show the results of various degrees of sharpening, going from no sharpening to 100% sharpening to 200% sharpening

Note the halos in the 200-percent-sharpened image, a sure sign of oversharpening. The amount of sharpening you should apply depends upon the resolution and content of the image as well as on the effect you want to create. In general, however, it's a good idea to zoom in on your image so you can view the actual impact of the sharpening before you commit to a specific set of sharpening values.

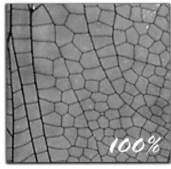

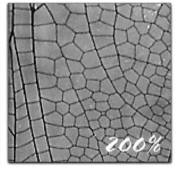

The Need for Sharpening and Controlling It

The truth about digital image capture, whether by scanner or digital camera, is that digitizing *softens* images. Lots of averaging goes on in the digitizing process — but the smoothing process is not uniform. High-contrast edges are softened more than low-contrast areas. High-contrast edges become wider and smoother. And it is the sharpness of the high-contrast edges in an image that controls the focus in a digital image. Sharpening is basically a process of enhancing edge contrast: Increasing the contrast in grayscale values between adjacent pixels increases image sharpness.

But because high-contrast edges are softened more than smooth areas, if you apply the same sharpening to smooth areas that you do to edges, you may oversharpen smooth areas, creating unwanted patterns. This is where the Threshold setting comes into play. When you set a minimum (threshold) value that must exist between two adjacent pixels before they can be affected by the sharpening process, you can restrict sharpening to just the higher-contrast edges.

Layers: An Example

Layering is one of the most powerful and useful tools you have for your makeover projects. You can create layers in various ways, isolate image sections, work on them, and then place them where you want them. The selection you made in the Kachemak Bay image is a handy basis for creating a layer we can use in a makeover.

1 Choose Window⇨Layers to activate the Layers palette.

2 With the last sky selection active, choose Layer⇨New⇨ Layer via copy (⌘+J or Ctrl+J).

Note that a new layer is added to the Layers palette.

3 In the Layers palette, choose Multiply from the Layer Blending Mode drop-down menu.

Doing so darkens the whole sky and makes the clouds pop out in contrast.

4 Click and drag the first multi-plied layer over the Make New Layer button at the bottom of the Layers palette.

This creates a second multiplied layer. The sky becomes even darker and the clouds stand out in even greater contrast.

Note how adding these multiplied layers changes the whole mood of this image. And the fact that you were very careful to create high-quality selections and masks means that the transitions between the various parts of the image will be gradual and natural looking.

Before

After

2 DIMENSIONAL MAKEOVERS

As you work with your digital images, often you'll discover that you simply *have* to change a key dimensional characteristic of your image to get it looking just right. You may want to change the width and/or height, crop your image, adjust its resolution, or even add additional canvas to the image. Or you may want to change the dimension of your image by combining multiple images together into a panorama view. All of these changes can be done in Photoshop with near-zero fuss and minimal damage to your images.

One of the keys to reducing the complexity of the dimensional makeover process — as well as minimizing image damage, including softening and reduction of image details — is to have a clear understanding of what is happening in your image when you adjust its dimensions. Some dimension adjustments involve changing the actual number of pixels in your image. If you are simply adding canvas area, and therefore pixels, you won't get any interpolation — and therefore no image damage. But if you are adjusting the number of pixels in an image through the Image Size dialog box, then interpolation — and with it image quality degradation — will occur. And if you know interpolation is bound to occur, you can at least reduce the number of times it does occur and therefore reduce the negative impact of that interpolation.

So, you'll definitely want to have a clear understanding of your image's starting condition, your final destination, and what will be happening to your pixels along the way. To help you get a handle on all these nuts and bolts of dimensional makeovers, this chapter goes over the key distinctions between image size and dimension as well as linear and square resolution.

Making Over the Width and Height of your Digital Image

Changing the width and height of your images is one of the most common adjustments to make — especially when you're dealing with images that come from your digital camera. But adjusting width and height can be fraught with image-damaging *interpolation* — literally a change in the number and values of pixels in your image — if you are not careful.

But before you leap into the makeover adjustments found in this chapter, please read the Photoshop Confidential (on image sizes versus dimensions) so we can be sure we're all talking the same language.

Image Size

Pixel Dimensions: 14.1M

Width: 2560 pixels
Height: 1920 pixels

OK
Cancel
Auto...

Document Size:

Width: 35.556 inches
Height: 26.667 inches
Resolution: 72 pixels/inch

Scale Styles
☑ Constrain Proportions
Resample Image: Bicubic

Photoshop Confidential

Coming to Terms with Image Size vs. Dimension

We Photoshop users often frustrate ourselves, and each other, by confusing terms like *image size, dimension,* and *linear resolution*. So let's clear the air and squelch the confusion before we go any farther. Photoshop's Image Size dialog box can act as a visual aid in our quest to sort out these characteristics. (Choose Image⇨Image Size from the main menu to call it up. Go ahead; I'll wait for you.)

Okay, first we need to clearly separate image *dimension* from image or file *size*. In the world of Photoshop, *image size (also known as file size)* always refers to the combined amount of digitized stuff, measured in bits and bytes, in an image — essentially, how much space it takes up in your computer. In the Image Size dialog box pictured here, the image size is 14.1MB (megabytes — that is *millions of bytes*). *Image dimension*, on the other hand, always refers to the how much actual area an image covers — most commonly measured in either pixels or inches. The Photoshop Image Size dialog box shown here

gives us those dimensions both ways: as 2560 pixels x 1920 pixels (the on-screen size), or as 35.556 inches x 26.667 inches (the size it would be if you printed it out). These two dimensional values are related to each other by the *linear resolution* number, which here is 72 ppi (pixels per inch). (***Note:*** If you divide 2560 pixels by 72 pixels per inch, you get 35.556 inches, and 1920 pixels ÷ 72 pixels per inch gets you 26.667 inches, which is all the math you'll need to figure out linear resolution.) You'll be using this dialog box many times — and after a while, you get very comfortable with it. Having a low linear resolution is fine for display on low resolution devices such as monitors, but having higher linear resolutions is pretty much essential if you want to reproduce your image with high quality on higher resolution output devices such as printers. (It's also important to know the resolution requirements of your output devices prior to creating and/or adjusting your images.)

Keep in mind that digital-camera images usually have relatively large physical dimensions (say, 2 inches by 3 inches) and low linear resolution, usually 72 ppi (but sometimes as low as 1 ppi — as in, "Yikes, instant eyestrain"). Of course, low resolution won't work with large size — for instance, a 2-x-3-inch, 72ppi image is a nearly useless combination of resolution and dimension. The linear resolution (72 ppi) is too low for printing (which typically requires 200–300 ppi) and the image dimension (2 in. x 3 in.) is way too large for use on the Web.

Here's how to make over your digital camera image's width and height while minimizing the damage to your image.

❶ Open a digital image.

Open the Arches_Juniper.tif file.

Note: All the images used in this book are available for download and training use from the Web site associated with this book.

❷ Choose Image⇨Duplicate to make a duplicate copy.

Don't take chances! Always make a duplicate copy of any image you work with. That way, you can always keep your original image safely tucked out of harm's way.

❸ Open the Image Size dialog box.

To view the starting dimension and resolution, choose Image⇨Image Size.

❹ Evaluate the image size values.

The starting image dimension (in inches) for "Arches Juniper," as seen in the Image Size dialog box pictured here, is 35.556 x 26.667 inches — close to the 2-x-3-inch standard for digital images — with a linear resolution of 72 ppi. In this project, you give both

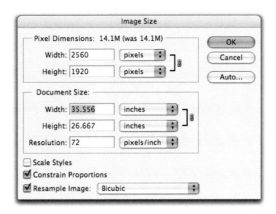

Making Over the Width and Height of your Digital Image *(continued)*

dimension and resolution a makeover for this image; you end up with an image approximately 5 x 7 inches, with a 200-to-300ppi linear resolution. Oh, by the way, you'll want to limit how many steps you do — that limits the amount of interpolation you run into — so you retain as much image quality as possible.

❺ Deselect the Resample Image check box.

The relevant check box is located in the lower-left corner of the Image Size dialog box. Using it as described here prevents any interpolation/alteration of the number of pixels.

Note: Deselecting the Resample Image check box disables the top half of the Image Size dialog box, preventing any alteration in the number of pixels in the image (our nemesis, interpolation).

❻ Change the dimensions of the image.

Type 7 as the number of inches in the Width field of the Document Size section.

Note that the height automatically changes to 5.25 inches if the Constrain Proportions check box is selected. With these new dimensions, the linear resolution now reads 365.714, which is a good result for printing at higher resolutions — much sharper.

You have changed the dimensions of the image from 35 x 26 inches to approximately 5 x 7 inches without altering the number of pixels — so no interpolation has occurred. The dimensions of the pixels themselves *have* changed — from 1/72 to 1/365 of an inch, and that's how the dimensions of the whole image have been so drastically reduced. (To see the differences in pixel dimensions, compare the two samples on the next page — a section of the original image at 72 ppi and the same section at 365 ppi.)

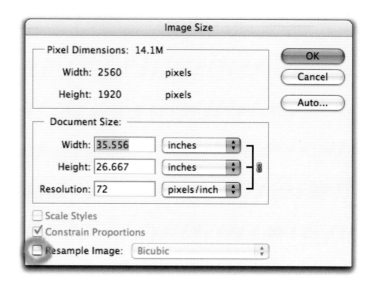

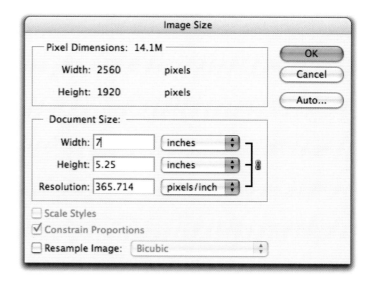

Taz's Take: You can just leave the image as is, with an appropriately stunning resolution of 365.714. If you'd like to see how to change the linear resolution using resampling, rather than by changing the image dimensions, continue with Step 7.

Adjusting the linear resolution without resampling the image will not change the pixel data in the image, just the dimensions of the pixels and therefore the overall dimensions of the image. Whenever you check the Resample Image check box, and make an adjustment to either the linear resolution or any of the image dimension values, you will be introducing image interpolation that will alter the pixel data and typically soften the image and reduce the image's clarity. So, if your target linear resolution is 300ppi (the standard requested resolution for commercial printing), and your non-resampled image resolution is close to 300ppi (as the 365ppi is here), you should typically just let the linear resolution stand. If your non-resampled resolution rises above 400ppi, though, you might want to consider resampling down to 300ppi.

❼ Select the Resample Image check box to activate image resampling.

Taz's Take: There's only one way you can achieve a linear resolution of exactly 300 ppi while retaining the same image dimensions: Reduce the number of pixels in the image, so each pixel can grow bigger while covering the same area.

❽ Type 300 ppi in the Resolution field of the Image Size dialog box.

Note: Doing so changes the dimensions for your image from 2560 x 1920 pixels to 2100 x 1575 pixels, and lowers the file size from 14.1MB to 9.46MB.

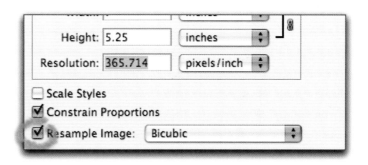

Making Over the Width and Height of your Digital Image *(continued)*

❾ Click the OK button to apply the changes.

The image actually shrinks a bit on-screen, as a result of your reducing the number of pixels in the image.

Taz's Take: I often apply a little Unsharp Mask after resampling like this to retrieve some of the image sharpness lost during the resampling. (Please see Chapter 9 for more info on using sharpening tools.)

Note: The use of resampling here discards unnecessary file size and the sharpening helps to restore some of the image clarity lost during interpolation. You will have to make the call as to whether the reduction in file size is worth a) the softening that will occur and b) the additional sharpening step that's now required.

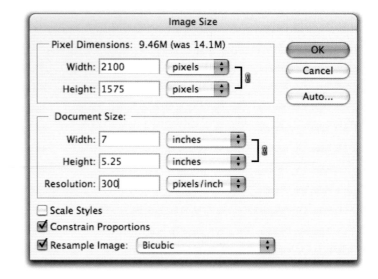

Making Over Print Images for the Web

Another common dimensional makeover you're likely to perform someday involves converting a high-resolution and large-dimension image — the kind you'd use for print — to an image you can use on the Web. Luckily, you can adjust the print image for use on the Web via the same procedure you'd use to change the dimensions of a digital-camera image for print. Here's how:

❶ Open a 5-x-7-inch, 300ppi print-based image.

The "Arches Juniper" image you converted to 300 ppi in the previous section would work just fine.

❷ Choose Image⇨Image Size.

Doing so activates the Image Size dialog box.

❸ Deselect the Resample Image check box in the Image Size dialog box.

For this task we don't want any interpolation — so toggle resampling off.

❹ Type in the width dimension you want in the Width field of the Document Size section.

A width of 3 inches would be nice.

Note: Be sure to select the Constrain Proportions check box; that changes the Height dimension automatically to 2.25 inches.

❺ Select the Resample Image check box in the Image Size dialog box.

You're going to want the significant reduction in file size accomplished by resampling in order to facilitate Internet transport and Web viewing. (The softening effect of the interpolation will just have to be taken in stride.)

Making Over Print Images for the Web *(continued)*

❻ In the Resolution field of the Document Size section, type either 72 ppi (to optimize for lower-resolution monitors) or 96 ppi (to optimize for higher-resolution monitors).

I'd try 72 ppi here.

Note how using 72 ppi reduces the image size to 102.5KB from 9.46MB. (You can view such info at the top of the Image Size dialog box.) I'd never use such a low-resolution image in print — a quick glance at the finished result (shown at the bottom of this page) will tell you why — but it could work just fine on the Web.

Stretching the Truth Makeover Method 1

In the previous two makeovers, you were very conscious of making sure that you maintained the proportionality of your images. But there may be times when distortion is your goal. Here is how to accomplish that.

❶ Open and duplicate an image you would like to distort.

For example, open ChickenRGB300.tif (downloaded from the Web site associated with this book) and Choose Image⇨ Duplicate.

❷ Deselect the Constrain Proportions check box.

Unchecking this box allows you to adjust image width and height independently, which frees you up to try for some distortion.

❸ Select Percent from the drop-down menu to the right of the Height field (labeled *inches* by default).

The default unit of measurement and adjustment in the Document Size section of the Image Size dialog box is inches. But you can use other units as well. If you're making distortion adjustments, you may find it more convenient to think in terms of percentages.

❹ Type 110 in the Height field to increase the height by 10 percent.

Doing so increases the height dimension by 10 percent while leaving the width dimension alone.

Taz's Take: If you want to affect more distortion, try a 25% value here.

❺ Click the OK button to complete the vertical distortion.

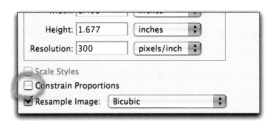

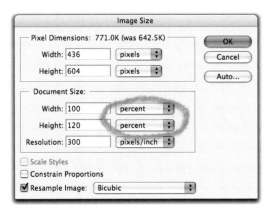

Before   *After*

Stretching the Truth Makeover Method 2

As long as you're in a distorting mood, here is another distortion method — one that concentrates on just a selection instead of the entire image.

① Open and duplicate an image you would like to distort.

For instance, open ChickenRGB300.tif and Choose Image⇨Duplicate.

② Click the Magic Wand tool in the toolbox to select it.

Doing so activates the Magic Wand Options bar.

③ In the Options bar, set the Tolerance to 10, deselect the Anti-Alias feature, and then select the Contiguous feature.

Using such a small Tolerance level — and no anti-aliasing — allows you to make a cleaner selection close to the edge of the chicken, so no stray anti-alias pixels are left behind when you distort the image.

④ Using the Magic Wand tool, click the white background.

The Magic Wand does its Magic thing, selecting everything except the chicken.

⑤ Choose Select⇨Inverse.

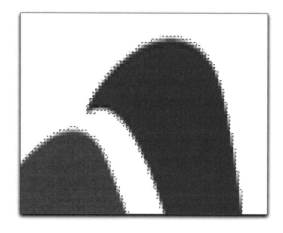

The Inverse command lets you select the chicken instead of the background.

Note that the selection is very close to the edge of the chicken's anti-aliased edge pixels. Make sure that all the pixels are selected or some may be left behind as an unsightly outline when you distort the image.

⑥ Use the Expand command (Select⇨Modify⇨Expand) to refine the selection.

To enlarge the selection, one pixel at a time, type **1** in the Expand By field of the Expand Selection dialog box.

⑦ Click OK to apply the selection expansion.

Your selection expands out in accordance with your settings.

⑧ Choose Edit⇨Transform⇨ Distort.

Note: There are other transformations available to be applied as well, such as scale, rotate, skew, perspective, and warp.

⑨ Click and drag up on the Transform box that appears around the chicken.

Keep at it until you have the distortion effect you're looking for.

⑩ Hit the Enter key to apply the distortion.

This method distorts the selected portion of the image rather than the whole image.

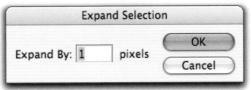

Cropping Makeovers

Cropping out unnecessary or distracting portions of an image can be one of the simplest and most effective makeover moves you can do. You can eyeball the cropping or you can do it by the numbers (using the Width and Height fields of the Crop tool's Options bar).

Note: With the Crop tool and its Options bar, you can crop, resize, and reset an image's resolution all at once. As you might suspect, this technique can bring in quite a bit of interpolation, so you'll probably want to sharpen up the image a tad when you're done.

❶ Open and duplicate an image that needs cropping.

For this example, use the Lonely_Moose.tif image — a photo taken in Denali National Park in Alaska. Compositionally, this image suffers from one of the most common mistakes made in wildlife photography . . . placing the subject smack in the middle of the image. This image screams out, "Crop me! Crop me!"

In addition to cropping the image, set the image dimensions to 4 x 3 inches and the resolution at 300 ppi.

❷ Choose the Crop tool from the toolbox and use the Options bar to set the Crop controls.

Press the Enter key to activate the first (Width) field. Type **4** inches as a width, and then press the Tab key to move to the next (Height) field. Type **3** inches, and then press the Tab key once again to move to the Resolution field. Type **300** as your ppi value.

❸ Using the Crop tool, draw the crop area.

Draw your crop from below and to the left of the Moose, up toward the upper-right corner of the image. This places the Moose in a better (out-of-center) position visually.

Width: 4 in   Height: 3 in   Resolution: 300   pixels/inch

Notice that the crop area is going to be constrained to the 4-x-3-inch ratio you designated. Also notice that after you release the mouse (after you've drawn the initial crop area), by default the portion of the image outside the crop darkens with a black screen (shield) to help you visualize what the final crop will look like.

Note: After you have made a crop selection, you can change the color and transparency of (or even deactivate) the crop shield using the Crop tool's Options bar.

❹ If necessary, click and drag within the crop margin to relocate the cropped area.

You can also click and drag on any side to adjust the dimensions of the cropped area.

❺ Press the Enter key to apply the crop.

The cropped-out portion of the image disappears.

❻ Choose Image➪Image Size to view the image's dimensions and linear resolution in the Image Size dialog box.

Notice that the image is a perfect 4 x 3 inches at a 300ppi resolution.

❼ Choose Filters➪Sharpen➪ Unsharp Mask to access the Unsharp Mask dialog box.

Applying Unsharp Mask helps compensate for some of the softening that invariably occurs during resampling. *Note:* SmartSharpen can work here as well.

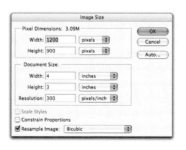

❽ Set the Amount field in the Unsharp Mask dialog box to 100 percent, the Radius to 1.0 pixels and the Threshold to 0.

Cropping Makeovers *(continued)*

Note: The Amount value determines how much sharpening will be applied, the Radius controls the width of the sharpened area, and the Threshold controls where the sharpening will be applied. Please See Chapter 9 for an in-depth discussion of sharpening.

⑨ Click OK.

The final image is cropped and sharpened with just the dimensions and resolution you wanted!

Adding Image and Background Acreage

One of the oh-so-cool features of working with digital images is that you can add to (and subtract from) the real estate they take up. Here's how you can add some extra canvas to your images (and even extend their backgrounds):

❶ Open and duplicate an image to which you want to add a footer.

Perhaps the Granite_lichen.tif file would do? I took this shot in the Inyo Mountains of California.

❷ Choose Image⇨Canvas Size.

This gets you to the Canvas Size dialog box.

❸ Change the settings in the Canvas Size dialog box.

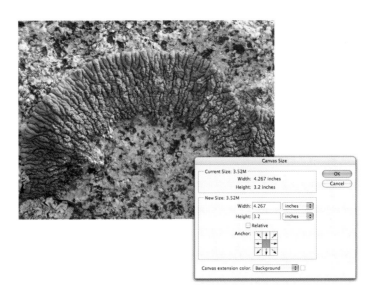

Let's say we want to add 0.5 inch to the top of the image — just the place for setting down a bit of added granite background. First, select the Relative check box. Then type **0.5** (inch) in the Height field. *Note:* If you don't check the Relative check box, you have to do math to figure out what to put in the Width field . . . Yuk!

In the Anchor area, click the middle square in the bottom row. This ensures that the whole 0.5 inch of added canvas gets added to the top of the image.

Click on the Canvas Extension Color drop-down menu located at the bottom of the Canvas Size dialog box to select a background color for the added acreage.

Taz's Take: Be sure to select a background color that highly contrasts with the image you want to extend; here you should select white, the default background color.

❹ Click OK to accept the settings.

Your 0.5 inch's worth of space is added to the canvas, ready to be filled in.

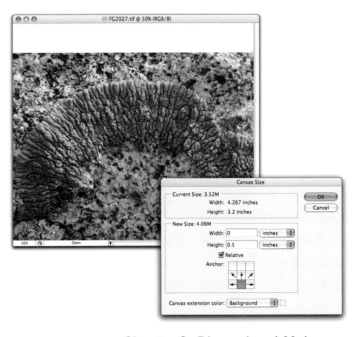

Adding Image and Background Acreage *(continued)*

⑤ Choose the Magic Wand tool from the toolbox.

Selecting the Magic Wand tool calls up the Magic Wand Options bar.

⑥ In the Magic Wand Options bar, set the Tolerance to 0, deselect Anti-alias, and then select Contiguous.

These settings are crucial — double-check to make sure they're right. They allow you to select just the added white canvas without any fringe pixels.

⑦ Click anywhere in the added white canvas.

The Magic Wand magically selects just the added canvas.

⑧ Click and drag the selection into place.

Move the selection from Step 6 straight down over the granite background until the top edge of the selection is *exactly* along the top edge of the granite.

Taz's Take: It's really helpful to zoom in so you can clearly see the top edge of the granite.

Note: Press the Spacebar and the ⌘/Ctrl key to activate the Zoom tool.

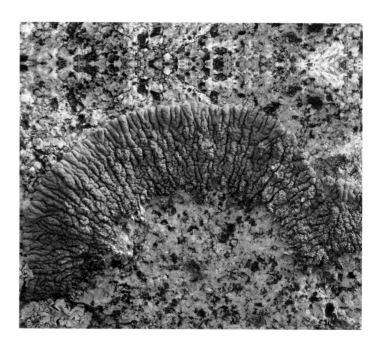

Keep in mind that moving your selection down does not cost you your 0.5 inch's worth of added canvas. That bit of real estate patiently stays behind, waiting to be developed.

⑨ Duplicate the selected granite background area.

Here you use a keyboard shortcut: Press Ctrl/⌘ + Alt/opt and then click and drag the Granite selection up into the added canvas area. It should fit exactly. Luckily,

Photoshop snaps the image into place when you get it close enough, but . . .

Don't deselect yet!

You'll note that the added canvas area is filled, but the edge of the duplicated area is painfully obvious . . . fixing that glaring error comes next!

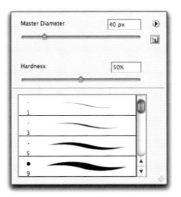

⑩ With the duplicated granite selection still active, choose Edit⇨Transform⇨Flip Vertical.

The granite selection flips vertically on its horizontal axis, creating a mirror image of the granite pattern — one that matches the granite pattern beneath it perfectly.

⑪ If necessary, select the Clone tool from the toolbox and use it to clean up any blemishes.

One slight blemish I can see in our example is the little bit of lichen that was duplicated and yet is not in the middle of the top edge of the image. Time to use the Clone tool.

Clicking the Brush Menu on the left side of the Options bar and creating a 40-pixel width brush with 50-percent hardness should get you the perfect Clone tool for the job.

Using the Clone tool's default 100-percent Opacity and Flow settings, press Alt/opt + click just underneath, but not on, the sliver of lichen at the top edge of the added canvas area. (The idea here is to grab a little piece of the granite pattern.) Release your keys and drag the Clone tool over the lichen. Doing so replaces the lichen with the cloned granite pattern.

If the mirroring of the flipped background is too obvious for your liking, use this same Clone tool and settings to replace some of the more obvious mirrored image components with random clone locations from around the granite background.

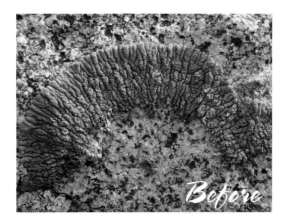

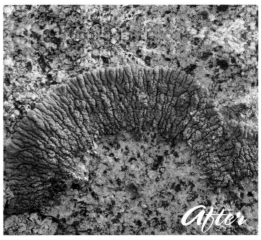

Making Over Multiple Images into Panoramas

If you try to capture a broad sweeping land-scape in one camera shot, the landscape fea-tures usually appear too small, and often lose their impact. A better approach is to capture the sweep of the landscape in sev-eral larger-scale image shots — and then stitch those shots together in Photoshop. Here's how it's done:

❶ Shoot a series of connected photos.

Shoot a series of photos that you'd like to stitch together into a panorama.

But before you shoot away, check out the Photoshop Confidential sidebar on how best to shoot panorama images.

❷ Sort and organize your images.

Sort through your images and select just the ones you want included in your panorama. Place these images in a separate folder.

Photoshop Confidential

 Building Panoramas One Step at a Time

The key to creating an awesome-looking panorama is *consistency*. Set up your camera on a tripod with the camera perfectly horizontal (use a level if you have one). **Note:** Keeping the camera in the same horizon-tal plane will make the images much easier to stitch together in Photoshop.

Start shooting images on the left side of your panorama and shoot from left to right. Overlap each image by about 10 percent. Also try to shoot all the images under the same lighting conditions and with the same exposure. I took the series of photos used in this chapter on a day when there were short-term vari-ations in the weather; lighting conditions caused some noticeable exposure variations from one frame to another, and I had to do some tweaking. The more consistency you have, the better.

When you're done shooting, download your panorama images to a dedicated folder on your hard drive. (I like to name my folder "Panorama," just to be different.) I create a second folder beginning with the same name but with the addition of the word *Removed* to indicate that these are images that I originally shot but later decided not to include in the panorama. I sometimes retrieve images from this Removed folder and add them to a panorama.

You can load individual images into Photomerge — Photoshop's own panorama tool — but here's a tip that can save you some hassle: Organizing only the images you want into a folder first and then selecting that folder in Photomerge is often the most efficient way to work.

③ Choose File⇨Automate⇨ Photomerge to activate Photoshop's Photomerge tool.

The Photomerge dialog box makes an appearance.

④ Choose Folder from the Use drop-down menu and then click the Browse button to browse to the folder containing your images.

All this browsing takes place in a Select Folder window.

Note: I've placed a number of images for you in a folder entitled Kenai Panorama Images on the Web site associated with this book.

⑤ After selecting your folder in the Select Folder window, click the Choose button to load the images into Photomerge.

Your images are loaded into Photomerge and you end up back in the Photomerge dialog box.

⑥ In the Photomerge dialog box, select the Attempt to Automatically Arrange Source Images check box.

This tells the Photomerge tool to match up and overlap the images in the correct order.

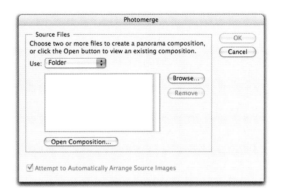

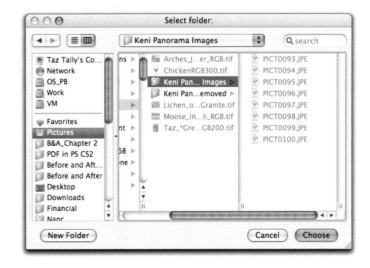

Making Over Multiple Images into Panoramas *(continued)*

❼ Click the OK button to initiate the opening and arrangement of your images.

This operation may take a moment or two as the Photomerge tool opens and evaluates — and then attempts to stitch together — your selected images.

The result of the automatic merging appears in the Photomerge window.

Taz's Take: The greater the consistency in the shooting, the better the results — and the less work you'll have to do to organize and line up your images. With my images of the Kenai Mountains, the shooting overlap was well done (if I do say so myself), as Photomerge was able to stitch the images together rather well. Anyone would notice, though, that the variation in lighting and exposure has created some inconsistencies across the panorama.

In Chapter 4, you'll find out how to fix these and similar exposure to exposure inconsistencies:

❽ Adjust the zoom to view the entire panorama.

Take a look at the Navigator window located in the upper left of the Photomerge window. You'll notice that the red view rectangle indicates that the whole panorama is not currently visible on-screen.

Click the slider located directly under the Navigator window to resize the view until you can see the entire thumbnail of the panorama in the Navigator view window, and/or the whole panorama in the main Photomerge window.

❾ Using the Select Image tool and the keyboard's various arrow keys, align the individual frames.

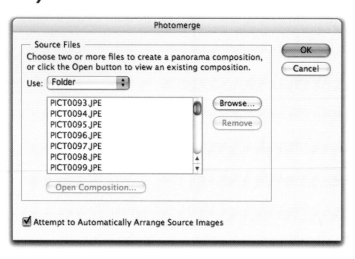

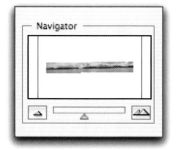

You'll find the Select Image tool arrow in the upper-right corner of the toolbox.

Aligning itself is pretty simple. Just click any individual image frame in the panorama to call up a red selection box around the image. Using the arrow keys (or by simply clicking and dragging), you can then move the image frame up, down, left, or right.

⑩ Select a Blending option.

If you're happy with the current look of the panorama, you can select the Advanced Blending check box in the Compositions Settings area. This tells the Photomerge tool to blend all the photo frames together into one image without further ado.

Note: If you select Advanced Blending, click the Preview button that becomes active to preview the results of that blending.

If you want to have a chance to tweak some of the individual image frames (as you definitely want to do in the Kenai example), then click the Keep as Layers check box located beneath the Composition Settings area. (Note that doing so deactivates the Advanced Blending check box.)

Please see the "Making Over Colors to Match" section in Chapter 4 to find out more about tweaking these kinds of exposure mismatches.

⑪ Choose a Perspective option.

In Photomerge, you have the option of viewing your panorama as a flat panel (the default view), in a curved perspective, or as a Cylindrical Mapping perspective. To view your panorama in a curved perspective, click the Perspective button located in the Settings section on the right side of the Photomerge window.

Making Over Multiple Images into Panoramas *(continued)*

You can experiment with the Cylindrical Mapping mode as well (using the Cylindrical Mapping check box located in the Composition Settings section) if you would like to create a more circular view perspective.

Taz's Take: Sometimes when you move between the various view modes, you may receive different (and not always pleasing) results. Don't try to move the image frames around manually if you want to return to another organization; instead, use Cmd/Ctrl+ Z to step backward in the view sequence.

⑫ Save or export the panorama.

When you are through manipulating your panorama, you can save your panorama either as a .pmg (Photomerge format) or as another file format.

I mention both options here for the sake of completeness, but trust me, you really don't want to save your panorama in Photomerge format. (Okay, if you simply *have* to know, you do that by clicking the Save Composition As button located in the upper-right corner of the Photomerge window.) What you *really* want to do is save your panorama in Photoshop format — that way you can edit it later in Photoshop if you so desire.

The Photomerge window makes exporting your panorama a snap. Simply click the OK Button — the one above the Save Composition As button mentioned previously — to export your image for opening and editing in Photoshop. This may take a few minutes; Photoshop will need to apply a transformation to each image.

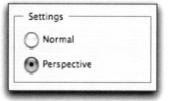

After this export is completed, your panorama opens as a multilayered Photoshop image.

⑬ Choose File⇨Save⇨Format⇨ Photoshop.

Save your panorama in Photoshop (.psd) format before you do anything else. Be sure to include the layers by checking the Layers check box.

Note: Such panoramas tend to be *large* files. To check the file size and dimensions of an image, choose Image⇨Image Size to call up the Image Size dialog box.

This particular panorama is a 62-x-8.5-inch, 300ppi, 136MB image. You will need 500MB of RAM and 2GB of Scratch Disk — every bit of that — to manipulate this image in Photoshop.

⑭ Crop the Panorama

After your image is open and saved in Photoshop, you'll likely want to crop the image to remove any uneven edges. But hold off on doing so until you have closely checked out all the frame boundaries to make sure the stitching is perfect. Use the Zoom tool to zoom in on the frame boundaries and look along all of them; make sure they match.

Tip: You can press the Shift + Cmd/Ctrl keys to activate the Zoom tool.

Select the Crop tool (C) and then click and drag it across your image to select the portion of the panorama you want to keep.

Note: You will want to zoom in on the edges of the crop to make sure you're keeping all the pixels you want.

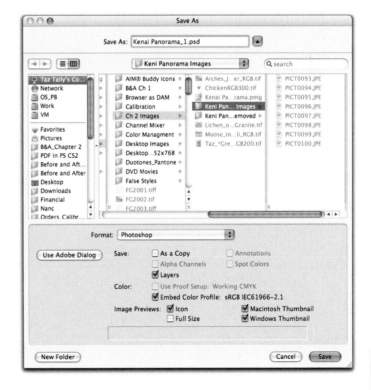

Making Over Multiple Images
into Panoramas *(continued)*

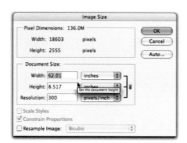

Before

After

3
EXPOSURE MAKEOVERS

Adjusting the exposure of images is a fundamental photo-editing skill — one you're sure to use day after day. The most common exposure adjustments involve setting highlight and shadow points as well as making overall brightness and contrast adjustments. Many scanned images — and most digital photographs — typically require at least some adjustments to these characteristics.

You can set highlight and shadow points either qualitatively (by eye), or quantitatively (by the numbers), or by using a combination of the two. If an image contains a diffuse, white highlight area, it's usually best to set the highlight by the numbers to make sure you get it correct. If no white highlight is available, then you can usually make an adjustment using just the naked eye — with a little help from the image data visible in the histogram.

Keep in mind that the order in which you perform your image adjustments is important as well. Typically, you'll want to adjust highlight and shadow points first and then move on to affect overall image brightness. Contrast adjustments will typically be fourth on your list. Whole image corrections typically precede any partial image (selected area) adjustments.

As a final note, this chapter focuses on applying your basic image exposure makeover skills to grayscale images. Chapter 4, on the other hand, shows you how to apply many of these same skills to making over color images.

Making Over Diffuse Highlights

One of the most common makeover adjustments you'll encounter involves the adjustment of the highlight value of an image that has a diffuse, white, highlight. Here is an example:

❶ Open the image Mark_ Tauna_Loomis_GS_300.tif image.

You'll notice that this image (available for download from the Web site associated with this book) looks a bit flat and the white area (Tanua's shirt) looks a bit dingy.

❷ Choose Image⇨Duplicate to make a duplicate copy.

Always, *always* work with a duplicate copy, rather than your original.

❸ Choose Window⇨Info.

The Info palette makes an appearance.

❹ Click the Eyedropper icon on the left side of the Info palette and select Grayscale from its contextual menu.

The Info palette can now measure grayscale values as percentages of K (as in CMYK, where "K" stands for "key" but really means "black) when you move the cursor over the image.

❺ Choose the Eyedropper tool from the toolbox and set its sample size to 3 by 3 Average in the Eyedropper tool's Options bar.

This allows the Eyedropper tool to measure and display an average grayscale value of nine pixels in a 3-by-3 matrix. Doing so gives you a clearer sense of how it looks than a single pixel would.

⑥ Move the Eyedropper tool over those sections of the image whose grayscale values you want to measure.

Here you're looking for sections of the image that display diffuse white highlights, rather than the bright white you'd need to display and print with detail. Tanua's shirt is an example of a diffuse white highlight.

If you move your cursor over the right side of Tauna's white shirt and measure its grayscale, you'll notice that the grayscale value averages around 26 to 27 percent.

These mid-to-high 20-percent-grayscale values are too high for this diffuse highlight area to appear bright white. (Such high values are one big reason why this image appears flat and dingy.)

⑦ Choose Image⇨Adjustments⇨ Levels to call up the Levels dialog box (with its accompanying Histogram).

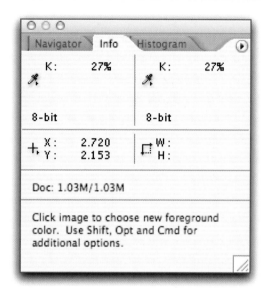

Photoshop Confidential

Most discussions of highlights don't mention that there really are *two* types of highlights: the specular highlight and the diffuse highlight. A *specular* highlight is one that is pure white — one with a K percentage value of 0 (or an RGB value of 255). A specular highlight contains no detail, and therefore will print with no halftone dot. The *diffuse* highlight, on the other hand, does contain detail — and those details are precisely what need to be preserved when you set a highlight value. When evaluating highlights in images, always look for diffuse highlights — the lightest portion of an image that still has detail. And if this highlight is supposed to be a white highlight, the Luminance value (whether K or RGB) should be set so that this white highlight "looks" white but still shows detail. For most commercial printers and high-quality desktop printers, a good, safe highlight setting is K=5 percent / RGB=242. If the detail is lost, the highlight will look flat or "blown out," as if the parts of the light exploded into a blur. (You can see this effect in newspapers when highlight values of less than 15 percent fail to print.) This results in a pure white area (sometimes referred to as a *blown-out area*) with no image detail present.

Making Over Diffuse Highlights *(continued)*

Note that the Input Levels Highlight slider on the right side of the histogram is located well to the right of the main image data in the histogram. This far-right location of the highlight pointer is a clear indication that the diffuse highlight value for this image is too high.

8 Use the Highlight slider to adjust the Highlight value.

Move the Input Levels Highlight slider in the Levels dialog box until it is under the beginning of the first major data peak.

9 With the Eyedropper of the Info palette positioned over the diffuse highlight on Tauna's shirt, fine-tune the position of the Levels Highlight slider.

I'd aim for a highlight value in the Info palette registering approximately 5 percent.

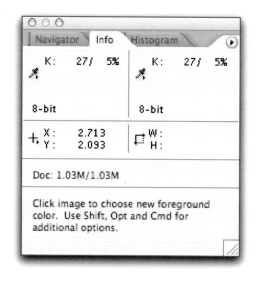

Now view the change in the image, after you have adjusted the highlight. Note how the image is lighter overall, the diffuse highlight is bright white (but detail is still present), and the contrast is improved as well . . . all just by adjusting the highlight point!

Before

After

Making Over Specular Highlights/ Increasing Overall Brightness

Learning to recognize and deal with a specular highlight is an important makeover skill. The following steps walk you through a particularly good (or bad, depending on how you look at it) example.

❶ Open the Kooteney_Hotel_ GS.tif image.

Notice that this image (again, available for download from this book's Web site) is dark for the most part — the only exception being the line of lights spaced along the front of the motel, which in this case happens to be a very light shade.

❷ Choose Image⇨Duplicate to make a duplicate copy.

As always, work only with duplicates; save your original as is.

❸ Choose Window⇨Info.

Doing so calls up the Info palette.

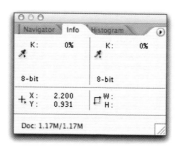

❹ Choose the Eyedropper tool from the toolbox and set its sample size to 3 by 3 Average in the Eyedropper tool's Options bar.

Ready for sampling!

❺ Position the Eyedropper tool over the middle of one of the lights and note that the K value = 0 percent.

This indicates that there is no data in this bright area — which pretty much defines what we mean when we say an image has a specular highlight.

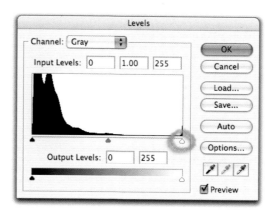

Making Over Specular Highlights/ Increasing Overall Brightness *(continued)*

6 Choose Image⇨Adjustments⇨ Levels to access the Levels dialog box.

Note in the dialog box how the Highlight slider is way right, similar to the starting position in the previous exercise. The difference here is that there is a small peak of image data at the highlight end in this image and histogram.

This small data peak at the highlight end represents the specular highlight area of the bright light bulbs. This area of the image is so much lighter, relative to the remaining image data, that nearly all the rest of the image data has been pushed far to the left of the midtone. When the specular highlight displaces histogram data this way, it reveals the reason why this image seems so dark and low-key.

7 Reset the highlight by moving the Highlight slider left until it is directly below the first bump-up in the image data in the histogram.

8 Click OK in the Levels dialog box to apply this change.

Note how the overall image brightness has improved . . . somewhat. There's still room for some improvement, however.

9 Choose Image⇨Adjustments⇨ Curves to call up the Curves dialog box.

What we're aiming for now is increasing the image's overall brightness.

10 Click the horizontal grayscale gradient bar (located under the graph) until the highlight end is on the right.

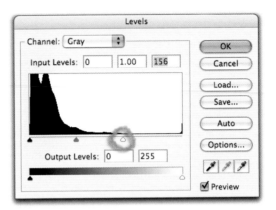

Note: If your Curves dialog box does not have the fine 10-percent grid seen here, Opt/Alt+click anywhere on the grid. Doing so changes the coarse grid to a fine grid.

⓫ Lighten the image by clicking and dragging the middle of the curve in the Curves dialog box up 20 percent (2 fine grid lines).

This move significantly lightens the mid-tones, showing progressively less impact toward the highlight and shadow ends.

Taz's Take: This lightening could be performed with the Midtone slider in the Levels dialog box, but the results are typically not as smooth and therefore not as high quality as I'd like.

⓬ Click OK in the Curves dialog box.

You see an immediate, overall brightening of the image.

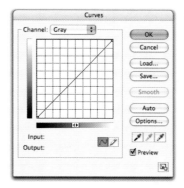

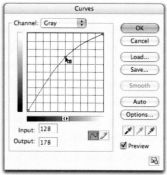

Making Over Contrast in an Image

The Levels and Curves dialog boxes can be used to give the contrast of an image a dramatic makeover. Here's how:

① Open, the Trees_Reflection.tif image.

You can download this image from the Web site associated with this book.

Note the very low contrast in this image. Low contrast per se doesn't make for a bad image — in fact, it's right for the image's original mood. But what happens if we make over this image with a higher-contrast look?

② Choose Image⇨Duplicate to make a duplicate copy.

The original image had a nice feel to it, so we don't want to lose that forever. Worth repeating: Always work on a copy.

③ Choose the Eyedropper tool from the toolbox and set its sample size to 3 by 3 Average in the Eyedropper tool's Options bar.

You'll again want to use the Eyedropper tool to sample color values.

④ Choose Image⇨Adjustments⇨ Levels, to call up the Levels dialog box and then Choose Windows⇨Info to bring up the Info palette.

Note that the Shadow slider in the Levels dialog box is set way to the left of the actual shadow data in the histogram. This setting shows why the image has such low contrast.

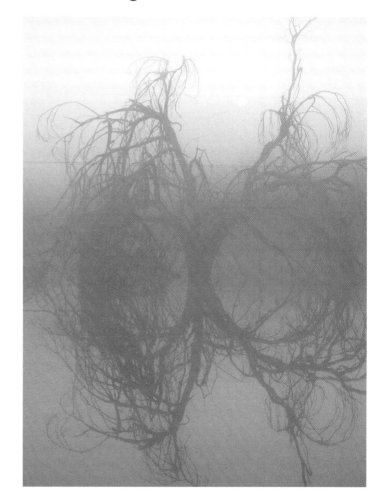

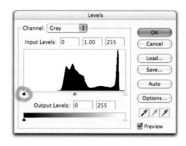

⑤ Reset the shadow point by moving the Shadow slider to the right.

You should end up just under the beginning of the data bump at the shadow end of the histogram.

⑥ Move the Eyedropper tool over the dark tangle of reflected limbs toward the left side of the image and measure the grayscale (K percent) of the image data here.

The grayscale percent will measure approximately 50–55% initially.

⑦ Fine-tune the position of the Shadow slider until the Info palette measures 95 percent.

Setting the dark shadow at 95 percent allows any available shadow detail to remain visible. If maintaining shadow detail is not important, experiment with moving the Shadow slider even farther in, which darkens the shadow portions of the image even more, creating more contrast.

⑧ Click OK to apply the Levels adjustment.

Looking good, but we could probably come up with a more effective image with the help of the Curves dialog box. Give it a try.

⑨ Choose Image➪Adjustments➪ Curves.

The Curves dialog box makes an appearance.

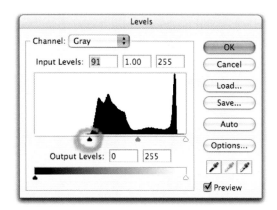

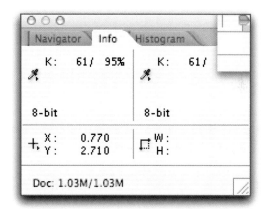

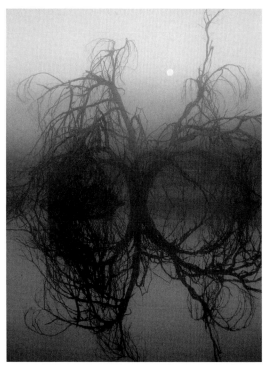

Making Over Contrast in an Image *(continued)*

⑩ Click the horizontal gradient bar (located under the graph) until the highlight end is on the right side.

⑪ Click the quarter-tone area of the curve and drag it up one to two horizontal lines. Similarly, click and drag the three-quarter-tone position on the curve down one to two horizontal lines.

The *quarter-tone* position on the curve is — you guessed it — a quarter of the way across the grid; you can find the *three-quarter-tone* area at three quarters of the way.

⑫ Click OK to apply this curve adjustment.

Note how the contrast of the image has increased again, in response to applying the "S-shaped" curve adjustment.

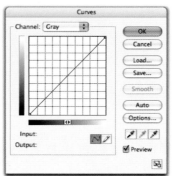
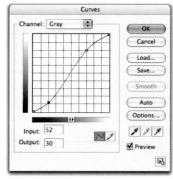

Before

After

Curve Shapes

The shape of a curve when you apply it to an image can dramatically affect the contrast of an image. Wherever a curve has a steep slope (as it is in the midtone in the preceding exercise), contrast is enhanced. More grayscale data is moved to the quarter-tone and three-quarter-tone areas of the image, thereby increasing the image's overall contrast. If a curve is flattened in the midtone (as in the following exercise), grayscale data are concentrated in the midtone aera of the image, which reduces contrast for the overall image. So the rule is: Steepening the curve increases contrast; flattening the curve decreases contrast.

Making Over Your Total Brightness and Contrast

Some images need it all . . . highlight and shadow adjustments as well as brightness and contrast help. For images that have multiple makeover issues, *the order in which you perform your adjustments is just as important as the adjustments themselves.* To show you what I mean, I'll walk you through the procedure for salvaging a particularly problematic image.

❶ Open the image Frances_and_Sheila.tif image.

This image is available for download from the Web site associated with this book.

❷ Choose Image⇨Duplicate to make a duplicate copy.

Even if the original image seems not much to look at, you still want to work on a copy.

❸ Choose Windows⇨Info.

Doing so calls up the Info palette.

A quick glance at the readings in the Info palette tells the tale: This image not only has poor highlights and shadows, but also poor contrast.

❹ Choose the Eyedropper tool from the toolbox and set its sample size to 3 by 3 Average in the Eyedropper tool's Options bar.

❺ Move the Eyedropper tool over the white blouse.

Note that it measures about 20 percent K — way too dark for a diffuse highlight.

❻ Move the Eyedropper tool over the right side of the black belt toward the right side of the image.

Note that the grayscale is around 70 percent, which is too light for a shadow area.

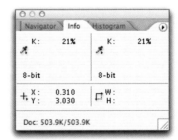

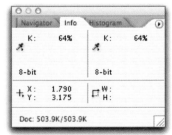

❼ Choose Image⇨Adjustments⇨ Levels to call up the Levels dialog box.

Note that both the Highlight and Shadow sliders are some distance away from the main image data.

❽ Move the Highlight slider to the left until it's directly under the significant data bump in the histogram.

Fine-tune the placement of the Highlight slider until the Info palette measures 5 percent in the sleeve area (the lightest area) of the diffuse highlight in the white blouse.

❾ With the Levels histogram still open, move the Shadow slider to the right until it is directly under the data bump in the Shadow end of the histogram.

❿ Using the Eyedropper tool, measure the right side of the black belt again.

Note that the K value is now around 80 percent — a marked improvement on the earlier 70-percent range, but still too light. The reason for this is that the background of the image is even darker than the black belts, so the dark background portion of the image is what's showing up in the far-left side of the histogram.

⓫ Move the Shadow slider further to the right until a measurement of the black belt in its darkest area reaches close to 95 percent.

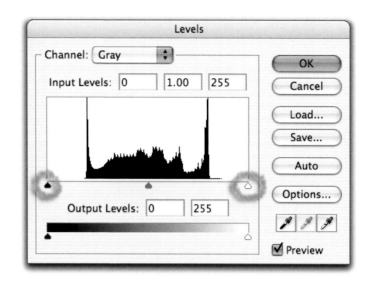

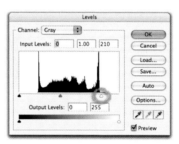

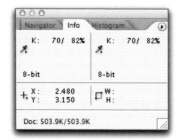

Making Over Your Total Brightness and Contrast (continued)

⑫ Click OK to apply final highlight and shadow adjustments.

Note how much the brightness and contrast of the image have improved.

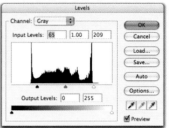

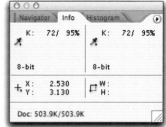

Examining Contrast Options: Darkening and Increasing Contrast

At this point, you have several options. You can leave the image as is or you can keep going — say, adjusting overall image brightness and/or further adjusting the image contrast. Use curves to make any of these brightness or contrast adjustments.

To see how this works, start out by darkening an image and increasing its contrast.

❶ Choose Image⇨Adjustments⇨ Curves.

The Curves dialog box appears.

❷ Click and drag the middle of the curve downward in the Curves dialog box.

Doing so darkens the image overall.

❸ First click and drag the quarter-tone portion of the curve slightly up; then click and drag the three-quarter-tone portion of the curve slightly down.

Remember, the quarter-tone area is a quarter of the way across the grid; the three-quarter-tone area is three quarters of the way across.

❹ Click OK to apply the adjustments.

Now the image is a bit darker and has a bit more contrast.

Before

After

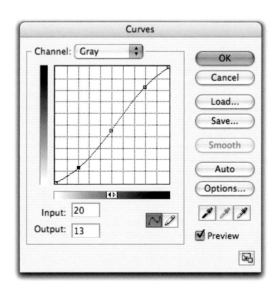

Examining Contrast Options: Darkening and Decreasing Contrast

From time to time, you'll want to darken an image and decrease its contrast. Here's how that's done:

❶ Choose Image⇨Adjustments⇨ Curves.

The Curves dialog box shows up on-screen.

❷ Click and drag down on the middle of the curve in the Curves dialog box.

Doing so darkens the image overall.

❸ First click and drag the quarter-tone portion of the curve slightly down; then click and drag the three-quarter-tone portion of the curve slightly up.

❹ Click OK to apply the adjustments.

Now the image is a bit darker and has a bit less contrast.

Comparing the two images — the one with more contrast and the one with less — you can see that a little bit of movement in the Curves dialog box goes a long way when you make any curve adjustments that affect contrast. Don't overdo it.

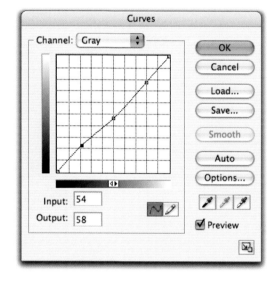

Making Over Your Total Brightness and Contrast *(continued)*

Before

After

Photoshop Confidential

Order in the Court!

As you can see in our Frances_and_Sheila example, the order in which we apply makeover adjustments is just as important as the adjustments we make. The proper order for any makeover involving multiple adjustments of highlight and shadow, as well as changes in overall brightness and contrast, is as follows:

1. Manipulate the Highlight and Shadow sliders in the Levels dialog box, guided by your Info palette for critical highlight and shadow values.

2. Move the curve in the Curves dialog box up or down at the midtone to affect overall brightness.

3. Fine-tune the overall contrast by adjusting the shape of the curve.

By adjusting your highlights first, you get a chance to first define the overall distribution of image data and then review your resulting image brightness and contrast prior to proceeding. If you start with a Curves adjustment of brightness and contrast, you could easily either over or under adjust your image.

It is also worth mentioning that each of these Levels and Curves adjustments are destructive to image data. Each time you make a Levels or Curves correction, more data is lost. So you will want to limit the number of Levels and Curves adjustments to one each if you can. If you are not very confident of the adjustments you are making, and you need to tweak them numerous times, you should consider making these adjustments initially in Adjustment layers.

Making Over Backlit Images

A common challenge with digital photographs is an image shot with backlighting, where the background has much better lighting than the foreground. Using a fill flash when you take the photo can help, but often even that is not enough. For a quick-and-dirty technique I've used many a time (with good results), check out the following:

❶ Open the Taz_and_Zip_Beach.tif image.

This image is available for download from this book's Web site; it's a self-portrait I took of my dog Zip and me on the beach in front of our house in Homer, Alaska. I had the camera on a remote control and I used a fill flash . . . but the bright sun on the white snow and glacier-covered mountains was just too much of a difference in exposure. The background is really okay, it's just Zip and me that need some rehab.

❷ Choose Image⇨Duplicate to make a duplicate copy.

The thought of losing a great Dog and Man shot is too much to bear, so be sure to work with a copy.

❸ Click the QuickMask icon (Q) — located at the bottom of the Photoshop toolbox — to activate the QuickMask tool.

Using the QuickMask tool in Photoshop is a fast way to make and/or edit a selection using one of the brush tools (particularly if the selection doesn't have to be perfect).

Activating the QuickMask allows you to paint in a selected area using a Brush tool. If you have already made a selection, that selection will appear as a 50% transparent red area.

Making Over Backlit Images *(continued)*

Note: The color and transparency of the QuickMask can be controlled by double-clicking on the QuickMask button.

You can quickly toggle between the Normal and QuickMask view of your selection by simply pressing the "Q" key.

④ Set the Foreground Color

Press the "D" (for Default colors) key to make sure the foreground color is black.

⑤ Double click the QuickMask icon to access the QuickMask Options dialog box.

The Quick Mask Options dialog box duly makes an appearance.

⑥ In the Quick Mask Options dialog box, click the Selected Areas radio button.

Doing so makes any QuickMask area an included (selected) area rather than excluded area.

⑦ Click OK to apply this option.

The Quick Mask Options dialog box closes, and you're ready to apply your mask.

⑧ First click the Brush tool (B) in the toolbox to call up the tool, and then click the Brush menu in the Options bar that appears.

A wealth of Brush options appears.

⑨ Select a medium-size brush (here 65 pixels) to start with; then use the slider to set the hardness to 0%.

Taz's Take: A soft-edged brush is crucial for the success of this technique.

Here's a really handy tip for performing this type of work. Use the bracket keys [ ] to increase and decrease the size of your brush on the fly as you work, so you don't always have to return to your Brush palette.

Brush control galore: You can exercise complete control over your brush size, shape, and an enormous variety of other characteristics with the help of the Brushes palette. Choose Window⇨Brushes (F5). You can drag the Brushes tab out as a separate palette if you want it to remain available as a floating palette (instead of disappearing after every use).

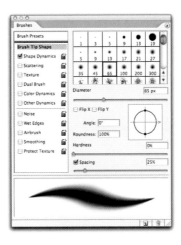

Making Over Backlit Images *(continued)*

➓ Using the soft-edged brush, paint a mask over the portion of the image you would like to adjust.

Remember that the QuickMask tool has been active all this time, just waiting for you to select your brush.

For our example, paint the mask on Zip and me. I recommend that you paint the interior areas of the selection with a big brush, and then work the edges with smaller brushes.

With some images — such as this one — you can get by with less precise selections, but typically you will want to be careful when you make your selections, because careful selections lead to better quality results.

Note: You can always undo a portion of the section using ⌘/Ctrl+Z, or by switching foreground colors from black to white (X) and unpainting the mask.

➓ Click the Normal selection tool in the Toolbox or type Q to deactivate the QuickMask.

You're presented with a normal selection on-screen, which can then be edited. (In this case, we want to lighten the selection.)

➓ Choose Image⇨Adjustments⇨ Curves.

The Curves dialog box shows up on-screen.

⓭ Click the middle of the curve in the Curves dialog box and drag up.

For this example I'd drag upward by two fine grid lines.

⓮ Click the OK button to apply the Curves correction.

Be sure to review the results; you might need to fine-tune your dragging of the curve here.

⓯ Choose Select⇨Inverse to select the background.

We're going to want to darken this selection to help with the contrast.

⓰ Choose Image⇨Adjustments⇨ Curves.

The Curves dialog box reappears.

⓱ Click the middle of the curve and drag down.

For our example, I'd recommend dragging downward by just one fine grid line.

⓲ Click the OK button to apply the Curves correction.

As always, check your results to make sure your execution matches your initial vision.

Using a pressure-sensitive cordless pen (for example, a Wacom pen) and a tablet can make selections such as these QuickMasks much easier and more accurate.

Taz's Take: The greater the difference in exposure you create between the foreground and background images, the tighter your QuickMask selection will need to be.

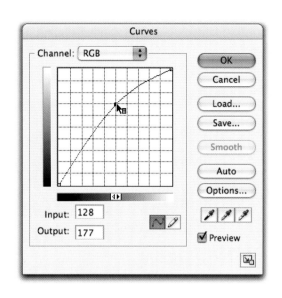

Making Over Backlit Images *(continued)*

Before

After

4

COLOR MAKEOVERS

Many people are intimidated by the thought of adjusting color images. No need to be. All the basic exposure-correction skills used in Chapter 3 to correct grayscale images apply here as well. The only difference is that when you work with color images you are adjusting multiple channels instead of just the one that you have in a grayscale image.

Other than that, you are still fighting the good fight by setting highlight and shadow points — whether qualitatively (by eye), quantitatively (by the numbers), or a combination of the two. If an image contains a diffuse, white highlight (or other neutral area), or color areas that people tend to recognize off the bat, such as skin tones (known as memory colors), it's nearly always best to make the correction by the numbers. (That way you can make sure the on-screen result is correct, and confidently prevent — or remove — unwanted color casts.) If no neutral or near-neutral area is available, then usually histogram data can help you do an accurate color correction (as with the grayscale images in Chapter 3).

As with correcting grayscale images, there is usually a preferred order in which to adjust color images. Image evaluation should always be your first task; you will want to determine which portion(s) of your image is (are) most critical to get right. Often one part of an image, such as a background, may be ignored, while a more important part of the image, such as a face or product, should receive most of your attention. You will nearly always look for neutral areas in your image, as correcting neutrals provides you with known values that you can use to correct color across your image.

Your actual correction sequence will typically be as follows: Highlight and shadow adjustment (often neutralization), midtone neutralization, memory color adjustment, brightness, contrast, and (finally) sharpening.

88

Performing a Basic Color Makeover

If you can find a white highlight in a color image, you have a double blessing: You can use the white highlight to set a diffuse highlight (as in Chapter 3) or to perform a color correction. Here's how to do both:

❶ Open the Florida_House.tif image.

You can grab this image from the Web site associated with this book.

Note that the walls of the house in this image are neutral, or at least should be.

❷ Choose Image⇨Duplicate to make a duplicate copy.

Remember my mantra from Chapter 3: Always work on a copy.

❸ Choose Window⇨Info.

The Info palette makes an appearance.

Photoshop Confidential

Measuring Grayscale versus Measuring Color

The makeover in Chapter 3 measures grayscale using the %K (0-to-100 *percent*) grayscale, where 0% = white and 100% = black. When you're working with RGB images, you use a different scale: 0-to-255 *shades of grayscale* values, where 0 = black and 255 = white; it's the inverse of the %K scale. We measure output RGB values by measuring the 0–255 grayscale values of the pixels on each of the three (RGB) channels that compose the RGB "color" image — *grayscale* values because all RGB color images are actually constructed from three grayscale channels, each of which is assigned to one of the three output colors: red, green, or blue. I stress *output* colors because the color isn't added until the image is actually output on an RGB monitor.

I know it sounds strange, but when you're capturing or editing a color image, you're really working with only grayscale values *to which color values are assigned on output.* So when you're measuring and reading RGB values with the Info palette in Photoshop grayscale, you're really measuring and reading grayscale values.

4 **Click the left Eyedropper in the Info palette and select RGB from its contextual menu.**

When that's done, moving any tool over your RGB images makes your Info palette measure and display the "RGB" grayscale values for each pixel on each of the three channels.

5 **Choose the Eyedropper tool from the toolbox and set its sample size to 3 by 3 Average (in the Eyedropper tool's Options palette).**

Doing so sets the Info palette to calculate and display RGB/Grayscale values, which are the average of a 3x3 matrix of pixels.

6 **Move your Eyedropper cursor over the (supposedly) white stucco front of the house, just to the right of the entryway.**

The idea here is that the RGB values should all be equal. If there is a color cast in this image, it will show up as unequal RGB values in such neutral areas. Also, these white walls represent a diffuse highlight — so set their grayscale value at approximately 5% (242 in RGB values).

Note that the Red value is okay at 241, but the blue and green values are way too high (253 and 251). This indicates a strong blue-green color cast in the highlighted area of the image.

7 **Click and hold the Eyedropper tool in the toolbox until the two "hidden" tools appear; select the "hidden" Color Sampler tool.**

The Color Sampler tool allows you to record the RGB values of up to four areas in the Info palette.

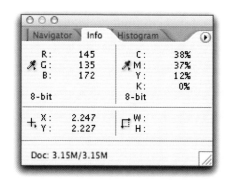

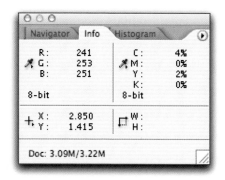

Performing a Basic Color Makeover *(continued)*

⑧ Using the Color Sampler tool, click the white stucco section of the image — the section with RGB values of R=241, G=253, B=251.

The Color Sampler tool records these values in the lower portion of the Info palette (the one showing the label *#1*).

⑨ Again using the Color Sampler tool, click the (black) pavement section of the image.

The driveway is another neutral or near-neutral area of the image.

Note that the RGB values saved here as Sample #2 are R=52, G=78, B=85. Once again, you see that a supposedly neutral area of your image is indeed not neutral.

You now have two sample points recorded for you in the Info palette — one in the highlight and one near the three-quarter tone. Time to put the info gleaned from these two sample points to good use.

R:	241	C:	4%
G:	253	M:	0%
B:	251	Y:	2%
		K:	0%
8-bit		8-bit	

| X: | 2.850 | W: | |
| Y: | 1.415 | H: | |

#1 R:	241		
G:	253		
B:	251		

Doc: 3.09M/3.22M

R:	50	C:	80%
G:	76	M:	58%
B:	83	Y:	52%
		K:	35%
8-bit		8-bit	

| X: | 2.213 | W: | |
| Y: | 2.800 | H: | |

#1 R:	243	#2 R:	52
G:	254	G:	78
B:	252	B:	85

Doc: 3.09M/3.22M

Photoshop Confidential

Neutralization

In my experience, the key to most color-correction decisions and techniques is to understand and work with *neutrals* — shades of gray. In RGB terms, neutral and gray are identical values. So an image area that measures 128R, 128G, 128B is a neutral-gray midtone value (*Note:* 128 is midway between 0 and 255). Similarly, an image area measuring 242R, 242G, 242B represents a neutral 5% highlight (0.95 x 255 = 242). And any other shade of gray in an image should also be neutral — that is, have equal RGB values. And since all RGB color images are really constructed as distinct sandwiches of three grayscale channels, all neutral or gray areas of such a color image should have the same grayscale values on all three channels.

Your basic color-correction techniques for neutralization take advantage of this sandwich effect. Suppose, for example, you measure an area that's supposed to be neutral gray (equal RGB values) but it isn't — that is, it has unequal RGB values. Then you know the color is incorrect because it isn't really gray — the image has a *color cast*. Now, if you make an image-wide correction so that all neutral areas have equal RGB values, then all the other (non-neutral) color areas should be corrected as well. That's easier to get a handle on as you gain more experience using the Info and color-correction tools . . . just remember: Think grayscale!

⑩ Choose Image⇨Adjustments⇨ Curves to call up the Curves dialog box.

The Curves dialog box duly appears.

⑪ Choose Blue from the Channel drop-down menu in the Curves dialog box.

You want to isolate the Blue channel because your Color Sampler tool has told you that the Blue value needs to be lowered.

⑫ In the Curves dialog box, click and drag the Highlight (right) end of the curve downward until the Blue value reads approximately 242 in the Sample #1 section of the Info palette.

You are adjusting the Highlight end of the curve because that is the area of the image you are measuring and correcting:

The idea here is to drag the curve downward while monitoring the changes to Sample #1 in the Info palette — so be sure to keep the Info palette open and on-screen.

Taz's Take: The number 242 didn't come out of the blue, as it were. You'll remember that Sample #1 dealt with the white walls — a diffuse highlight that should read approximately 242 in RGB values. Also keep in mind that, if your sample point is slightly different than your initial measuring point, your RGB values may vary slightly.

⑬ Choose Green from the Channel drop-down menu in the Curves dialog box.

RGB stands for Red Green Blue, so you're going to have make sure all three colors are set at approximately 242.

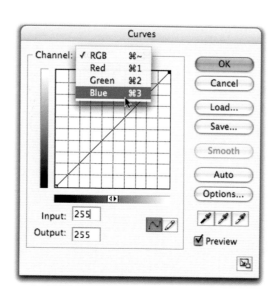

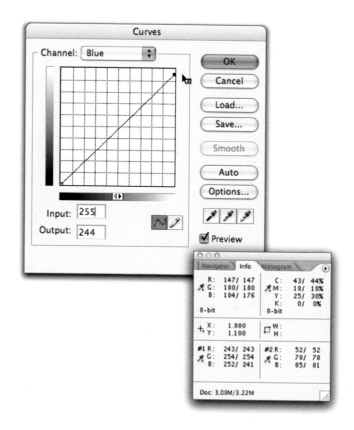

Performing a Basic Color Makeover *(continued)*

⑭ Click and drag the Highlight (right) end of the curve down until the Green value reads approximately 242 in the Sample #1 section of the Info palette.

You are adjusting the highlight end of the curve as that is the portion of the image you are measuring and correcting.

Again, keep your eye on the Info palette.

⑮ View the Color Sampler tool to review the RGB values of the driveway.

You'll discover that, even after your use of the Curves dialog box, your driveway RGB values are R=52, G=78, B=81 — they're definitely still not neutral — which means that your image is still in need of some color correction.

Since you do not have a specific target value for the driveway (such as the 242 value for the diffuse highlight), a good rule to follow in a circumstance like this is to use the intermediate value (the Green value of 75) as your target value

⑯ Choose Red from the Channel drop-down menu in the Curves dialog box.

When working with this channel, keep your eye on Sample #2 in the Info palette.

⑰ While monitoring the Red value in Sample #2 in the Info palette, click and drag the middle of the curve upward until the Red value reads approximately 75.

Note: Here you are moving the middle of the curve rather than specifically the three-quarter-tone portion because you're assuming that this color imbalance exists throughout all the internal tones of your image.

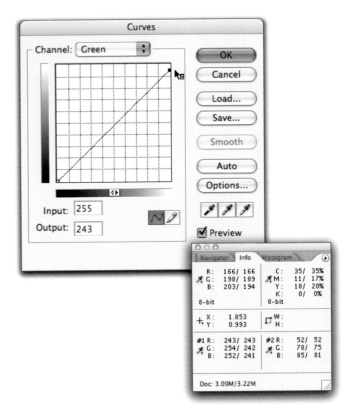

⑱ Choose Blue from the Channel drop-down menu in the Curves dialog box.

Green is the benchmark, so you can skip him and go to Blue.

⑲ While monitoring the Blue value in Sample #2 in the Info palette, click and drag the middle of the curve up until the Blue value reads approximately 75.

⑳ Click the OK button in the Curves dialog box to apply all the curve-based neutralization corrections.

This completes your neutrals-based color correction, a simple but effective makeover. Contrast your final image with your starting one. Note how the stucco is whiter, the blacktop is blacker, and the image contrast and color saturation are much improved.

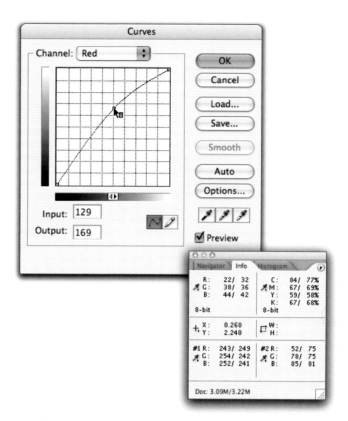

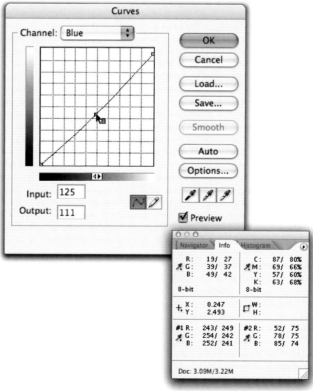

Memory-Color Makeovers

In addition to using neutral grays to affect your color makeovers, the other key category of color correction values involves what are known as memory colors. *Memory colors* are certain kinds of colors that your human memory "just knows" are right or wrong — intuitively — by glancing at them. The colors we associate with (for example) blue skies, green grass, red stop signs, and skin tones are common memory colors. When such colors seem "off" in an image — even just slightly off — you tend to notice it right away. (For you portraitists out there, note that skin tones are especially important when the focus of the image is someone's face.)

Here you can see some examples of memory colors where you can tell right off that they are not quite right. You don't need an info tool to tell you that these color are wrong!

Unlike a neutral gray (where a specific numeric value, such as a 5% highlight, is the goal), skin tones require you to focus on ratios of red to green to blue (rather than specific numeric values). No matter if you're viewing a skin tone in the highlight, midtone, or shadow zone, the ratio of the RGB values should remain the same — even when the specific numbers vary.

Now, whole books have been written about skin tones, but I have a simple ratio you can use to make sure that people in your images look like humans and not Klingons. The RGB ratio I use most often when measuring and adjusting skin tones is R>G>B in a ratio of 5/4/3.

Here is how this works mathematically: If your skin tone Red value is 100, your Green value should be approximately 80 and your Blue should be approximately 60. To determine your Green and Blue values, do some quick arithmetic:

Divide your Red value by 5: $100 \div 5 = 20$.

Multiply 20 x 4 to determine your target Green value: 20 x 4 = 80.

Multiply 20 x 3 to determine your target Blue value: 20 x 3 = 60.

To see how this ratio works in the "real world," make your way through the following steps:

❶ Open the image entitled Taz_Portrait_RGB_300.

Here you'll use a portrait of the Taz with some serious color problems. (Taz Portrait_ RGB_300 is available for download from the Web site associated with this book.)

❷ Choose Image⇨Duplicate to make a duplicate copy.

As bad as the original may be, always work on a copy.

❸ Choose Window⇨Info.

The Info palette makes an appearance.

❹ Click the Eyedropper icon on the left side of the Info palette and select RGB from its contextual menu.

You'll be working with RGB values again.

❺ Choose the Eyedropper tool from the toolbox and set its sample size to 3 by 3 Average in the Eyedropper tool's Options bar.

As before, you'll want to work with an average matrix size of 3x3 pixels.

❻ Move your Eyedropper cursor over the sunlit (image-left) side of the forehead.

The RGB values measured here are R=203, G=177, B=172.

Memory-Color Makeovers *(continued)*

Immediately you can see that the Green and Blue values are almost identical — which signals a color problem immediately: Blue values should be approximately 25% lower than Green values if they are supposed to be in a 4/3 ratio (around 121, let's say); using our 5/4 target ratio of red to green, the Green values should be approximately 161 instead of 177.

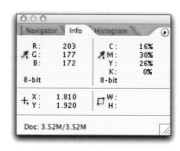

⑦ Click and hold the Eyedropper tool in the toolbox until the two "hidden" tools appear; select the "hidden" Color Sampler tool.

The Color Sampler tool allows you to record the RGB values of up to four areas in the Info palette.

⑧ Using the Color Sampler tool, click the sunlit (image-left) side of the forehead.

Using the Color Sampler tool, sample and record the initial color value of 203/177/172.

⑨ With the Color Sampler tool still active, sample and record a second set of RGB values on the cheek.

Here your RGB values should read 194/165/152 — also not within the range associated with our 5/4/3 ratio. To get these numbers in line, we need to move them to 194/155/116.

Taz's Take: It's always a good idea to work with at least two sets of RGB values. Doing so ensures that you're working with representative RGB values. Also avoid sampling areas in shadows; sample the lighted areas whenever possible.

⑩ Choose Image➪Adjustments➪ Curves to call up the Curves dialog box.

The Curves dialog box appears.

⓫ In the Curves dialog box, choose Green from the Channel drop-down menu.

You might like to work in order from Red to Green to Blue, since that is the ratio order.

⓬ ⌘/Ctrl + click sampled point #1 and then ⌘/Ctrl + click sampled point #2; this adds control points associated with skin-tone values to your curve.

Since you are very specifically targeting the skin tones in this image, it is appropriate to locate the skin-tone areas on the curve and use those points for making the curve adjustments.

Note: Since both points end up being so close together, you can click and drag one of the points off the curve graph, so that just one point remains for adjustment purposes. The second point stays in place.

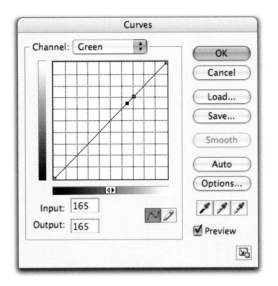

⓭ While monitoring the sampled values in the Info palette, click and drag the sampled point on the curve downward until the #1 sample Green value is approximately 163.

Note that the Green value at the #2 sampled point is now 152 — very close to your #2 target value of 155.

⓮ In the Curves dialog box, choose Blue from the Channels drop-down menu.

One more color to go.

⓯ Press ⌘/Ctrl + click the #2 sampled point to add a control point associated with that skin-tone value to the Blue curve.

Again, it makes sense to use a control point associated with skin tones here.

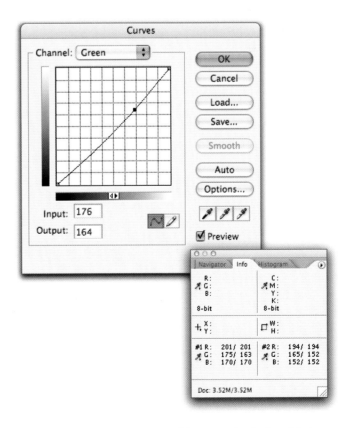

Memory-Color Makeovers *(continued)*

⑯ While monitoring the #2 sample point in the Info palette, click and drag the sampled point on the curve downward until the #1 sample Blue value is approximately 116.

Note that our #1 sampled point did not quite make it down to the projected Blue value of 121 — and if you pulled the curve down until the Blue value *did* equal 121, the image would appear too yellow. This sometimes happens where one of the values may not be exactly on the money. That's why you use at least two points (I often use three). Multiple sets of RGB data to monitor improve the consistency of your results. One of the values may be off if the data in the image vary widely; if you have several data points, you can ignore any blatantly anomalous values.

⑰ Click the OK button to apply the color corrections to this image.

When you compare the final image with the initial image, you'll see that a (relatively simple) color makeover has made a huge difference.

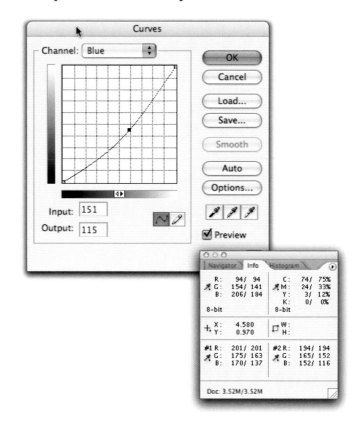

Doing a Quick-and-Dirty Color Makeover: To Neutralize or Not to Neutralize

Some color corrections can be done qualitatively, with no specific color-target values in mind. You might aim for a general "look" rather than for precise values. And neutralization is not always the goal. For example, here's an image with two makeover adjustments you can do using just your two eyes and the Levels dialog box:

1 Open the Kooteney_RGB.tif image.

As is the case with all the images I feature in the text, this image is available for download from the Web site associated with this book.

On-screen, you'll note that this image is not only very dark, but also has an obvious yellow color cast.

2 Choose Image⇨Duplicate twice to make two duplicate copies.

In one copy, you keep the color cast; in the other, you take it away. More about why in a moment.

Instead of going the numbers-and-channels route to this makeover, we're going the quick-and-dirty route: using only the visual assist of histograms in the Levels dialog box. Why? Well, for one thing, it's faster (you may want to go kayaking); for another, frankly, there are times when quick-and-dirty is good enough.

No Neutralization — Keep the Color Cast

Here you lighten the image while retaining the color cast.

1 With one copy of the image open, choose Image⇨ Adjustments⇨Levels.

The Levels dialog box makes an appearance. (Make sure that RGB is showing in the Channels drop-down menu.)

Doing a Quick-and-Dirty Color Makeover: To Neutralize or Not to Neutralize (continued)

The histogram here tells a pretty clear story: You've got a specular highlight (the lights) in this image, which shows up as the small data peak on the far-right side of the histogram. It is this bright, blown-out area of the image that forces the remainder of the image into the three-quarter-tone and shadow tonal ranges.

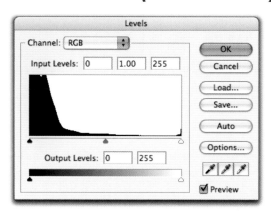

② Click and drag the Highlight slider to the left until it is directly under where the image data begins to bump up in the histogram.

Doing so brightens the image but retains the color cast.

③ Click and drag the Midtone slider until it just enters the steep slope of the main data peak in the histogram.

If you simply must have numbers, slide until you get around 2.0 in the midtone's Input Levels field — the middle one of the three fields.

④ Click the OK button to complete this adjustment.

Brightening the Image and Saying Adios to the Color Cast

Here you lighten the other image while reducing the color cast.

① With the second copy of the initial image open, choose Image⇨Adjustments⇨Levels.

In this example, you work on the individual channels (instead of the master RGB channel) to reset the highlight.

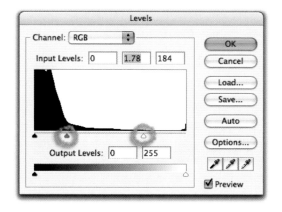

② **Choose Red from the Channel drop-down menu.**

Doing so isolates the Red channel for adjustment.

③ **Drag the Highlight slider to the left until the slider is directly under the first bump in the image data.**

The middle figure here to the right gives you an idea where to stop.

④ **Choose Green from the Channels drop-down menu.**

Doing so isolates the Green channel for adjustment.

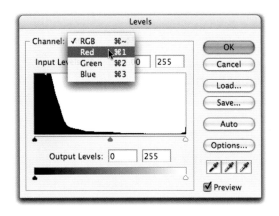

⑤ **Drag the Highlight slider to the left until the slider is directly under the first bump in the image data.**

Note how much farther left you have to drag to get to the Green channel's significant data than you do for the Red channel. And contrast this histogram with the one displaying the Blue channel. (See the next step for details.)

⑥ **Choose Blue from the Channels drop-down menu.**

Doing so isolates the Blue channel for adjustment.

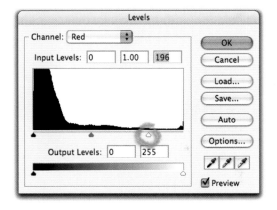

⑦ **Drag the Highlight slider to the left until the slider is directly under the first bump in the image data.**

Note that the beginning of the significant data in the Blue channel is way farther left than was the case in either the Red or the Green channel. Such offsets in the highlight data (seen here in these histograms) are the root cause of the color cast.

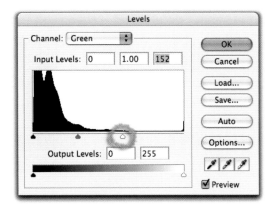

Doing a Quick-and-Dirty Color Makeover: To Neutralize or Not to Neutralize *(continued)*

⑧ Choose RGB from the Channel drop-down menu.

We're going to use the RGB channel to adjust midtones.

⑨ Drag the Midtone slider to the left until the Input Levels midtone value is about 2.0.

This is the same Midtone level we used in our previous example.

Note: Since you've already removed the main color cast with your channel-by-channel Highlight adjustment, you can make the Midtone adjustment by using the master RGB channel.

⑩ Click the OK button to apply the correction.

Contrast this image with the final image in the example you get in the "No Neutralization — Keep the Color Cast" section. Note how the image has been brightened by about the same amount, but the color cast has been largely removed.

Keep in mind that there's no absolute right or wrong way to do this adjustment. Either result is acceptable, depending upon your preferences. Option One — retaining the color cast — is what you might use for a honeymoon-hotel brochure. Option Two — removing the color cast — works for (say) a family-vacation-motel brochure.

If you want to fine-tune the colors, you can use your Curves dialog box, your Info palette, and the techniques we used in the previous Florida House exercise. (Well, sure . . . but I'd rather go kayaking!)

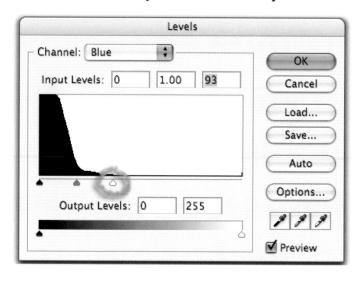

Before

After

Doing More Complex Color Makeovers: Neutrals and Skin Tones

When you are faced with an image that has both neutrals and memory colors, you will really want to adjust the neutrals first to color correct the entire image. Then you can address the memory colors to see if they need more work. Often, performing a neutralization will take care of any memory color problems as well . . . but not always.

❶ Open the Woman_with_ Wine.tif image.

Note that the shirt in this image (available for download from the Web site associated with this book) is a neutral — or at least should be: The RGB values should all be equal. If there is a color cast in this image, it will show up as unequal RGB values in neutral areas such as this shirt. Also, the lightest portion of the shirt — which includes the collar and sleeve facing the light source — represents a diffuse highlight, which should be set at approximately 5% (242 in RGB values). In addition, we have skin tones in this image — critical memory colors that we want to be correct.

❷ Choose Image⇨Duplicate to make a duplicate copy.

Always, always work on a copy.

❸ Configure the Info palette and Eyedropper as in the "Performing a Basic Color Makeover" section at the beginning of this chapter.

Same approach: Set the Info palette to measure RGB values and set the size of the Eyedropper tool to 3 by 3 Average.

Doing More Complex Color Makeovers: Neutrals and Skin Tones *(continued)*

❹ Move your Eyedropper cursor over the light side of the collar and shoulder of the shirt (image-left) to measure the white highlight.

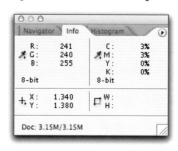

Note that the RGB values in the Info palette measure 241, 240, 255. We are looking for two things here: (1) equal RGB values, and (2) a highlight value of 242, which is the RGB equivalent of 5%.

The Red and Green values are okay here, but the Blue value is way high — a sure sign of a strong Blue color cast in the highlight area of the image.

❺ Click and hold the Eyedropper tool in the toolbox until the "hidden" tools appear; then select the "hidden" Color Sampler tool.

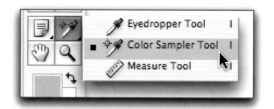

The Color Sampler tool allows you to record the RGB values of up to four areas in the Info palette.

❻ Using the Color Sampler tool, click the white shirt's collar.

The Color Sampler tool records the RGB values (240, 241, 255) in the lower portion of the Info palette and gives it the label of #1.

❼ Still using the Color Sampler tool, measure and sample the RGB values in a darker area of the shirt.

Try sampling just to the image-right side of the collar. Note that the RGB values here are approximately 156, 141, 190.

Here, the Red and Green values (156 and 141) are not as close as they were in the highlight, but the Blue value is still significantly higher (190) than both of them — indicating that the blue color cast does indeed extend throughout the image.

8 **Click with the Color Sampler tool to record this RGB value as well.**

You now have two sampled points.

9 **Using the Color Sampler tool, click the right (image-left) side of the woman's face and capture the current RGB values.**

We'll need these values to evaluate the skin tone.

Note: This sampled area will initially be sample #3 but will become sample area #2 after you remove the temporary #2 sample location you create.

10 **Choose Image⇨Adjustments⇨ Curves.**

The Curves dialog box makes an appearance.

11 **In the Curves dialog box, choose Blue from the Channel drop-down menu.**

Doing so isolates the Blue channel for correction. (You've isolated the Blue channel because the Blue value is the one most in need of correction.)

12 **While watching the #1 sample in the Info palette, click and drag the Highlight (right end) of the Blue channel curve downward until the Blue value is about 241.**

The idea here is to change the Blue highlight value to equal the Red and Green highlight values. (You color-correct the highlight by neutralizing it.)

Taz's Take: Neutralizing the highlight is a critical makeover adjustment, because the human eye is particularly sensitive to seeing colors in bright white areas.

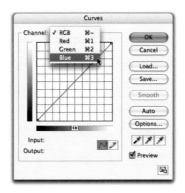

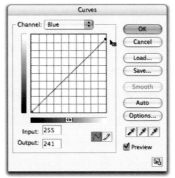

Doing More Complex Color Makeovers: Neutrals and Skin Tones *(continued)*

⓭ Click and drag the middle of the Blue channel curve downward until the Blue value for Sample #2 in the Info palette is = 156.

You want the Blue value in Sample #2 to be the same as the Red value.

Note: You are now working in the midtone area of the image since you have changed locations from a true highlight (the brightly lit collar of the shirt) to an area of the shirt that is in a casted shadow.

⓮ Using the Color Sampler tool, measure and sample the RGB values on the right (lighted) side of the woman's face.

You'll get figures such as R=205, G=173, and B=159 — after the Blue highlight adjustment — which will be saved as Sample #2. The trouble is, if we apply the 5/4/3 ratio rule, these numbers should be approximately R=205, G=164, B=123. The next step takes care of that.

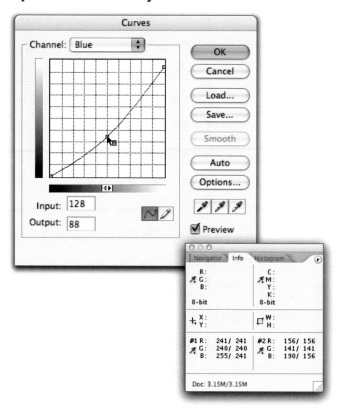

Photoshop Confidential

Those Pesky Numbers

The numbers in the Info palette point out a problem — and in this case, numbers don't lie. After neutralizing the Blue value, we end up having to move the Green value quite a distance — from 141 to 156 — if we want to neutralize the darker shirt areas. Doing so will create far too much of a green color cast in this image, making the woman a bit too envious — of what, we are not sure.

Two points to be made here:

1 Be careful of working with neutrals in color-casted shadow areas (as compared with straight tonal shadow areas, although sometimes these may be the same), as they often have color casts that are different than the color balances in the well-lit portion of the image. You will have to look at the image to judge whether you think the dark area is in a casted shadow (as it is here) or whether the dark area is simply a shadow zone in the image. Note that this casted shadow area is not a shadow area in terms of tonal range, it is too light.

2 You should focus your attention on the most important areas of your image — in this case, the white highlight and the facial skin tones. Never mind the color balance of color-casted shadow areas; that's of minor importance. Go to work on the important stuff, such as the skin tones.

15 **In the Curves dialog box, choose Green from the Channel drop-down menu.**

You want to isolate the Green channel here so you can adjust the Green values separately.

16 **While monitoring your sampled color values in the Info palette, drag the midtone of the curve until the Green value in Sample #2 is approximately 164.**

Here you are working in the midtone region of the image rather than the highlight area of the shirt.

17 **In the Curves dialog box, choose Blue from the Channel drop-down menu.**

The idea here is to now isolate the Blue channel for correction.

18 **While monitoring your sampled color values in the Info palette, drag the midtone of the curve until the Blue value in Sample #2 is approximately 123.**

19 **Click OK to apply the whole range of curve-based corrections.**

Now contrast the starting and finished images. Notice how your makeover image has a brighter, whiter shirt, how the colors pop more, and how the skin tones look healthier.

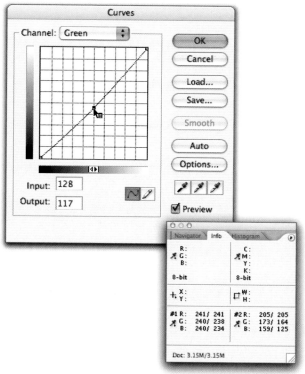

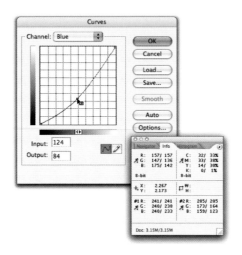

Making Over Colors to Match

Photoshop has several tools for matching colors between images — including a truly dandy one called (surprise, surprise) Match Color. (Choose Image⇨Adjustments⇨ Match Color to check it out.) But for this makeover you'll use one of the more old-fashioned techniques for matching color across images. (Nothing wrong with using tried-and-true methods now and again, is there?)

Taz's Take: Photoshop has a specific tool for making these types of adjustments. It is called the Match Color tool, which you can access by Choosing Image⇨Adjustments⇨ Match color. This tool often works just fine . . . but not always. If you try the Match Color tool here, you'll see that this is one of those circumstances where it does not work. Using the method I describe here, you'll have more specific control over sampled and affected areas across two images you are trying to match.

Flip to Chapter 2 for a look at that rather nice panorama image. Nice, but not without its flaws. The Photomerge tool used to create that panorama had a hard time stitching the constituent images together because their lighting conditions were so different. But help is on the way: These steps show how the color in the two panels in this panorama (or, for that matter, any two images) can be made to match seamlessly.

❶ Open Kenai_94.tif and Kenai_95.tif, make duplicate copies of both, and then designate your source and destination images.

Both images are available for download from the Web site associated with this book.

When using this matching technique, you must decide which image you'll use as your source image (the one whose colors will stay the same) and which image you'll want to

Making Over Colors to Match *(continued)*

use as your destination image (the one whose colors you'll want to change). I recommend using Kenai_94 as the source and Kenai_95 as the destination.

② Overlap these two images as shown on the previous page (with Kenai_94.tif on the left and Kenai_95.tif on the right).

③ Click on Kenai_95 to make sure it is the active window.

It should be in the foreground anyway, given the overlap, but it never hurts to check.

④ Choose Image⇨Adjustments⇨ Levels to call up the Levels dialog box.

⌘/Ctrl+L works, too.

Make sure RGB is selected in the Channel drop-down menu.

⑤ Double-click the White Point eyedropper in the Levels dialog box.

Doing so calls up the Color Picker dialog box.

⑥ Using the White Point eyedropper, click in the source image (Kenai_94) in the cloud area just to the left of the overlap.

The color values of the sampled clouds are numerically captured in the Color Picker dialog box — as well as displayed graphically.

⑦ Close the Color Picker dialog box.

No need to have excess stuff open on-screen. My advice: Always close what you don't need.

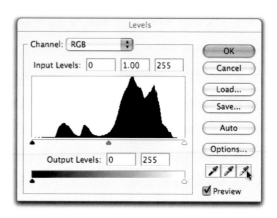

8 Click a part of the sky in the destination image just to the right of the overlap between the two images.

The idea here is to try to match the source and destination locations as closely as possible.

9 Click the OK button in the Levels dialog box to apply the source colors to the destination image.

You can see how the two images match each other much more closely now.

Note: Such image-matching tweaks should be done before you process any images through the Photomerge tool.

Before

After

5

COMPOSITION MAKEOVERS

Sometimes a makeover involves changing the content or composition of an image rather than simply adjusting what is there. A *composition makeover* changes what is there — and it may be as simple as cropping out an unwanted portion of an image or as dramatic as replacing an entire background or completely removing an element from an image. Other composition makeovers may be subtler, such as *desaturating* (otherwise known as "removing the color") or blurring one portion of an image to focus attention on another part of the image.

When you capture images with your digital camera, you can think ahead as to how you might later change the composition of an image. Since you're restricted to capturing an image with a specific dimension, such as 1600x1200 pixels (4x3 ratio), you can concentrate on capturing the critical portion of a scene in which you're interested — knowing that the image may contain elements you want to remove (or alter) later. Digital image capture provides you with this image morphing/altering capability — which opens up to you a whole world of creativity.

Many projects may consist of making more than one composition alteration to the image. You may want to crop, remove, and/or replace elements, apply selective sharpening and/or burring, and apply vignetting. When you want to effect multiple changes, you'll first want to determine the order in which you apply those changes so that you can have the best results for your image without having to redo many steps.

If this sounds complicated, don't worry. You've already seen many of the skills covered here — element selection, histogram reading and editing, curve tool adjusting, and color correction skills — in previous chapters. Now you get a chance to put them together to creatively change your images.

Doing an Image Extraction and Addition Makeover

Zeroing in on an image to isolate (through selection) a portion you want to use is a key skill in *extraction makeovers* — performing soft-edged extractions and placing the extracted image segments in other images. Fussiness counts: Pay special attention to the edges of your selection to make sure that the extraction will blend seamlessly into its new background.

1 Open Arches_Juniper.tif.

This image is available for download from the Web site associated with this book.

The idea here is to remove a juniper tree from one image ("Arches_Juniper") with the intent of placing it in another ("Red_ Rocks") — without making a royal mess of things.

2 Choose Image⇨Duplicate to make a duplicate copy.

You're doing some radical editing here, so work only on copies.

3 Using Spacebar+⌘/Ctrl, zoom in on the juniper tree so you can see what kind of selection job you've gotten yourself into.

Okay, the juniper tree looks like a fairly difficult extract — the tree has all those open spaces of varying sizes and opacities. Add to that the patches of sky (and those clouds with various colors and luminance values showing through the branches) and you've got yourself a bit of a selection headache.

Luckily for you, Photoshop provides several tools you can use to select the juniper tree. You could use the Magic Wand tool to get started, or perhaps the Color Range tool — and Photoshop even has a specific Extraction tool (Filter⇨ Extract) — all of which you might, and

could, use here. For this particular makeover, however, you'll want to use one of my favorite tools for making selections and extractions of complex images: the Background Eraser tool.

④ Crop the image.

Select the Crop tool (C) from the toolbox. Then click and drag over the portion of the image you want to retain, in this case the juniper tree.

Photoshop Confidential

Secrets of the Background Eraser Tool

Given the fact the Background Eraser tool is one of my fave Photoshop tools of all time, I suppose I should linger a bit over how it works. Just to warn you: The Options bar for the Background Eraser tool has several different settings . . . and understanding how these settings work will help you achieve successful selections.

The Background Eraser's brush is adjustable for size, shape, and softness — and its three eyedroppers offer three ways to sample and remove the background:

Continuous: This eyedropper (no surprise here) continuously samples the background for removal as you move the Background Eraser tool across your image.

Sampling: Once: This eyedropper uses only the pixel values for sampling and removal that you get from the pixel on which you first click.

Sampling: Background Swatch: This eyedropper uses the current background color in the Photoshop palette to control any removal.

The Limit drop-down menu determines which pixels will be removed. Choosing Contiguous here means only those pixels touched by the crosshair get removed; choosing Discontiguous here removes pixels across the full width of the brush; choosing Find Edges here means (instead) that the tool looks for high-contrast pixel boundaries to determine where to stop the removal.

The Tolerance value determines the range of pixels to be sampled and removed; the Protect Foreground color looks for pixels that have the current foreground color and protects those from removal.

I know all this may look like a lot to get your mind around at first, but try out the Background Eraser tool with the makeovers in this chapter. I'm sure you'll become a fan as well.

Doing an Image Extraction and Addition Makeover *(continued)*

❺ Click and hold down on the Eraser tool in the Toolbox until all three Eraser tools are visible; then select the Background Eraser tool.

The Background Eraser tool appears as a brush shape with a "+" in the middle. The "+" sign is the *sampling location,* which determines which pixel values will be sampled and removed.

❻ Configure the Background Eraser tool, using the tool's Options bar.

I'd recommend a Brush diameter of 30 pixels with a hardness around 90%. As for your Tolerance setting, I'd push it up to 25–30% to be sure you remove all the light sky-related pixels from the edge of the tree trunk.

Turning to eyedroppers, be sure to use the Sampling: Continuous one (Eyedropper # 1) so that your Background Eraser tool adjusts to the changing background as you move along the edge of the tree. But be careful to keep the "+" away from the tree pixels.

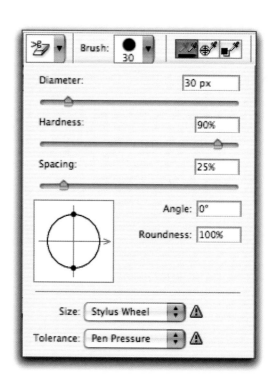

Finally, choose Discontinuous from the Limits drop-down menu so you can overlap the edge of the brush onto the tree to remove background (sky and cloud) pixels, up to the edge of the tree.

❼ Using Spacebar+⌘/Ctrl, zoom in so you're viewing just a short segment of the tree trunk.

Start with a tight zoom so you can try various Tolerance settings until you have a feel for what will work for this image area.

Note: You can change the Tolerance setting on the fly by typing in numbers on the numeric keypad: 2 = 20, 3 = 30, 35 = 35, and so on. You can also change the Brush size on the fly by pushing the square-bracket keys: [ ].

8 Point the crosshair at the center of your brush at the sky background, with the edge of the brush overlapping the tree trunk.

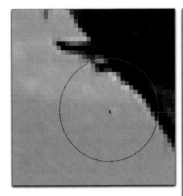

Starting out with the high contrast outside edge when experimenting with various Eyedropper choices and Tolerance values will provide you with good experience for working with the lower contrast edge differences that exist in the interior areas of the tree.

9 Click and drag the brush along the edge and monitor how effectively the pixels are being removed.

It may take a couple of passes to get the effect you want, especially with a semi-soft-edged brush.

The edge of the tree trunk should now be free of any blue sky or white clouds, but still have a semitransparent, anti-aliased edge.

10 Work your way along the edge changing the brush size, and threshold value as needed.

Use the Spacebar to activate the Hand tool to allow you to move around without having to change tools.

Photoshop Confidential

Edge Secrets

The secret to any good extracted edge is that it should be free of any background colors (blue sky or white clouds, in our example) *but* not diminish its own pixel values too much (for example, the lovely woody pixels in our image). In addition, the finished edge should be *anti-aliased* (made gradational) from the opaque tree trunk to clear transparent pixels. This clean, gradational edge is critical to being able to place your finished extracted image onto another background, because any remaining background color is going to stand out like a sore thumb on another background. (The gradational edge is also important for allowing the extracted image to blend in with another surrounding area.) So, for each edge, experiment with Tolerance settings and brush softness till you get the look (and the removal) that results in a clean, semitransparent edge.

Doing an Image Extraction and Addition Makeover *(continued)*

⑪ In the Options bar, change to the Sampling: Once eyedropper.

With the Sampling: Once eyedropper, you can click a background color and then drag the Background Eraser across many branches to remove that background color.

⑫ Still in the Options bar, change the Tolerance setting to 30–35% and make sure that Discontiguous is selected in the Limits drop-down menu.

You're gong to want to select and remove a wider range of pixels here. (The interstices have a wider range of background pixel values because all the branches are so close together.)

⑬ Using Spacebar+⌘/Ctrl, zoom in on an interior area, and then click with the crosshair of your brush on the middle of a representative background color for that area.

The idea here is to sample this background area.

⑭ Click and drag across the area.

Pixels corresponding to the background color you sampled are selected and removed.

⑮ Using the Spacebar to activate the Hand tool, move around the inside area of the tree branches — clicking the background colors and then dragging to remove those pixels.

Change your Tolerance settings as needed to suit the range of pixel values that need to be sampled and removed. (In areas where the

sky is barely showing through, you may want to drop your Tolerance setting to as low as 10%.)

Taz's Take: Stay zoomed in so you can monitor the quality of your sampling and removal. If you oversample and remove too much, just use ⌘/Ctrl+Z to undo any misstep. If you undersample and underremove, just sample and remove the same pixels, changing your Tolerance settings (using the keypad) as required.

⑯ Back in the Options bar, set your eyedropper to Sampling: Continuous, select a larger brush, and set Tolerance to 100%.

After completing the initial edge and interior sampling and removal, scrub the area outside the boundaries of the tree to remove any missed pixels. Do the same with the surrounding background.

⑰ Using the brush with the new settings, scrub around the tree.

When you're finished, your tree should be completely isolated from its original background.

⑱ Open and duplicate the Red_Rocks.tif image, then rename it Red_Rocks_Plus_Juniper.tif.

As usual, you can find this image on the Web site associated with this book.

Be sure to place this image on-screen so you can see it when you return to the Arches_Juniper image.

⑲ With the Arches_Juniper image once again active, select the Rectangular Marquee tool from the Toolbox.

Doing an Image Extraction and Addition Makeover *(continued)*

⓴ Using the Rectangular Marquee tool, draw a selection around the portion of the tree you want to transfer.

Be sure to select all of the tree, but none of the (remaining) sky background.

㉑ While holding down the ⌘/Ctrl key, click and drag the marquee-selected juniper tree over into the Red_Rocks image.

When you drop the juniper tree image, it's placed in the Red_Rocks image, right where you dragged it. (Here it's shown near the middle of the image.)

Keep in mind that the juniper tree gets added to the Red_Rocks image as a separate layer — which you can verify with a quick glance at the Layers palette.

㉒ Double-click the name of this layer in the Layers palette and rename it *Juniper*.

I strongly recommend that you get into the habit of giving descriptive names to your layers — rather than sticking with the default Layer 1, Layer 2, and so forth. It'll help you keep track of what the layers show when you start adding them to your images.

㉓ Back in the main image, select the Move tool from the Toolbox, and then use it to click and drag the tree into position.

I'd move the tree toward the left side of the image, between the two sections of the buff-colored sandstone.

Note that the tree looks out of place, just kind of sitting on top of the image. We're going to take care of that right now, by moving a section of the sandstone outcropping in front of the tree.

24 Using Spacebar+⌘/Ctrl, zoom in on the base of the tree; then use the Move tool to fine-tune the tree's placement.

Place the tree near the top of the foreground sandstone outcrop, making sure that you can still see some blue sky on each side of the tree.

25 Select the Magnetic Lasso tool from the Toolbox and, in the tool's Options bar, check the Anti-Alias box, and set the Feather to 1 pixel.

The Magnetic Lasso tool works well because it was designed to make it easy for you to make selections with high contrast edges.

26 In the Layers palette, click the Background layer to activate it, and then toggle off the juniper tree view by clicking the eye on the left side of the Juniper layer.

The juniper tree disappears, for now — but keep in mind the tree's placement in the image.

27 Using the Magnetic Lasso tool, select the section of sandstone outcropping you want to place in front of the juniper tree.

I recommend starting at the top of the foreground outcrop to the left of where the tree will be, tracing an irregular path through the sandstone below the bottom of the tree, drawing the path up to the top of the outcrop, then running along the top of the foreground outcrop until the lasso path gets close to the starting point. When you've reached that point, double-click to close the path and complete the selection.

Doing an Image Extraction and Addition Makeover *(continued)*

28 Choose Layer➪Layer➪Layer via Copy to make a copy of the sandstone selection and place it on its own layer.

The Layers palette makes a note of the new addition.

29 In the Layers palette, double-click the layer label and rename the layer *SS*.

Always go with descriptive names when naming layers. (Here SS stands for *sandstone*.)

30 Still in the Layers palette, click and drag the SS layer above the Juniper layer and then toggle on the view that shows the Juniper layer.

The juniper tree now appears behind the sandstone outcropping.

Taz's Take: The anti-alias and 1-pixel Feather settings create a natural-looking transition from outcrop to tree trunk.

The juniper tree now fits in (somewhat) better with its surroundings, but you'll notice that the original Arches_Juniper image had the tree in shadow, whereas the Red_Rocks surroundings are fully exposed to the sun. We'd better lighten the tree a bit to make it fit with its new (sunnier) surroundings.

31 Click the Juniper layer in the Layers palette to make it active.

32 Choose Image➪Adjustments➪Curves.

The Curves dialog box makes an appearance.

33 Click and drag the midtone point of the curve up 20–30% to lighten the tree.

The idea here is to make the tree's luminance more in line with that of the surrounding area.

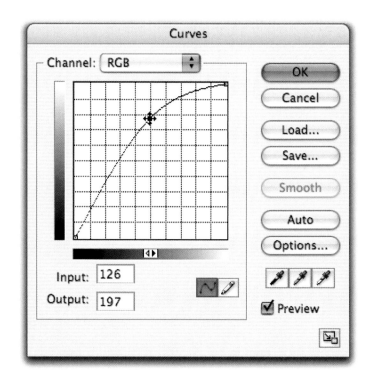

The finished product (check out the image below) shows Red Rocks with a (rather solitary) juniper tree added to its outcroppings.

A Picture-Within-a-Picture Makeover

You don't necessarily have to add or remove content to change an image dramatically; in fact, you can achieve some pretty stunning effects by doing a (relatively) simple crop. The important skill here is not the cropping technique itself, which (truth to tell) is a simple one-step process. The real trick is the ability to see the new image in your mind . . . the ability to see the picture within a picture.

Cultivating this ability to predict a picture within a picture is what can allow you to salvage dramatic images from otherwise-ho-hum photos. After a while, don't be surprised if you start putting this picture-within-a-picture vision to use right away in your work with new images — even in the initial image captures, as you're shooting the image. Once you get in the habit of seeing the picture within a picture, you'll start to pre-think your crops as you shoot your photographs.

To give you a sense of how this whole picture-within-a-picture thing works, check out the following makeovers.

Note: Cropping an image so dramatically requires that you have enough resolution to support the image dimension you want to create with just the cropped image. So always consider the cropping you intend to affect when you select your original image-capture resolution.

Changing the Balance

When you work on balance in an image, you manipulate where the various image elements are located and how they relate to one other. For instance, in situations where large masses of background mask the importance or significance of a smaller middle ground or foreground image, removing a competing element can shift the balance of significance to another portion of the image. The following makeover illustrates what I mean.

① Open the Kenai_South.tif.

This image is available for download from the Web site associated with this book.

② Choose Image⇨Duplicate to make a duplicate copy.

Again, you're doing some radical editing here, so only work on a copy.

This photo of the Southern Kenai Mountains along the edge of Kachemak Bay is one of those ho-hum images I was just talking about — ho-hum for a number of reasons. First, the beautiful mountains are smack in the middle of the image . . . boring. Second, the large expanse of water in the foreground has little character to it; not only does it fail to add interest to the image, it actually detracts from the drama of the mountains. The sky has some interesting features, but again, the large expanse of dull water detracts from that too.

The solution here, clearly, is to lose the water. (A lot of it, anyway.)

On this page are several versions of this image showing various amounts of water and sky — and any one of them is a vast improvement over the original image.

③ Delineate your crop by selecting the Crop tool from the Toolbox and then clicking and dragging over the portion of the image you want to keep.

Time to use that picture-within-a-picture vision thing.

④ Press the Enter key to apply the crop.

Doing so gives the *adios* salute to those parts of the image you don't want around anymore — most, if not all, of that water.

You can see several, but by no means all, crop options, on this page.

A Picture-Within-a-Picture Makeover *(continued)*

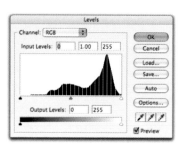

Taz's Take: Don't ignore the horizontal crop! When you're looking for the picture within a picture, don't forget to consider cropping in both directions. In the photo for this particular makeover, the obvious crop is vertical (as in the previous step) — but you can apply a horizontal crop as well.

⑤ **Choose Image➪Adjustment➪ Levels to access the Levels dialog box.**

Always check your image's histogram after you perform a crop, just to see whether you may need to adjust the lighting. Often a previous highlight or shadow area may have been given the boot during the crop.

Note, for example, how the Shadow Point slider here is way to the left of the image data. This means the shadow data in the image will be much lighter than it could (or should) be, and therefore present a lower contrast with the rest of the image elements.

⑥ **Click, hold, and drag the Shadow Point slider until it's snuggled up under the start of the significant shadow data in the histogram.**

You can see how this improves the overall contrast here: The shadow areas of the image darken.

Foregrounds, Middlegrounds, and Backgrounds

Good image composition is often about managing the relative importance of (and the relationship between) the foreground, middleground, and background areas of your image. For instance, if all three have the same significance or characteristics (such as lighting), an observer's eye may be confused about where to look. This can result in a less interesting image.

① Open the Illiamna.tif image.

This image is available for download from the Web site associated with this book.

② Choose Image⇨Duplicate to make a duplicate copy.

As always, stick to working on a copy.

The interesting parts of this image are the mountain (Mt. Illiamna, an 11,000-plus-foot volcano on the west side of Cook Inlet in Alaska) and the water taxi. The image lacks drama for two reasons: 1) Both the mountain and the water taxi are in the middle-ground, and 2) the current foreground (the water), and background (the sky) are boring, boring, boring.

③ Select your Crop tool from the Toolbox, and then click and drag to mark out the boring parts for elimination.

I'd recommend marking most of the current foreground and background (water and sky) for destruction.

④ Press Enter to apply the crop.

Note how the foreground components have completely changed. The interesting parts of the image now occupy different positions and have an altered degree of prominence. Initially, both the water taxi and Mt. Illiamna were in the middleground. Now, the water taxi is in the foreground, and Mt. Illiamna is in the middleground. And the really boring background sky is now reduced, as it should be, to a minor player.

Alternate Method: "But wait!" you say, "I *like* the water. It creates a nice foreground." Okay . . . try this crop where the water is retained but most of the sky is tossed out.

Either image is a marked improvement over the original . . . the creative choice is yours.

A Picture-Within-a-Picture Makeover *(continued)*

Changing the Emphasis

Sometimes you have an image that is well composed, but you just want to emphasize part of the image. Here, cropping will allow you to completely alter the content and emphasis of the image.

① Open the Sanford_Chistochina. tif image.

Here you have a very well composed image with an interesting foreground, middle-ground, and background, asymmetrically arranged. There's even a powerful eye line to boot — the Chistochina river — leading the viewer back through the image to the volcanoes (Mt. Sanford and Mt. Wrangle in Alaska) in the background.

As always, this image is available for download from the Web site associated with this book.

② Choose Image➪Duplicate to make a duplicate copy.

This is a nice image, so don't take any chances; as always, be sure to work on a copy.

Photoshop Confidential

Shooting with Cropping in Mind

The picture showing Mt. Illiamna and the water taxi illustrates what happens when you shoot a picture with cropping in mind. You may have taken this photo with the key elements — the mountain and the water taxi — in the middle of the photo in order to capture the breadth of the mountain scene, from right to left. If (when making the original shot) you had zoomed in to create an initially better composition, you would not have been able to capture the breadth seen here. So part of seeing the picture-within-a-picture is seeing beyond the extra stuff you have to capture (due to the format constraints of your camera): In this case, you pick up a lot of excess, unwanted sky (and perhaps water) so you can capture the desired breadth of image. So you take the whole scene, planning to pull out the picture within a picture with your Crop tool later. It's like cropping in imagination before cropping in the real world. Pretty smart, huh?

Okay, you might wonder why such a nice image has popped up as a cropping candidate at all, right? Well, the point here is that cropping is not just for rescuing a poorly composed image. You can also crop a nice image so you end up with another image with a totally different focus . . . not necessarily a better image, but just a different one.

③ Select your Crop tool from the Toolbox, and then click and drag down from either upper corner to include only a small portion of the middleground.

Bottom line: You're going to want to crop out most of the river.

④ Press the Enter key to apply the crop.

Note that the emphasis is now totally on the mountains rather than on the river. And the spatial eye-line focus is now horizontal — rather than vertical, as it was in the original image.

A Crooked Makeover

Some images refuse to be straight no matter how long you look at them! Thankfully, such crookedness is easy to fix in Photoshop. Here's how it's done.

❶ Open and duplicate the Book_ Photo image.

This photograph of a page from a book represents a common circumstance where *off-axis* (crooked) images are created. Often, due to the interference of the binding, when pages from a document are scanned or photographed, what's on them ends up crooked in the image. Here's an easy way to square up such images:

❷ Find a line and then draw a parallel line.

Look for a line in your image that should be either horizontal or vertical. Here the square boxes represent both of these. Select the Measure tool, which is located in the same tool set as the Eyedropper (I).

Starting at the upper-left corner of the left square, click and drag the Measure tool out past the upper-right corner of the right square.

Note: The longer the distance you draw to create your straight off-axis line, the more precise a measurement of the off-axis angle you get. This is why using the two horizontal lines in the square is a better choice than using a single vertical line.

Take a look at the Options bar and you will see that it will register the angle of this line to a within a tenth of a degree, here 1.4°.

signals is required to reproduce those actual colors on the destination device. You can think of the source profile as telling the CMS where the color came from, and the destination profile as where the color is going to.

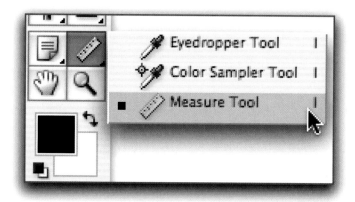

Figure 3-3
Profiles

A profile contains two sets of values, RGB or CMYK device control values, and the corresponding CIE XYZ or CIE LAB values that they produce.

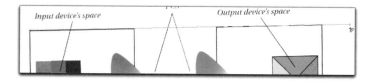

③ Rotate the image.

Choose Image⇨Rotate Canvas⇨Arbitrary.
The Rotate Canvas dialog box appears, and
here is the really good news: The off-axis
angle of 1.43° is automatically input into the
Angle field — precise to ¹⁄₁₀₀ of a degree, no
less! As a bonus, the CW (Clockwise) rotation
direction is also correctly selected for you.
Click the OK button to apply the rotation.

So if you're just awake enough to draw a
straight line (with the Straight Line measuring tool), and can locate the Rotate menu
choice, Photoshop will do the rest for you.

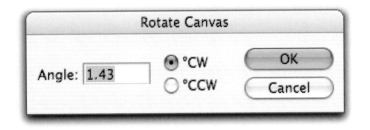

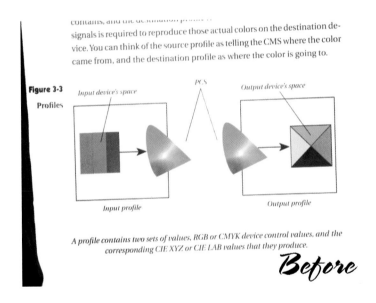

signals is required to reproduce those actual colors on the destination device. You can think of the source profile as telling the CMS where the color
came from, and the destination profile as where the color is going to.

Figure 3-3
Profiles

Input device's space   PCS   *Output device's space*

Input profile   *Output profile*

*A profile contains two sets of values, RGB or CMYK device control values, and the
corresponding CIE XYZ or CIE LAB values that they produce.*

Before

signals is required to reproduce those actual colors on the destination device. You can think of the source profile as telling the CMS where the color
came from, and the destination profile as where the color is going to.

Figure 3-3
Profiles

Input device's space   PCS   *Output device's space*

Input profile   *Output profile*

*A profile contains two sets of values, RGB or CMYK device control values, and the
corresponding CIE XYZ or CIE LAB values that they produce.*

After

Making Over to Remove Distractions

Being able to remove distracting or unwanted image elements is always a handy makeover skill. Photoshop is there to help, offering numerous tools — such as the Rubber Stamp tool (actually the Clone Stamp tool . . . but most people use the Rubber Stamp name), Healing and Spot Healing Brushes, and Patch tools — for doing just that. (Even the good old-fashioned Copy and Move commands can help in a pinch, so don't forget them.) The following makeover puts a few such tools through their paces, while highlighting "best practice" tips to help you put these tools to their best use.

① Open the Zip.tif image.

You'll immediately notice a very common unwanted distraction: the polygon-shaped *lens flare* that often occurs when you shoot a photograph at too high an angle to the sun.

Note: This image is available for download from the Web site associated with this book.

② Choose Image⇨Duplicate to make a duplicate copy.

Always, always work on a copy.

③ Choose Window⇨Info.

The Info palette makes an appearance.

④ Click the Eyedropper icon on the left side of the Info palette and select Grayscale from its contextual menu.

Set the Info palette to measure %K values.

⑤ Choose the Eyedropper tool from the Toolbox and set its sample size to 3 by 3 Average in the Eyedropper tool's Options bar.

This setting allows the Eyedropper tool to measure and display a grayscale value based on *nine* pixels in a 3x3 matrix, rather than on just a single pixel, which can often be misleading.

6 Move the Eyedropper tool over the image till it's just to the right of the flare.

The %K values appear on the left in the Info palette.

Note: The %K value is in the low 70s (73% here).

7 Now move the Eyedropper tool over the image till it's just to the left of the flare.

You'll see that the %K value that shows up in the Info palette is in the low 60s (61% here), a good 10% lower than on the right side of the flare.

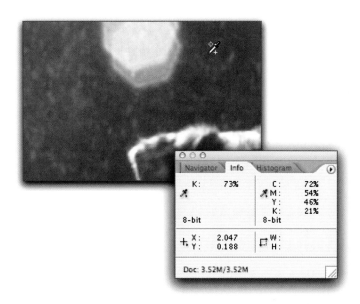

This difference in luminance value prevents you from simply covering up the lens flare by taking the Rubber Stamp tool and cloning from one side or the other — you'll end up with obvious edges if you go that route. And while you can sample multiple areas with a Feather brush and get the job done with the Rubber Stamp tool, the real tool of choice here — in my humble opinion — is clearly the Healing Brush tool. The Healing Brush does an especially good job of cloning content in an image that has significant differences in luminance values.

8 Select the Healing Brush tool from the Toolbox, and then use the tool's Options bar to configure the brush.

You'll want a large, hard-edged brush (70 pixels or so) with the Mode set to Luminosity and with the Sampled option checked as your Source.

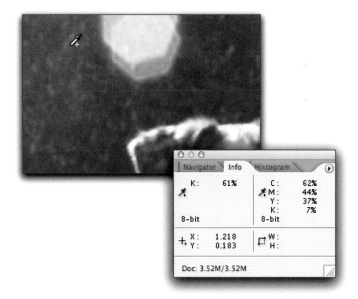

Making Over to Remove Distractions *(continued)*

9 Press the Opt/Alt key and then — using the Healing Brush tool — click the area you would like to clone.

As with all clone tools, first sample the area you'd like to clone and then paint the area to be replaced.

Here, pick an area far enough from the flare so you can paint the entire flare with a single set of painting strokes. Try your sample off to the right of the flare.

10 After sampling, release your keyboard keys — and then click, hold, and drag as you paint across the flare with *one* continuous set of back-and-forth strokes

Be sure to start your click-and-drag operation outside the flare, and continue until the flare is covered.

11 When finished, release your mouse button.

The painted pattern is going to look obvious while you're actually manipulating the Healing Brush, but the strokes disappear — along with the flare — when you're done using the tool.

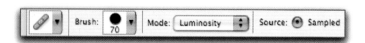

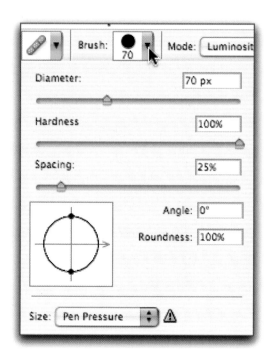

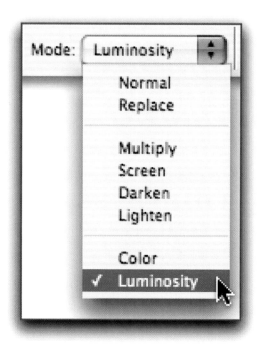

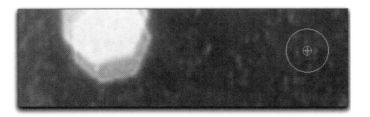

Before

After

Working with Clone Tools

Photoshop has a variety of Clone tools, including the Rubber Stamp tool, the Healing Brush, and the Spot Healing Brush. When you use one of these tools, pay attention to the Options bar settings, as these often determine the success or failure of an attempt to use a tool — as well as how hard you must work to achieve your results. More often than not, you'll find that using soft brushes with multiple strokes provides better results than trying to clone in one fell swoop. But there are always exceptions to any rule. In the makeover I

highlight here, you use a hard-edged brush with one application and the results are very good — better than, or at least as good as (and much faster than) those you'd get if you used a soft brush with multiple strokes. Be sure to experiment with your Mode settings — if one mode is not providing the results you want, try another. (Switching back and forth between Luminosity and Normal is a good strategy.) In other words, don't be afraid to try various settings or to break the rules once in a while.

Making Over Your Foreground Focus

The challenge for you as a rescuer of not-so-great photos is that many come to you with too much depth of field, that is, too much of the image in focus. If you pay close attention during shooting, you can defocus a portion of an image — often the background — during the image capture. But if (for whatever reason) this doesn't happen, you can do the defocus trick from within Photoshop. Here's an example:

1 Open the Joshua_Bloom.tif image.

Here you have two beautiful Joshua tree blooms captured in morning sunlight. (This image is available for download from the Web site associated with this book.)

The blooms here are in good focus. The background is somewhat out of focus (the result of an attempt to defocus the background by using a small f-stop value), but it isn't blurred enough to get the full defocus effect. In addition, the background is very busy — look at all those rock cliffs sporting interesting colors and shapes.

The cliffs, as nice as they are, tend to steal attention away from the blooms. The result is an image that is too confusing, with not enough focus on the Joshua tree blooms themselves — supposedly the image's main subject. The solution here is to defocus the background (as the photographer was trying to do in the first place).

2 Choose Image⇨Duplicate to make a duplicate copy.

You're doing some radical editing here, so only work on a copy.

3 Using the Lasso tool from the Toolbox, draw a rough outline offset from the entire Joshua tree.

You're setting this up to make a very feathered selection of this background content.

Taz's Take: Of course, the selection method you use depends on the image. Here, because there is so little contrast between the blooms themselves and the background (even on the individual channels), it's best to work with the standard Lasso tool. If you need a very tight selection and the image has poor contrast between subject and background, then the Magnetic Lasso tool is a dandy helpmate.

④ Choose Select⇨Inverse to inverse the selection.

The idea here is to select the background instead of the blooms.

⑤ Press the Q key (or click on the QuickMask button located at the bottom of the main Photoshop tool palette) to activate the QuickMask view.

Notice the hardness of the selection edge. This needs to be softened so the transition from the focused to the unfocused sections of the image will not be so abrupt.

⑥ Press the Q key again (or choose View⇨Normal) to return to the normal selection view.

⑦ Choose Select⇨Feather from the main menu and then type 100 in the Feather Radius field of the Feather Selection dialog box.

⑧ Click OK to apply the feather.

⑨ Choose View⇨QuickMask (or press the Q key) to reactivate the QuickMask view.

Now notice the softness of the selection edge. With the softer edge, you can provide

Making Over Your Foreground Focus *(continued)*

a gradual transition area in which to apply the defocusing.

⑩ Press the Q key again (or choose View⇨Normal) to return to the normal selection view.

⑪ Choose Select⇨Save Selection to save the feathered selection.

The Save Selection dialog box appears, at your service.

⑫ In the Name field of the Save Selection dialog box, type 100 Feather Background.

It's always a good habit to name your selections with info about how you created them, to help remind you later just what the heck you did!

⑬ Choose Window⇨Channels.

The Channels tab of the Layers palette appears, letting you know that, yes, indeed, your selection has been saved as an alpha channel. That done, you can recall it at any time — and/or duplicate it and edit it. Speaking of which, now is as good a time as any to duplicate the background layer.

⑭ Click the Layers tab in the same palette.

You'll note that the Background layer is locked — as the little Lock icon makes clear.

⑮ Double-click the Background layer listing in the Layers palette.

Doing so calls up the New Layer dialog box.

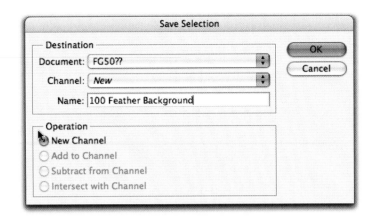

16 In the New Layer dialog box, type No Blur in the Name field and then click OK to apply this new name and unlock this layer.

The No Blur layer takes its place in the Layers palette.

17 Click and drag the No Blur layer over the New Layer Icon at the bottom of the Layers palette.

Doing so creates a brand-spanking-new copy of the No Blur layer. This is the layer you're actually going to feather.

18 Double-click the No Blur Copy layer in the Layers palette and then use the New Layer dialog box to rename it Blur.

19 Press Enter to apply the new name.

The Blur layer joins its kissing cousin (the No Blur layer) in the Layers palette.

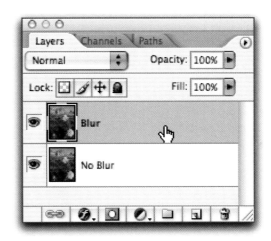

20 Click the Blur layer (to be sure it is selected) and then choose Select➪Load Selection.

The Load Selection dialog box makes an appearance.

21 In the Load Selection dialog box, choose the 100 Feather Background selection from the Channel drop-down menu, and then click OK to load that channel.

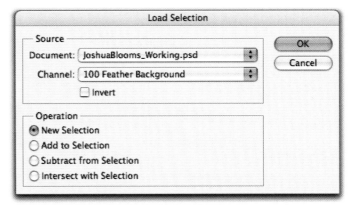

The 100 Feather Background selection you created (in Steps 7 and 8) loads into the Blur layer, creating a feathered (gradational) selection of the background on the Blur layer.

Making Over Your Foreground Focus *(continued)*

㉒ Choose Filter⇨Blur⇨ Gaussian Blur.

The Gaussian Blur dialog box makes an appearance.

Gaussian blurs are great for softening the image and creating a slightly out-of-focus look, which is exactly what we want here.

㉓ Press ⌘/Ctrl+H to hide the selection edge.

The idea here is that you want to see clearly how the blur affects the image and the feathered edge.

㉔ In the Gaussian Blur dialog box, type 5 in the Radius field, and then click OK to apply the blur.

A radius of 5 is a good choice here because it softens the image enough to decrease its emphasis but not so much that it creates a distraction. But feel free to use another value if you prefer.

Taz's Take: You can experiment with various combinations of feathering and blurring your selection to get a wide range of results. With the settings used here, the blur looks pretty good on the far background but it's a bit extreme in the near foreground. Not to worry. We planned ahead by creating two layers — Blur and No Blur — to mitigate this over-the-top blurring in the foreground.

㉕ Press ⌘/Ctrl+D to deselect the selection.

You're faced with a top layer with a blurred background and a bottom layer with no blurring. The trick now is to blend those two layers so they look natural together.

㉖ With the top Blur layer selected, click the Add Layer Mask icon located at the bottom of the Layers palette.

A white layer mask appears next to the Blur thumbnail in the Layers palette.

We're going to use the layer mask to blend the Blur layer from foreground to background with the underlying No Blur layer, to create a more realistic progressive increase in out-of-focus appearance as the eye travels into the background.

27 Click to select this layer mask, and then select the Gradient tool from the Toolbox.

The idea here is to use a gradient to gradually increase the blur as the image progresses into the background. Pure white in the layer mask will apply 100% of the Blur layer. Pure black will allow 0% of the Blur layer or 100% of the No Blur layer.

28 In the Gradient tool's Options bar, choose the White to Black gradient from the Gradient Picker.

White to Black is the default gradient, so this one is a no-brainer.

Note: You can also create your own custom gradient if you prefer.

29 With the layer mask selected, drag the White to Black gradient downward, from the middle of the image down to the top of the lower-left bloom.

Doing so causes a gradient to appear across the layer mask.

You'll notice that the blur grades from a maximum in the far background to a minimum right next to the lower-left bloom. Guess what? You've just blended the two images together. Now all you have to do is improve the contrast a bit by darkening the background.

Taz's Take: You can experiment not only with various kinds of gradients, but also

Making Over Your Foreground Focus *(continued)*

with various starting and ending points for applying those gradients.

③⓪ To darken the background, first click the Blur layer to be sure it's selected.

You are darkening the Blur layer rather than the No Blur layer because the layer mask is forcing this Blur layer to be visible in the background.

③① Choose Select⇨Load Selection.

The Load Selection dialog box reappears.

③② In the Load Selection dialog box, choose the 100 Feather Background selection from the Channel drop-down menu and then click OK.

The 100 Feather Background selection created in Steps 7 and 8 loads into the Blur layer.

③③ Click the Create New Fill or Adjustment Layer icon at the bottom of the Layers palette and then select Curves from the contextual menu that appears.

Doing so brings up the Curves dialog box.

Note: While it's true that you could just activate and use the Curve tool here directly, creating and using the Adjustment layer will provide nondestructive editability.

③④ In the Curves dialog box, click and drag the middle of the curve downward by two lines.

Doing so darkens the Feather Background selection.

③⑤ Click the OK button to apply this adjustment to the Blur layer.

Note that the background is slightly darkened, which further highlights the lighter

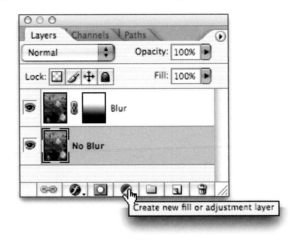

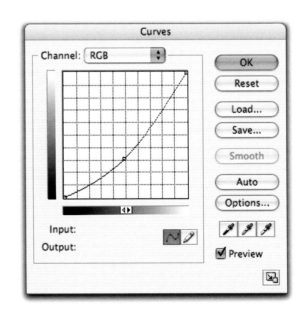

blooms in the foreground. (The effect will be even more impressive after you sharpen the blooms a bit.)

Also note that a Curves Adjustment layer has been added to the Layers palette. You can double-click this Curves Adjustment Layer icon at any time to adjust the effect of this Curves tool without making any permanent changes to the image. Only after the layers are ultimately flattened (on a *copy* of this image!) are the effects permanent. Adjustment layers provide safe, unlimited editablity to your layers.

36 **In the Layers palette, click the Blur layer to be sure it's selected, and then choose Select⇨Load Selection.**

Doing so calls up the Load Selection dialog box once again.

37 **In the Load Selection dialog box, choose the 100 Feather Background selection from the Channel drop-down menu and then click OK.**

The 100 Feather Background selection created in Steps 7 and 8 loads into the Blur layer.

38 **Choose Select⇨Inverse.**

Doing so shifts the selection to the foreground blooms.

39 **Choose Filter⇨Sharpen⇨ Unsharp Mask.**

The Unsharp Mask dialog box appears.

40 **In the Unsharp Mask dialog box, set the Amount to 100%, the Radius to 1.0 pixels, and the Threshold to 3.**

41 **Choose Image⇨Duplicate to make a duplicate copy of this image.**

Okay, two more steps.

Making Over Your Foreground Focus *(continued)*

㊷ With the Layers tab active, Choose Layer➪Flatten.

Doing so combines all the visible layers into one layer.

㊸ With the Channels tab active, drag each alpha channel to the palette's Trashcan icon.

Flattening this image (combining all the layers into one layer) and removing the alpha channels will significantly reduce the complexity and file size of this image, making it easier to display and print on all output devices.

Taz's Take: You can flatten your image and remove the alpha channels on the fly by choosing File➪Save As and deselecting the Layers and Alpha Channels check boxes in the Save As dialog box.

Now view your final makeover image and compare it to the original. Notice how the blooms are so much more prominent in the made-over image.

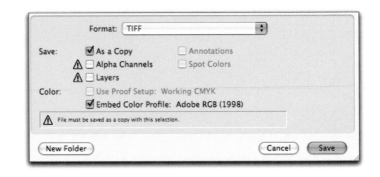

Doing a Vignette Makeover

Vignettes are a wonderful way to focus attention and communicate a soft feeling. There are lots of ways to create vignettes; here's one approach you can try, along with some general tips to think about.

① Open the Lavender_Birthday.tif image.

In this image — available for download from the Web site associated with this book — the flowers are a super-nice backdrop for the birthday greeting, but the greeting itself gets kind of lost in those big, bold flowers. One solution would be to make the type bigger, but a nicer solution is to make a vignette around the flowers.

Note that the type is on a separate smart layer. And while standard vignette procedure might include flattening the layers prior to making the vignette, in this case you keep the type as its own layer — while you're creating the vignette — so the type keeps all of its strength.

② Choose Image⇨Duplicate to make a duplicate copy.

Whatever editing you do, do it on a copy.

③ In the Layers palette, click the Background layer to select it.

④ Select the Elliptical Marquee tool from the Toolbox.

I think the Elliptical Marquee tool creates a pleasing vignette shape, but you can also use the rectangular marquee or create a custom selection using the Lasso tool.

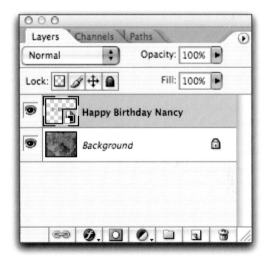

Doing a Vignette Makeover *(continued)*

⑤ Move your cursor over your image, park it in the middle of the type, press and hold the Opt/Alt key, and then click and drag your mouse out to form an elliptical selection from the center.

The idea here is to capture the text in the center of your ellipse.

⑥ Release your mouse button and Opt/Alt key when your selection is the size you want.

Be sure that you don't draw the edge of your initial vignette selection too close to the edge of the image — you want to avoid having your final vignette bump up abruptly against the edge of the image border.

⑦ Choose View➪QuickMask (or press the Q key) to activate the QuickMask view.

The QuickMask view lets you accurately view the edge of your selection.

Unless you've assigned a feather in the Marquee Options bar before creating your selection, you'll have a sharp-edged selection (like the one shown here).

Taz's Take: Normally you'll want to wait until you've drawn your selection before you feather the edge; after all, the size and shape of the selection influence which feather you assign. However, if you know in advance the feather you want to assign, then by all means assign it in the Options bar before you draw your selection — and you won't have to do it in the next step.

⑧ Press the Q key again or click on the QuickMask icon located at the bottom of the Toolbox to call up the normal selection view.

⑨ Choose Select⇨Feather.

The Feather Selection dialog box pops up.

⑩ In the Feather Selection dialog box, enter 20 pixels in the Feather Radius field.

A Feather Radius of 20 pixels is a good starting point, as this will create a significantly wide edge to the vignette. But feel free to experiment!

⑪ Press the Q key to reactivate the QuickMask view.

You're going to want to accurately view the edge of your newly feathered selection. (Looks pretty good, doesn't it?)

Note: You can experiment with various amounts of feathering and preview the results in QuickMask mode.

⑫ Choose View⇨Normal (or press the Q key again) to return to the normal selection view.

⑬ Choose Select⇨Invert to change the selection to everything *outside* the type area.

These are the parts (outside the type area) that you'll want to cover with a fill.

⑭ Choose Edit⇨Fill to activate the Fill dialog box. (Shift+Delete gets you here as well.)

Whichever method you choose, the Fill dialog box duly appears.

⑮ In the Contents section of the Fill dialog box, choose White from the Use drop-down menu.

White is a good choice to start with, as it is a bright neutral color that focuses all attention on the vignetted image. But feel free to experiment with other colors.

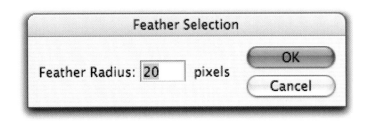

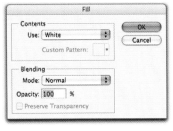

Doing a Vignette Makeover *(continued)*

⑯ In the Blending section of the Fill dialog box, choose Normal from the Mode drop-down menu and keep the Opacity at the default 100%.

Normal mode and 100% Opacity will apply the white color without an interaction with any underlying layer.

⑰ Click the OK button to fill the vignette mask with white, and then view the results.

This image should bring a smile to someone's lips.

One more thing to deal with: If you intend to print this vignette, you're going to want to test the edge of the vignette near the edge of the image to make sure the edge of the vignette peters out to a "0" value *before* it reaches the actual edge of the image. If it does not measure "0" before it gets to the edge, you'll likely see an abrupt termination when it prints.

And how do you test values near the edge? Why, with the Info palette, of course.

⑱ Choose Window⇨Info to activate the Info palette.

The Info palette stands to attention, ready to help.

⑲ Click the Eyedropper icon on the left side of the Info palette and then select Grayscale from its contextual menu.

⑳ Choose the Eyedropper tool from the Toolbox and set its sample size to 3 by 3 Average in the Eyedropper tool's Options bar.

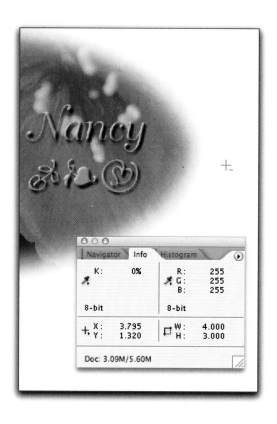

This allows the Eyedropper tool to measure and display a grayscale value based on an average of nine pixels in a 3x3 matrix, rather than on just a single pixel, which can often be misleading.

㉑ Move the Eyedropper tool around the edge of the vignette at the border of the image.

Make sure that the values in the Info palette measure K=0% or RGB=255.

㉒ Select the Crop tool from the Toolbox, drag it across your image, and resize it to your liking.

㉓ When you're satisfied with what you see, press the Enter key to apply the crop.

We still need to flatten a copy of your final image prior to using the duplicate image for output.

㉔ With the Layers tab active, Choose Layer⇨Flatten.

Doing so combines all the visible layers into one layer.

㉕ With the Channels tab active, drag each alpha channel to the palette's Trashcan icon.

Flattening this image (combining all the layers into one layer) and removing the alpha channels will significantly reduce the complexity and file size of this image, making it easier to display and print on all output devices.

Taz's Take: You can flatten your image and remove the alpha channels on the fly by choosing File⇨Save As and deselecting the Layers and Alpha Channels check boxes in the Save As dialog box.

150

What a Difference a Day Makes Makeover

Sometimes there is just no accounting for the weather . . . the day you take the picture of your house for the real-estate brochure, it's dark and moody and raining. (Yuck.) Here is how to change the day!

① Open the House.tif image.

This image is available for download from the Web site associated with this book.

Note that the sky in this image is pretty much nonexistent, except for a few nondescript gray clouds in the lower-right corner of the sky. The house and rest of the foreground end up just plain dull-looking. (Not a selling point at all.) So we need to add some good sky and liven up the house as well.

② Choose Image⇨Duplicate to make a duplicate copy.

You're going to do some major editing here, so do it on a copy.

③ Use Spacebar+⌘/Ctrl to zoom in on the lower-right corner of the sky — the part containing those boring gray clouds.

These guys add nothing to this image, so it's time to take them out.

④ Select the Magic Wand tool from the Toolbox and — using the tool's Options bar — set the Tolerance to 10 and enable the Anti-Alias and the Contiguous features.

⑤ Using the Magic Wand tool, click near the top edge of the gray clouds, and then press the Shift key and click your way down through the clouds until all are selected.

Make sure that you've selected all the gray cloud pixels — but *only* the gray cloud pixels.

Taz's Take: Use the Shift key and the Lasso tool to fine-tune your selection by adding or subtracting small areas. (Use the Shift key to add to, and the Opt/Alt key to subtract from, your selection as needed.)

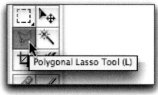

6 When you're finished, press the Delete key to remove the selected pixels.

Note how the anti-alias setting leaves a thin row of semitransparent pixels along the edge of the deleted selection. These transparent pixels are going to be important when you fit in your new sky.

7 Using the Polygonal Lasso tool from the Toolbox, draw a selection around the outside of the upper half of the camper.

The Polygonal Lasso tool makes straight-line selections, which is great for selecting straight-line, boxy things like campers.

8 Choose Select⇨Save Selection.

The Save Selection dialog box makes an appearance.

9 Type Camper in the Name field of the Destination section of the Save Selection dialog box.

10 Click OK to save the selection.

This saved selection takes its place in the Channels tab of the Layers palette, where it appears as alpha channel #4.

With this selection bagged and stored, it's time to make another selection.

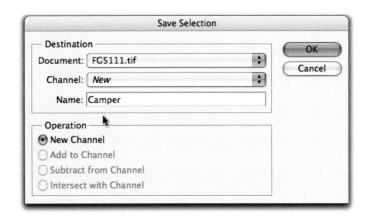

What a Difference a Day Makes Makeover *(continued)*

⓫ Select the Magic Wand tool from the Toolbox and — using the tool's Options bar — set the Tolerance to 30, enable the Anti-Alias feature, and *disable* the Contiguous feature.

Disabling the Contiguous feature allows you to select all the open spaces you see in the trees.

⓬ Using the Magic Wand tool, click the white sky background.

Doing so selects all of the sky, part of the truck, much of the white camper, a few sections of the dog run, and the white part of Zip the dog.

⓭ Select the Lasso tool from the Toolbox, press and hold the Opt/Alt key, and circle the selected portions of the truck, the dog run, and Zip.

The idea here is to *deselect* these particular pixels (areas of white that aren't sky) while leaving the white sky pixels selected.

⓮ Choose Select⇨Inverse to switch the selection to the house and the remainder of the foreground.

The idea here is to select the main (non-sky) portion of the image you want to edit.

⓯ Choose Select⇨Load Selection.

The Load Selection dialog box makes an appearance.

⓰ In the Load Selection dialog box, choose the Camper selection from the Channel drop-down

menu, click the Add to Selection button, and then click OK to load that channel.

Doing so adds the camper to the foreground selection.

17 With the Lasso tool and your Shift or Opt/Alt keys, clean up any stray areas that need to be added or subtracted from the selection, and then Choose Select➪Save Selection.

The Save Selection dialog box makes an appearance.

18 Type Foreground in the Name field of the Destination section of the Save Selection dialog box.

19 Click OK to save this selection.

This saved selection takes its place in the Channels tab of the Layers palette, where it appears as alpha channel #5.

20 In another image, use your favorite selection tool to select a more appealing (rectangular) bit of sky.

I'd use the sky in the Red Rocks_RGB.tif image, available for download from the Web site associated with this book.

21 Pressing the ⌘/Ctrl key, drag this selected portion of sky from your chosen image onto the house image.

The selection gets placed on its own layer (Layer 1) in the house image.

22 In the Layers palette, double-click this layer and rename it Sky.

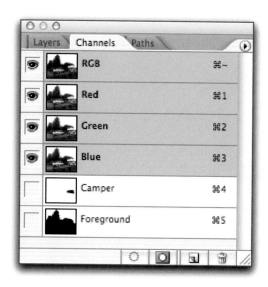

What a Difference a Day Makes Makeover (continued)

㉓ With the Sky layer selected, Choose Edit⇨Free Transform.

Four option points appear, one at each corner of the Sky layer.

㉔ Click and drag the four corners of the Sky layer until the layer covers all of the sky in the original House image.

㉕ Press the Enter key to apply the Resize transform.

The Sky layer takes on its new shape.

㉖ With the Sky layer selected in the Layers palette, click the drop-down menu in the upper-left corner of the Layers palette — where the current selection is Normal — and then select Darken.

Note how the sky fits nicely into the background of the old sky. Now the only problem is the white section of the camper.

㉗ Click the Sky layer in the Layers palette to select it and then choose Select⇨Load Selection.

The Load Selection dialog box makes an appearance.

㉘ In the Load Selection dialog box, choose the Camper selection from the Channel drop-down menu, click the New Selection button, and then click OK to load that channel.

The camper selection loads into the Sky layer.

㉙ Opt/Alt+click the Add Layer Mask button, located at the bottom of the Layers palette.

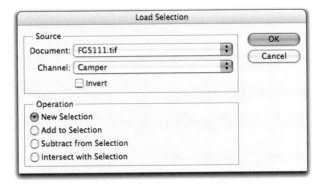

Doing so adds a layer mask to the Sky layer, with a knockout of the current camper selection. (The knockout is there to take the sky out of the camper.)

Looking good, but we still have some touchup to do.

③⓪ Click the Background layer in the Layers palette and then choose Select⇨Load Selection.

The Load Selection dialog box reappears.

③① In the Load Selection dialog box, choose the Foreground selection from the Channel drop-down menu, click the New Selection button, and then click OK to load that channel.

The entire foreground is now selected.

③② Click the Create Adjustment Layer icon (located at the bottom of the Layers palette) and then select Curves from the contextual menu.

The Curves dialog box makes an appearance.

③③ In the Curves dialog box, drag the midpoint of the curve up approximately 1.5 lines (about 15%).

③④ Click the OK button to apply the Curve adjustment to the foreground portion of this image.

Note that the foreground image area is much brighter now. Also note that a Curves Adjustment layer has been added to the Layers palette. This adjustment layer can be edited at any time — with no impact on image quality — simply by double-clicking the Adjustment Layer Curve icon. The effects of this layer are not applied until the image is flattened.

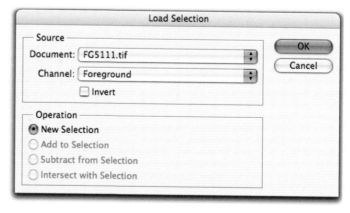

What a Difference a Day Makes Makeover (continued)

35 Now compare the finished image with the starting image . . . looks like a whole new day.

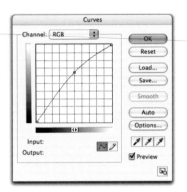

Before

After

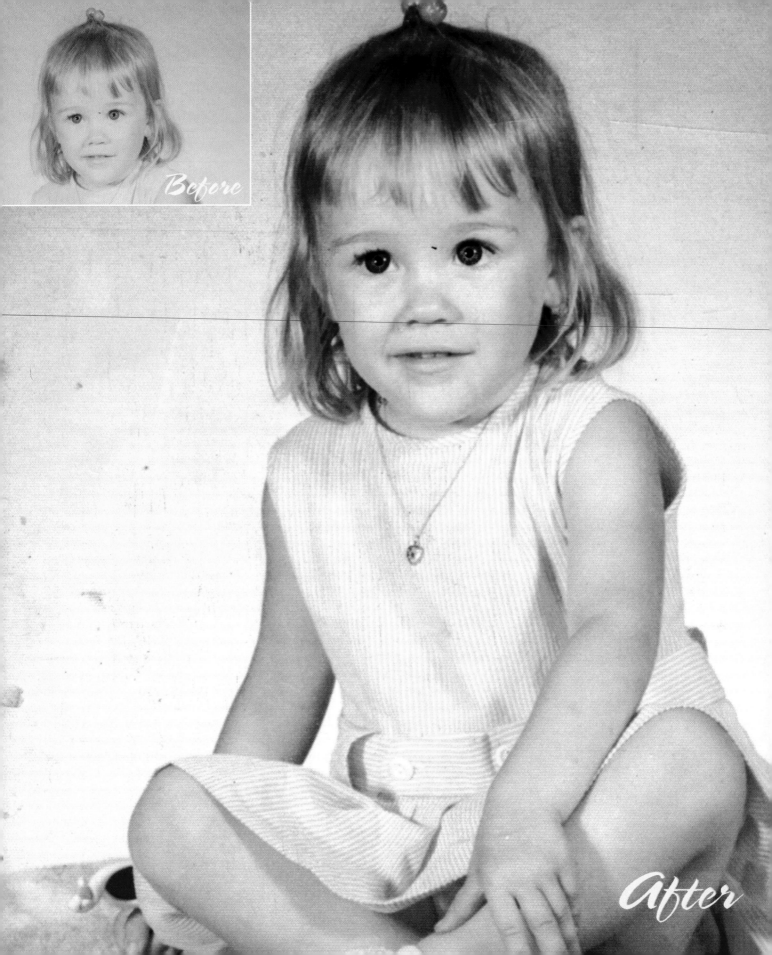

Before

After

6

REPAIR
MAKEOVERS

Life just has a way of doing damage to our images — and what's worse, you can't really just man the perimeters in hopes of keeping your images pristine, because this damage can attack from many different places. Dust and scratches can happen when film is mishandled. Blemishes can occur naturally or result from physical damage to photos. File compression — the scrunching of files when you convert an image to JPEG format , for example — can be a major source of image damage, as can "pushing" images using too high an ISO (or sensitivity) setting . Improper scanning — or even a slip when using an image editing application such as Photoshop — can impose some damage. And even the photographer's friend, the sun, can do some severe damage after the fact to your images. Every repair challenge is unique. Here you get a look at some approaches as well as specific skills that you can apply to many repair challenges.

One of the first steps in repairing a damaged image is to properly assess *what* the damage is. Then you will want to accurately identify *where* the damage is. And then you'll want to decide *which* adjustments and tools are best suited to repair the images, and finally work out the best order to perform your repair(s). Using the wrong tool or technique at the wrong time may result in more image damage. For instance, if you have an image that looks grainy, that graininess may be due to JPEG compression damage or it may be due to ISO push-related noise. Plus, the noise or graininess may be more on one channel than the other, which means you should focus your image repair on that one channel — thereby limiting the negative effects of the repair to just one channel. If your image is soft as well as grainy and you perform sharpening prior to mitigating the noise, the sharpening will only exacerbate the noise.

Faded-Image Makeover

Sunlight and oxygen can do some serious overall damage to photographic images. And if it's the color images in your portfolio under attack, you're going to see some very ugly color shifts as well, as the various pigments or inks that make up your images all get affected at different rates. (Talk about unpleasant surprises!)

Not to worry. With the help of Photoshop, you can deal with almost any surprise that sunlight and oxygen throw your way. Consider, if you will, the following example:

Fixing the Basics

❶ Open the Faded_Color.tif image.

As always, you can download this image from the Web site associated with this book.

This particular image has a number of repair challenges. It is obviously faded, its contrast is way too low, it has an enormous color cast — and it may be too soft or fuzzy and appear to be out of focus for some preferences, although that is a bit hard to really discern initially (due to the impact of all the other challenges).

❷ Choose Image⇨Duplicate to make a duplicate copy.

As problematic as this image is, you still want to work on a copy.

❸ Choose Window⇨Info to activate the Info tool.

The Info palette makes an appearance.

❹ Click the Eyedropper icon on the left side of the Info palette and select Grayscale from its contextual menu.

The Info tool can now measure grayscale values on %K (as in CMYK, where "K" stands for "key" but really means "black") when you move the cursor over the image.

⑤ Choose the Eyedropper tool from the Toolbox and set its sample size to 3 by 3 Average in the Eyedropper tool's Options bar.

This allows the Eyedropper tool to measure and display an average grayscale value of nine pixels in a 3x3 matrix, rather than just a single pixel, which can often be misleading.

⑥ Click and hold the Eyedropper tool in the Toolbox until the two "hidden" tools appear; select the "hidden" Color Sampler tool.

The approach here is to use the Color Sampler tool to measure an initial diffuse highlight and then use the measured and recorded grayscale values to create a reference point.

⑦ With the Color Sampler tool, click to sample the top of the sock in the image, which should be a neutral white. (RGB values of approximately 242,242,242.)

Clicking the top of the sock creates Color Sample Reference Point #1, which you'll see displayed in the lower-left corner of the Info palette. You can then refer back to this point when you adjust the image.

As you might have guessed, the RGB values here are way off of neutral, reading R=215, G=201, and B=163.

⑧ Choose Image⇨Adjustments⇨ Levels.

The Levels dialog box makes an appearance. You can see that the composite RGB histogram shows a major flat area on the shadow end and a small flat area on the highlight end.

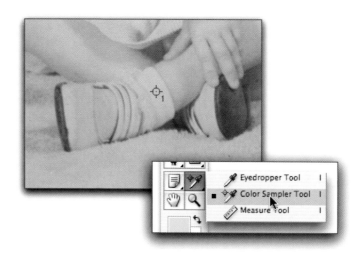

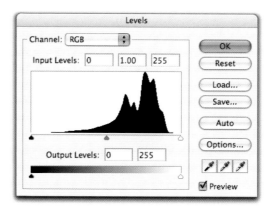

Faded-Image Makeover *(continued)*

Taz's Take: You *could* start by simply adjusting this histogram, but that would really miss the mark. The real image correction should occur on the individual channels. Channel-by-channel manipulations provide you with much more control over the data adjustment by allowing you to control each color channel separately. And many color casts are created by data that is offset from one channel to the next (as you will see below). Composite RGB channel adjustments maintain the relative positions of the data in all three channels, while channel specific adjustments allow you to move the data in each channel separately.

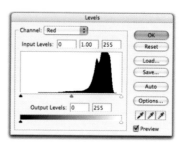

⑨ Take turns selecting the individual channels (Red, Green, and Blue) from the dialog box's Channel drop-down menu.

The idea here is to check out the histograms for each channel.

You can see that, in addition to large, flat gaps at the ends of both the highlights and the shadows, the starting and ending positions of each individual histogram are offset from the others.

First and foremost, let's dump the color cast by resetting the highlight and shadow points on Red, Green, and Blue channels, respectively.

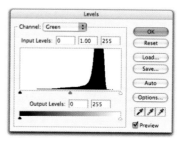

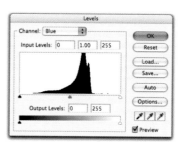

⑩ Choose Red from the Channel drop-down menu in the Levels dialog box.

The histogram for the Red channel appears in all its glory.

⑪ Slide the Highlight slider to the left until it's just under the place where the image-data values begin to rise.

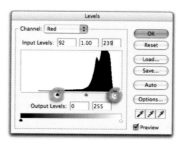

⑫ **Now slide the Shadow slider to the right until it's just under the place where the image-data values begin to rise.**

⑬ **Choose Green from the Channel drop-down menu in the Levels dialog box.**

Time for the Green channel histogram to make an appearance.

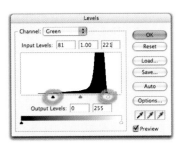

⑭ **Move the Highlight and Shadow sliders into positions analogous to where you placed the Red channel sliders.**

⑮ **Choose Blue from the Channel drop-down menu in the Levels dialog box.**

The ever-patient Blue channel histogram makes an appearance.

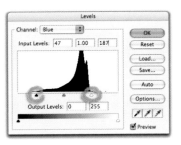

⑯ **Move the Highlight and Shadow sliders until they mirror where you placed the Red and Green channel sliders.**

We're making progress, but don't close the Levels dialog box yet.

In images with less damage, a simple realignment of the individual histograms is usually enough to neutralize at least the highlight of the image — and often the entire image as well. Here, the color casts are far more complex. To see what I mean, take another look at our diffuse highlight area and see what has happened.

⑰ **Examine Color Sample Reference Point #1 in the Info palette. (If the palette is not on-screen, choose Window⇨Info to call it up.)**

Faded-Image Makeover *(continued)*

No need to resample. The Info palette automatically pairs your new values resulting from the changes you've made alongside the old values, with the new values on the right.

The values here (R=221, G=228, B=217) are an improvement over the initial RGB ratios (R=215, G=201, B=163), but they're still not neutral — which implies a complex color cast in the image. To take care of that, you'll need to make this diffuse highlight neutral.

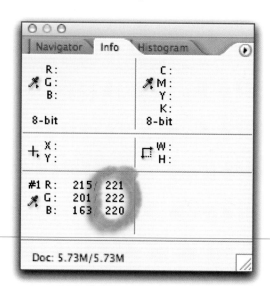

⓲ Choose Green from the Channel drop-down menu in the Levels dialog box, then slide the Highlight slider to the right until the G value in the #1 Color Sampler in the Info palette reads 221.

Since this is not a 5% highlight (242 on the 0–255 scale) — and making it so would blow out other areas of this image — you'll want to choose a target value. As a rule, the intermediate value (in this case 221, the Red value for Color Sample Point #1) is your best bet.

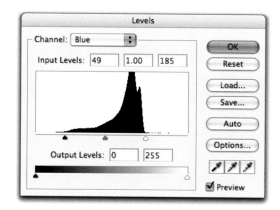

⓳ Choose Blue from the Channel drop-down menu in the Levels dialog box, then slide the Highlight slider to the right until the B value in the #1 Color Sampler in the Info palette reads approximately 221.

⓴ Click the OK button to apply the Levels changes.

You'll immediately notice a marked improvement in the image.

Zeroing In on Skin Tones

Any Photoshop professional out there will tell you that getting skin tones correct is a key goal in any makeover. Repair makeovers are no exception, so it wouldn't hurt to

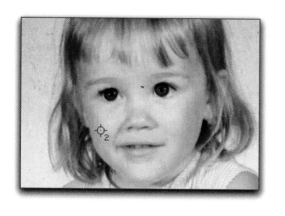

evaluate skin tones in our Fade_Image.tif example:

① With the Info palette visible, first move the Color Sampler tool over the middle of the right side (image left) of the face, then click to establish Color Sample Point #2.

Note that the RGB values here are R=216, G=201, B=152.

These values meet the basic requirement for normal Caucasian skin — a set 5/4/3 ratio between the Red, Green, and Blue values — but because there's not enough separation between the values themselves, the skin still looks a bit sallow.

R: 196	C: 23%	
G: 205	M: 12%	
B: 218	Y: 7%	
	K: 0%	
8-bit	8-bit	
X: 0.473	W:	
Y: 1.273	H:	
#1 R: 221	#2 R: 216	
G: 222	G: 201	
B: 220	B: 152	

Doc: 5.73M/5.73M

Photoshop Confidential

Skin Tones

Obviously, people of different nationalities and/or racial backgrounds have different skin colors. But the good news is that if you're dealing with a human being, the general ratio of R>G>B will hold true. Now, a red-headed Irishmen will likely have more red and less green than an Asian female whose skin tones will likely contain a bit more green than the Irishman. So, if you want to adjust your image to have a bit more or less red based upon the nationality (or degree of sunburn present) you can do this. A couple of other tips to keep in mind: a) the darker the skin, the less separation you will typically see between the RGB values, and b) babies tend to have redder skin than adults — adults tend to have higher blue+green (yellow) values.

There is not just one set of skin-tone values that work in all circumstances and lighting conditions. Try this the next time you are walking through an airport: Find a newsstand and stand in front of the woman's magazine section of the magazine rack. Now take a gander at the range of skin tone values that you see. They are all different and they all look human, and in all of them, R>G>B. Many magazines have their own sets of skin-tone values that they prefer — it's a way to create a consistent look and feel in their images — and I often ask a publication if they have a distinct ratio in mind when I am creating images for them. If you have multiple skin values in one image, pick one with which you are familiar and correct your image for that. The differences in the other skin tones will automatically take place as they will be captured differently from each other to begin with. So if you get one right, the other will usually follow. You can of course always make selections of individual skin-tone areas and correct them individually. (Now, if you have photos of Klingons or Cardassians . . . well, all bets are off on the R>G>B.)

Faded-Image Makeover *(continued)*

Taz's Take: You'll find that meeting the RGB 5/4/3 ratio is going to be difficult in images with both severe and complex color casts. Don't despair — you can adjust things so you get an increased separation between the RGB values, even if it means ending up with a different ratio. In images with large color casts, you may want to try a 6/5/4 RGB ratio or even a 7/6/5 ratio.

② Choose Image⇨Adjustments⇨ Curves.

Doing so calls up the Curves dialog box.

Again, the standard 5/4/3 RGB ratio isn't helping in this particular situation, so it might pay to try a 7/6/5 RGB ratio. If you leave the Red value alone at 216, that would leave you with 186 as your Green value and 155 as your Blue value.

Here's where you can check my math:

$216 \div 7 = 31$

$31 \times 6 = 186$ = target Green value

$31 \times 5 = 155$ = target Blue value

Taz's Take: You may want to create two (or even three) Color Sampler measurement locations, or at least sample around a bit with the normal Eyedropper, to make sure you're using representative skin-tone color values.

③ In the Curves dialog box, choose Green from the Channel drop-down menu.

Doing so calls up the adjustment curve for the Green channel.

④ With the Info palette visible, pull the Green curve down until the G value in the #2 Color Sampler reads approximately 185.

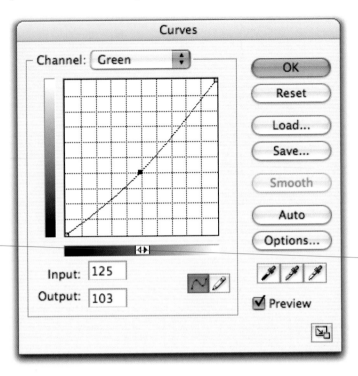

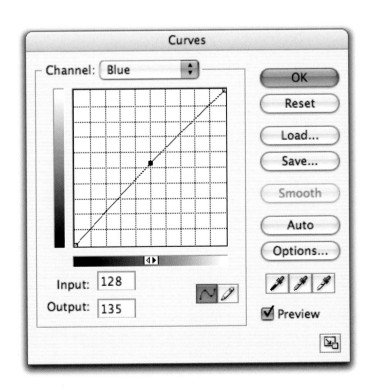

⑤ Back in the Curves dialog box, choose Blue from the Channel drop-down menu.

The adjustment curve for the Blue channel appears on-screen.

⑥ With the Info palette visible, pull the Blue curve down until the B value in the #2 Color Sampler reads approximately 155.

⑦ Click the OK button to apply the Curves adjustments.

Now when you check out the image you'll notice that it no longer looks too sallow. The skin tones have a healthier red tone to them, as a comparison with our starting image makes clear.

The Challenges Remaining: Revisiting the Neutrals

If you're under the impression that there's always something left to tweak, you're probably right. For example, in our Faded_Image.tif image, after you complete the adjustment of the skin tones, you'll notice that the RGB values of Color Sampler #1 are no longer equal. The Red value (221) and the Blue value (223) are now greater than the Green value (214). This is because the luminance range of the skin is actually close to that of the shoes.

No doubt about it — color-correcting the skin tones threw the neutrals out of whack. This is due to the complexity and extent of the color cast in the image, and can best be fixed by isolating (either mechanically with a feathered selection or by using the Color Range selection tool) and color correcting several portions of this image separately. If you do not have the time for this type of isolation and correction, then you may decide that the skin tones are the most important feature of the image and focus on correcting those.

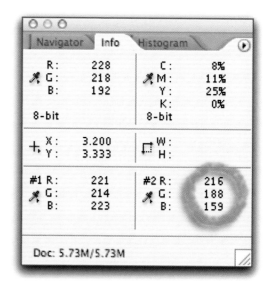

Color Blemish-Removal Makeover

Not surprisingly, many makeovers involve the removal of unwanted flaws and blemishes. Photoshop provides numerous tools to help with this task — including a set of brush tools that are especially good at it. To put these tools through their places, let's take another stab at Faded_Image.tif.

❶ Open the (corrected version of) Faded_Color.tif image.

For this exercise, start out with the version resulting from all the hard work we did in the first part of this chapter. You're going to want to adios the numerous blemishes plaguing this image — many of which now have an unpleasant red cast.

❷ Choose Image⇨Duplicate to make a duplicate copy.

We worked long and hard on this image, so play it safe and work on a copy.

❸ Select the Healing Brush tool from the Toolbox.

Doing so calls up the Options bar for this tool.

❹ Using the Options bar, select a soft-edged brush large enough to cover most of the blemishes.

Note that you can change the size of the brush on the fly by using the [ ] keys.

❺ Still in the Options bar, choose Lighten from the Mode drop-down menu and then click the Sampled radio button in the Source section.

You're selecting Sampled as your source here because you want to use an unblemished area of the image as the source for your correction data. As for Lighten, you choose that because blemishes here tend to be darker than the unblemished area.

⑥ Press Opt/Alt and then use the Healing Brush tool to click a blemish-free area close to one of the blemishes.

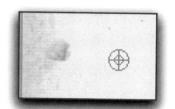 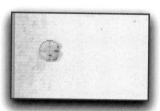

The idea here is to sample the color values of an area close to a blemish.

⑦ Release the Opt/Alt keys and then click once with the Healing Brush tool on a blemish.

The clicked area lightens momentarily, and then the blemish disappears.

Going the Spot Healing Brush Route

Among the numerous tools that Photoshop provides for removing flaws and blemishes from color images, the Spot Healing brush is especially well suited to this type of restricted blemish repair. To check out its effectiveness, do the following:

① Select the Spot Healing brush from the Toolbox.

As you'd expect, doing so calls up the tool's Options bar.

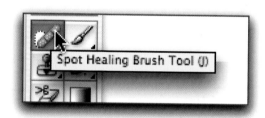

② In the Options bar, make sure the brush size is 50% larger in diameter than the blemish you intend to remove.

Doing so ensures ample sampling data.

③ Still in the Options bar, choose Normal from the Mode drop-down menu and set the Type to Proximity Match.

Lighten mode will work here as well, but Darken and Multiply definitely won't, and Luminance *almost* works. The mode you select depends upon the relationship between the blemish and the surrounding

Color Blemish-Removal Makeover *(continued)*

area. I typically start with Normal (which works in most circumstances) and then select another mode depending upon what does or does not happen when I apply the Normal setting. For instance, if my Normal repair results in a color shift, I try Luminance next. Proximity works here because you want the area surrounding the blemish to supply the repair data.

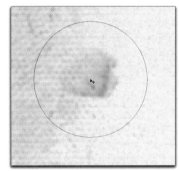

④ Now just move the Spot Healing brush over a blemish and click it once.

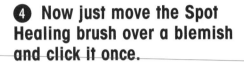

Using the Spot Healing brush is a single-step process — the brush samples and then removes the blemish all in one step.

Photoshop Confidential

Healing with Healing Brushes

All the Healing Brush tools (the Healing Brush proper, the Spot Healing brush, the Red Eye tool, and the Patch tool) are terrific choices when editing blemish areas like those seen in this particular makeover. The Healing Brush tools are at their best and most useful when you want to make (at times significant) changes in the hue and saturation of small areas, while maintaining local luminance values. Just keep in mind that Healing Brush tools work best when used on *small* areas, using either the point-and-click method I demonstrate in this makeover or going with small strokes. Avoid making long strokes, as streaking may sometimes result.

Scratch-Removal Makeover

Okay, the Healing Brush tool is a seemingly all-powerful tool that you'll find yourself using a whole lot. But variety is the spice of life, so let me show you one more blemish-removal technique you might find useful.

① Open the Little_Taz.tif image.

Note that this image (available for download from the Web site associated with this book) has several blemish challenges — including a scratch across the tie, a disruption of the background, and a crease across the forehead.

② Choose Image⇨Duplicate to make a duplicate copy.

As problematic as this image is, you still want to work on a copy.

③ Using Spacebar+⌘/Ctrl, zoom in on the scratch across the tie, and then select the Clone Stamp tool from the Toolbox.

As is the case whenever you select a tool, calling up the tool also calls up the tool's Options bar.

④ In the Options bar, set the Brush size so it is slightly larger then the scratch is wide, choose Normal from the Mode drop-down menu, and set the Opacity to 75%.

The reduced Opacity setting here is important; it helps ensure that the stamped edges don't look too obvious.

Note: You can adjust your brush softness and opacity to achieve the results you like.

Scratch-Removal Makeover *(continued)*

⑤ Hold down the Opt/Alt key and then click with the tool on a spot away from the scratch, to establish a source for the cloned image data.

Try to choose an area with similar luminance and texture.

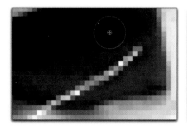

⑥ Release the Opt/Alt key, move the cursor over the right end of the scratch, and then click and drag over a short segment of the scratch.

You're going to make this repair in stages, so go over only a short segment.

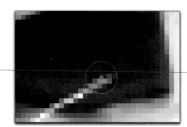

⑦ Resample from a slightly different source location and repeat the clone procedure.

You'll need to work over each section more than once, but doing so reduces the likelihood of creating any obviously cloned edge.

⑧ Repeat this cloning process along the entire length of the scratch (paying close attention to choosing good clone source locations) until the scratch is removed.

You may want to use single point-and-click clone steps — rather than dragging over segments — to prevent/remove any possible cloned edges. Also, it's a good idea to frequently change your cloning source to prevent the creation of any visible patterns.

Note: I often try both the Clone Stamp tool and one of the Healing Brush tools to see which type works best on any given challenge.

Background-Repair Makeover

For repairing consistent backgrounds, sometimes the simplest, low-tech tools and techniques are the best. Here's an easy way to fix the background in the Little_Taz.tif image.

❶ Using the Spacebar+⌘/Ctrl, zoom in on the background area.

❷ Select the Lasso tool from the Toolbox.

As expected, calling up the tool also calls up the tool's Options bar.

❸ In the Options bar, set the Feather to 3 pixels and enable the Anti-Alias feature.

The 3-pixel feather is essential if you want to create an undetectable edge.

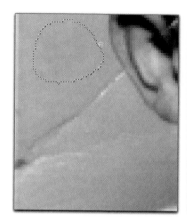 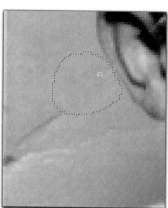

❹ Using the (feathered) Lasso tool, draw an irregularly shaped area over an undisturbed section of the background.

Again, try to choose an area with similar luminance and texture.

❺ Press ⌘/Ctrl+Opt/Alt and then click and drag the feathered selection over a portion of the disturbed background.

⌘/Ctrl+Opt/Alt are the keyboard shortcuts for the tried-and-true Duplicate and Move functions.

❻ Repeat this Duplicate-and-Move process until the background disruption is repaired.

I'd recommend overlapping the cloned and duplicated (or moved) areas.

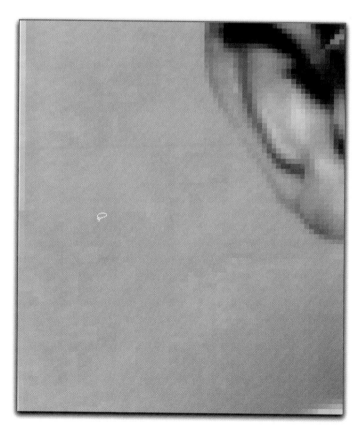

Crease Repair

Here's a little trick for those hard-to-repair cases like the nasty crease in the Little_Taz.tif image. (Want a hint? You're using a combination of an old technique and new tool.)

❶ Choose Window⇨Layers to activate the Layers palette.

The idea here is to create a Little Taz Blur layer.

❷ In the Layers palette, click and drag the Background layer over the Make New Layer icon.

Doing so creates (surprise, surprise!) a new layer.

❸ Again in the Layers palette, double-click the name of the new layer and rename it Blur.

❹ With the Blur layer selected, choose Filter⇨Blur⇨Gaussian Blur.

Doing so calls up the Gaussian Blur dialog box.

❺ In the Gaussian Blur dialog box, type 1.0 in the Radius field and then click the OK button.

The blur is applied to the layer.

❻ Select the Healing Brush tool from the Toolbox.

As expected, calling up the tool also calls up the tool's Options bar.

Note: You can try this with the Clone Stamp (also know as the Rubber Stamp) tool as well.

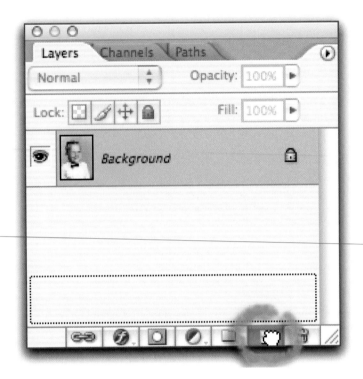

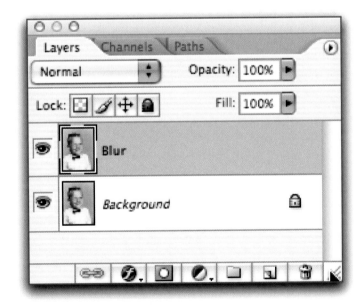

7 In the Options bar, set the Brush size so that it is slightly larger in diameter than what you want to clone, choose Normal from the Mode drop-down menu, choose Sampled in the Source section, and enable the Aligned option.

 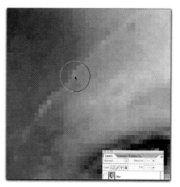

8 Using the Spacebar+⌘/Ctrl, zoom in on the crease on the Blur layer.

9 Press Opt/Alt and click the blurred crease.

Doing so samples the blurred zone of the pixels.

10 Back in the Layers palette, first hide the Blur layer (by clicking the eyeball on that layer to toggle off its visibility) and then click on the Background layer to activate it and zoom in on the crease.

You'll want to zoom in on the same area of the crease you sampled when you were working on the Blur layer.

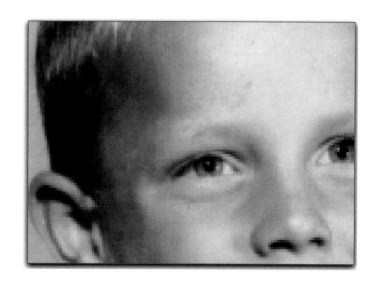

11 Drag the Healing Brush tool across the crease to remove it.

Use a combination of short strokes and single point-and-click strokes.

You can also try sampling the Background layer directly, if the Blur layer sampling does not work in all cases.

Note: On some segments in some images, you may want to switch to the Clone Stamp tool and work from the Blur layer as well, with the Clone Stamp tool set at 50% to 75% opacity.

Now compare the final repaired image with the initial one.

Before   *After*

"Removing the Years" Makeover

One of ways nature inexorably affects us — in the process effectively highlighting the steady march of time — can be seen in the lines and wrinkles that mark our faces (especially around the eyes). Now, Photoshop can't do anything to heal the actual effects of time's ravages, but it can do a lot to wipe away some of those years from a photographic chronicle. This makeover shows you how.

❶ Open the Age_Repair.tif image.

As always, you can download a copy of this image from the Web site associated with this book.

❷ Choose Image⇨Duplicate to make a duplicate copy.

Always, always work on a copy.

❸ Using Spacebar+⌘/Ctrl, zoom in on the left eye (image right).

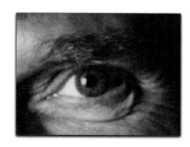

You'll notice a number of age-based wrinkles, just crying out to be removed. (Be sure to zoom in tight so you can see the wrinkles in detail.)

Photoshop Confidential

The Blessing of Unsharpened Images

When you're editing an image to remove stuff like age wrinkles, it's just better all around if you work with an image that hasn't been sharpened. Sharpening increases contrast along edges in an image — edges much like, well, wrinkles. This increase in contrast makes these features even more prominent — and therefore more difficult to excise. This is one of many reasons *not* to apply sharpening to your original image. (If you absolutely *must* sharpen an image, be sure to save an unsharpened version that you can use later for editing purposes if you have to make some adjustments.)

4 **Select the Healing Brush tool from the Toolbox.**

Doing so automatically calls up the tool's Options bar as well.

5 **In the Options bar, set the Brush size to 15 pixels, choose Lighten from the Mode drop-down menu, choose Sampled from the Source section, and then enable the Aligned feature.**

If you look closely, you'll see that the large horizontal wrinkle is created by a darkening of the skin; choosing Lighten as your mode should remove this dark crease.

6 **Press Opt/Alt and then click to sample on the light skin area, just above the wrinkle.**

7 **Release your mouse button and Opt/Alt key, then click and drag over the dark horizontal wrinkle.**

Be sure to use short strokes, working your way through most of the horizontal wrinkle until it begins to thicken significantly at its right end.

8 **Press Opt/Alt again, and this time click to sample the area below the wrinkle.**

9 **Release your mouse button and keys, and then continue the healing strokes over the right side of the wrinkle.**

10 **Now select the Clone Stamp tool from the Toolbox.**

Doing so calls up the tool's Options bar.

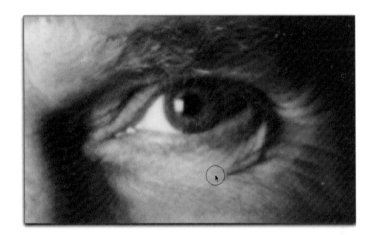

"Removing the Years" Makeover *(continued)*

⓫ In the Options bar, select a small, soft-edged brush, choose Normal from the Mode drop-down menu, set the Opacity to 75%, and engage the Aligned option.

Setting the opacity to 75% helps prevent any obvious clone duplications. You will find that using multiple passes with several clone sources will help you achieve good results with no obvious repeating areas.

⓬ Using the Clone Stamp tool, sample the small, fine-line wrinkles just below the eyes.

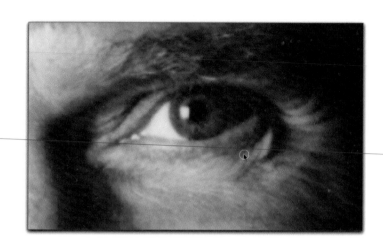

⓭ Clone these small fine lines through the area you just "repaired" using the Healing Brush tool.

The idea here is to add some natural-looking skin texture to the area.

⓮ Repeat this same procedure with the small fine-line wrinkles, targeting the area below where you worked with the Healing Brush tool.

Doing so removes some of these wrinkles as well and provides a more gradual transition to the surrounding skin area.

⓯ Repeat Steps 3 through 14, this time targeting the right eye in the image.

After taking care of the right eye, you've probably done as much wrinkle removal as you can get away with. If you take away too much, it won't be credible.

Now compare the finished version of the image with the initial version. As you can see, you've managed to remove the wrinkle effects of quite a few years.

Before

After

Alternate Method

In some cases, it's best to darken rather than lighten when you're doing wrinkle removal. For example, in the Age_Repair.tif image, as you approach the left side of the left eye (image right), the average luminance values darken considerably. Here, you'd want to switch form lightening to darkening adjustments. Here's how:

❶ Select the Healing Brush tool from the Toolbox and choose Darken from the Mode drop-down menu in the tool's Options bar.

❷ Using the Healing Brush tool, sample from the dark area of the wrinkle and then darken the lighter areas.

Try using short strokes as well as a simple point-and-click technique.

Work from both the darker (image right) and lighter (image left) side to blend these two areas together.

❸ Select the Clone Stamp tool from the Toolbox.

As always, doing so calls up the tool's Options bar.

❹ In the tool's Options bar, select a small, soft-edged brush, choose Normal from the Mode drop-down menu, and set the Opacity to 75%.

❺ Sample the small, fine-line wrinkles just below the eyes.

They're the ones that trend from the lower right up toward the left.

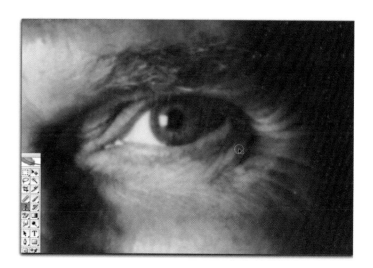

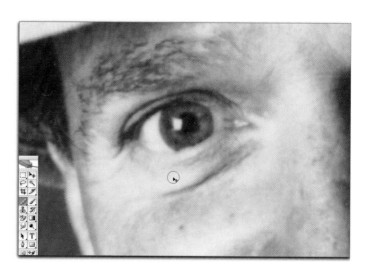

"Removing the Years" Makeover *(continued)*

6 **Clone these small fine lines through the area where you used the Healing Brush tool.**

Again, you want to create some natural-looking skin texture.

7 **Repeat this same procedure with the small, fine-line wrinkles near the corner of the eye.**

These trend from lower left to upper right, into the darker area.

8 **Repeat Steps 1 through 7, this time targeting the right eye in the image.**

The only trick here is to remember that you have to switch back to Lighten mode in the Options bar when you use the Healing Brush tool.

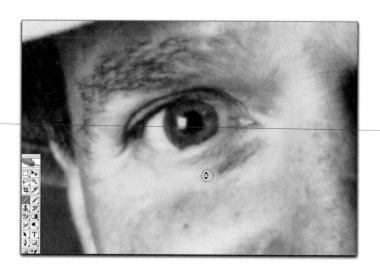

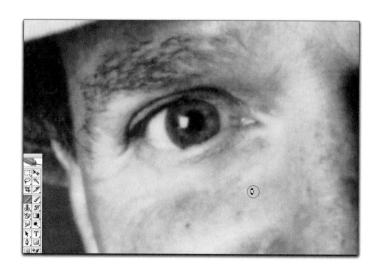

Making Over to Remove JPEG Posterization

Most images that digital cameras create in default automatic-capture mode are saved in JPEG file format. That usually makes sense, but keep in mind that saving images saved in JPEG format are automatically compressed — in a manner that removes image data — so the image loses some of its quality. (For the curious out there, the compression technique used in JPEG conversion is called *lossy* because of this loss.) Depending on the camera's quality setting, this compression can be significant — and its impact quite severe. Application of too high a level of JPEG compression can cause *posterization*, which creates a noticeable pattern in the image . . . and applying sharpening filters to highly compressed images only makes things worse.

Check out the following makeover for a better way to reduce JPEG-related posterization.

❶ Open the JPEG_Damage.tif image.

Feel free to download this image from the Web site associated with this book.

❷ Choose Image⇨Duplicate to make a duplicate copy.

As true now as it was ten minutes ago: You really want to be sure to work on a copy.

❸ Using the Spacebar and ⌘/Ctrl, zoom in on the area of JPEG damage.

The area in question is situated around the left eye (image right) of the strapping young man in the photo (my cousin Mark).

With the help of the Zoom feature, you can clearly see a rectangular pattern on the image — consisting of a 12x12 group of pixels. This is the posterization pattern created

Making Over to Remove JPEG Posterization (continued)

by the JPEG compression — and that's what we want to get rid of.

❹ Choose Filter⇨Blur⇨Gaussian Blur.

Doing so calls up the Gaussian Blur dialog box.

❺ In the Gaussian Blur dialog box, set the radius initially to 0.1, and then click the OK button.

Monitor how the adjustments affect your image.

❻ Start to raise the radius in 0.1 increments.

At about 0.3, you'll see a dramatic visual change as the blurring smooths the pixels out, dramatically reducing posterization.

You'll want to apply just enough blur to remove the posterization pattern . . . and no more. If you apply too much blur, image sharpness suffers. Even here, applying this 0.3-radius Gaussian Blur has noticeably softened the image. Time to fix that.

❼ Choose Filter⇨Sharpen⇨ Unsharp Mask.

The Unsharp Mask dialog box makes an appearance.

The idea here is to restore some of the image sharpness that was removed by the application of the Gaussian Blur.

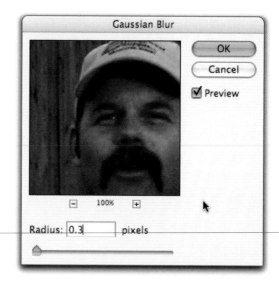

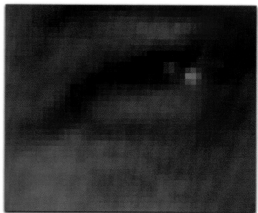

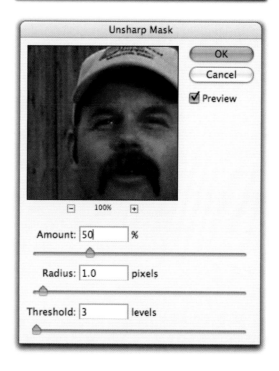

⑧ In the Unsharp Mask dialog box, set the Amount at 50%, the Radius at 1 pixel, and the Threshold at 3 levels, and then click the OK button.

Notice how the posterization has not returned.

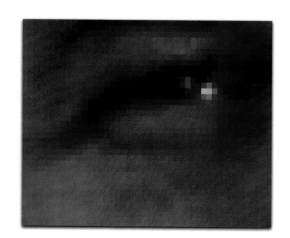

Photoshop Confidential

JPEG, Blurring and Sharpening

Posterization caused by JPEG compression can be very severe . . . and sharpening the image only makes it worse. The reason for this is that in a JPEG image, posterization forms high-contrast edges along the borders of the 12 x 12 groups of pixels, as well as *between* the individual pixels. These high-contrast edges are then thrown into even higher contrast by the application of the sharpening, when tends to "look" for high-contrast edges and make them even more so. Bottom line: Don't apply sharpening to a highly JPEG compressed image unless you have removed most of the posterization *first*.

The Threshold value in the Unsharp Mask dialog box also helps prevent the return of the posterization by limiting the sharpening (that is, contrast enhancement) to only those pixel pairs and edges that have at least 3 pixels of difference in their grayscale values — and that's prior to applying any sharpening. So the order in which you apply the blurring and softening (blurring first, and then sharpening . . . NOT sharpening and then blurring) is indeed critical. You may get into the habit (as I have) of just not using sharpening on images that have had significant amounts of compression applied to them . . . that way you avoid the sharpening-related posterization altogether.

Of course, from a quality, and workflow, standpoint, you're better off avoiding JPEG images altogether (if you can — some cameras don't give you that option) and saving your initial image in a lossless format (camera raw, of TIFF). You can always compress your image later, after you've worked over your image, if you do need a JPEG version.

Before

After

7 COLOR-MODE MAKEOVERS

One very handy — dare I say fundamental? — makeover skill is making effective, well-chosen changes to the color mode of an image. One such technique involves changing from color to grayscale for the purposes of printing in grayscale/B&W. Sure, you could just print a color image on a B&W printer — and the paper emerges in B&W, but typically the results are not satisfying. The same can be said for converting 24-bit RGB print images to 8-bit Web images. Achieving the results you want is all about controlling the makeover process, rather than just accepting a default or random result.

So, in this makeover chapter you'll find out about several makeover techniques for converting color images to grayscale. (Why several? Because knowing more than one makeover method allows you to choose the version that best suits your fancy.) I'll also walk you through several makeover methods for converting grayscale images to color, another handy tool set to have. And, for good measure, I'll introduce you to desaturation — and show you how you can use it to create some eye-catching images.

Making Over Color to Grayscale

If you don't much care how things turn out, you can certainly move from color to grayscale just by choosing Image⇨Mode⇨ Grayscale and taking what Photoshop gives you — or you can do the job right by taking control of the color-to-grayscale process, and get the results you really want. I'll show you both methods and let you decide.

Default-Mode Conversion

This is the Take-What-Photoshop-Wants-to-Give-You method. Sometimes you'll end up with acceptable results, but often not (and personally, I'm not a Settle-for-What-They-Give-You kind of guy). Nevertheless, here's what it looks like:

❶ Open the Sunset_RGB.tif image.

As always, you can download this image from the Web site associated with this book.

❷ Choose Image⇨Duplicate to make a duplicate copy.

Name this first copy Sunset GS Mode.

❸ Choose Image⇨Mode⇨ Grayscale.

The resulting grayscale image is Photoshop's default conversion to grayscale.

This may be an okay image for your immediate needs, but perhaps the overall contrast is a bit less than what you'd want. Let's see what else we can create without digging too deep into Photoshop's bag of tricks. (We don't want to have to call up all those Curves and Levels dialog boxes right this minute.)

Single-RGB-Channel-Mode Conversion

Here you can take your pick from among the three (already-existing) grayscale images that make up the RGB color channels.

❶ Open the original Sunset_RGB.tif image and make another copy by choosing Image⇨ Duplicate.

Name this second copy Sunset GS Red Mode.

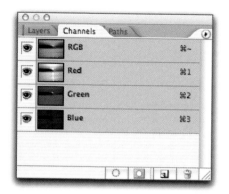

This image has a strong color cast, which means we could probably come up with *several* distinct grayscale-image versions simply by working with the individual channels.

❷ Choose Window⇨Channels.

Doing so activates the Channels palette.

❸ In the Channels palette, click the Red channel.

The Red channel appears on-screen.

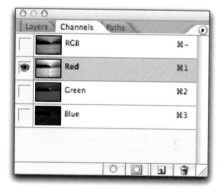

❹ Choose Image⇨Mode⇨ Grayscale, then respond Yes when Photoshop asks whether you want to discard the other channels.

You have just created a single-channel grayscale version image based on the Red channel.

Note: You can opt to turn that prompt about whether or not you want to discard the other channels off so it will stop pestering you.

I like the look of this here, but having more options out there never hurt anyone, so let's try for another grayscale image version, this time based on another channel.

Making Over Color to Grayscale *(continued)*

⑤ Repeat Steps 1 and 2.

This time, make another copy of the original RGB image and name the copy Sunset GS Green Mode.

⑥ In the Channels palette, click the Green channel.

The Green channel appears on-screen.

⑦ Choose Image⇨Mode⇨ Grayscale, then respond Yes when Photoshop asks whether you want to discard the other channels.

You have just created a single-channel grayscale version image based on the Green channel.

Note: Again, you can opt to turn off that prompt about the other channels.

Okay, with Red and Green out of the way, it's time to turn to Blue.

⑧ Repeat Steps 1 and 2 and name your new copy Sunset GS Blue Mode.

Repeating Step 5 works as well.

⑨ In the Channels palette, click the Blue channel.

The Blue channel appears on-screen.

⑩ Choose Image⇨Mode⇨ Grayscale, then respond Yes when Photoshop asks whether you want to discard the other channels.

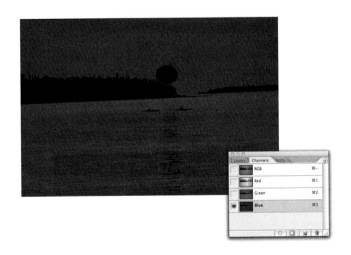

You have just created a single-channel grayscale version image based on the Blue channel.

Now compare and contrast all three RGB-channel-based grayscale images and select the one you like best . . . or (if you decide not to) continue with later sets of steps to see more conversion options.

Lab Mode Conversion

Unlike an RGB color image in which the luminance values are spread across all three channels, Lab mode is a three-channel color image mode in which all the luminance values are isolated on one channel, the L or luminance channel. The color values are concentrated on just two channels, the a and b channels. In this makeover technique, you'll only be concerned with the L channel, as the a and b channels just provide weird looking grayscale images.

Taz's Take: When you're working in Lab mode, you can isolate all the grayscale values on one channel, which provides you with another option for creating a grayscale image — an option that produces different results than any of the individual RGB channels, or than the straight mode conversion.

❶ Open the original Sunset_RGB. tif image and make another copy by choosing Image⇨Duplicate.

Name this new copy Sunset Lab GS.

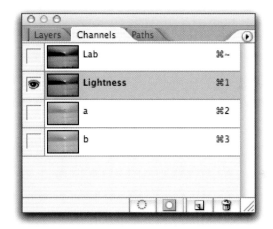

❷ Choose Image⇨Mode⇨Lab Color.

Doing so converts your image to Lab mode, which concentrates all the luminance

Making Over Color to Grayscale *(continued)*

(grayscale) values on one channel, the Lightness channel. (The color values are actually mixed together on the a and b channels, but just now we're only interested in the Lightness channel.)

If your Channels palette is not already visible, click on the Channels tab in the Layers palette to view the Lab channels.

③ In the Channels palette, click the Lightness channel.

④ Choose Image⇨Mode⇨ Grayscale, then respond Yes when Photoshop asks whether you want to discard the other channels.

You have just created a single-channel grayscale version image based on the Lightness channel.

Note: You can again opt to turn that warning off (in fact, if you haven't already checked that Don't Show Again box, you have a greater tolerance for annoying messages than I do).

So you have yet another version of the grayscale image, but we're not quite done yet.

Desaturate-Mode Conversion

Going the Desaturate route simply tosses out all the color values.

① Open the original Sunset_RGB. tif image and make yet another copy by choosing Image⇨ Duplicate.

Name this copy Sunset Desaturate GS.

② Choose Image⇨Adjustments⇨ Desaturate.

Doing so desaturates your image — and in the process, creates three identical channels.

Before

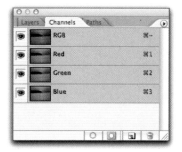

❸ Choose Image⇨Mode⇨ Grayscale.

The three identical channels merge into one (grayscale) channel.

Often, when you desaturate a typical RGB image, you end up with results not much different from what you'd get from a Mode or Lab conversion. But when you desaturate an image with a high degree of color cast — such as the sunset image you see here — you may achieve some interesting results.

Channel-Mixing Conversion

To make this conversion happen, you mix the characteristics of the three distinct channels. The steps go like this:

❶ Open the Gladiolus.tif image.

As always, you can download this image from the Web site associated with this book.

❷ Choose Image⇨Duplicate to make a duplicate copy.

Name this copy Glad Mix GS.

If you try to create a grayscale image here using one of the four methods covered earlier in the chapter, you won't be pleased with any of the results. The gladiolus would end up too dark or too light, and the native contrast of this particular image in grayscale mode isn't good. It turns out, though, that each channel has something to recommend it, and (luckily for us) we can easily mix them so the final result ends up more than decent. (Take a look at the three individual channels to see what I'm talking about.)

❸ Choose Image⇨Adjustments⇨ Channel Mixer.

Doing so calls up the Channel Mixer, a dialog box you can use to mix the RGB channels according to any set of percentages you can come up with.

Red channel

Blue channel

Green channel

Making Over Color to Grayscale *(continued)*

❹ Configure the Channel Mixer.

Given that the Red channel has the brightest version of the main gladiolus — so bright that it's blown out in the lightest area — you'll want to let the Red channel serve as the major component. The Green version would be good to mix with the bright glad on the Red channel. The Blue channel is very dark and low-contrast by itself, but can offer some good dark contrast.

Note: Before proceeding though, be sure to check the Monochrome button located at the bottom of the dialog box.

So, experiment with various percentages to see the effects. You may want to start out by trying Red at 70%, Green at 30%, and Blue at 10%.

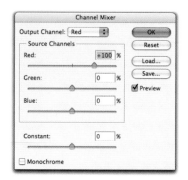

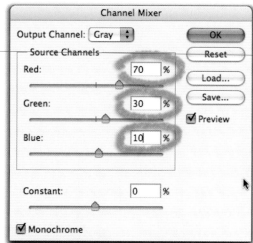

❺ Click the OK button in the Channel Mixer dialog box to apply your percentages.

Doing so creates a three-channel image with three *identical* channels.

The 70/30/10 combination gets you the results you see in the margin here — not bad at all, much better contrast than you would have gotten using any of the other methods I've shown you so far in this chapter.

Taz's Take: Please keep in mind that my version here isn't the only "good" version out there; you may find other mixing percentages you prefer.

❻ Choose Image⇨Mode⇨ Grayscale.

With this command, you merge the three identical channels into one.

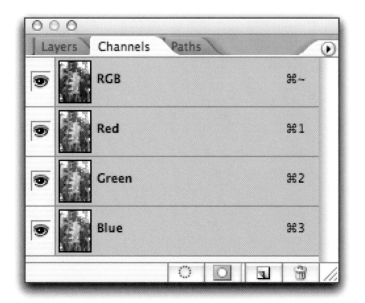

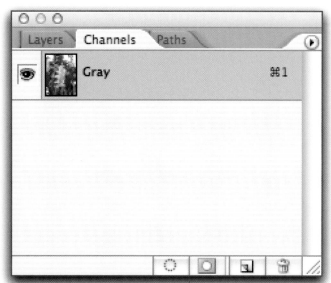

Photoshop Confidential

Grayscale vs. Color Capture

People often ask me the following question: "If what I really want to end up with is a grayscale image, shouldn't I capture in grayscale rather than color?" Well, after working through the makeovers in this chapter, you can answer this question as well as I; the answer looks like this: "Capture in color, or more specifically RGB color, because if you capture in grayscale, all the choices have already been made for you. If you capture in RGB color, YOU get to decide what to keep and what to toss."

Taz's Take: You should always start this conversion process from RGB and not from CMYK. CMYK channels are not conducive to creating grayscale images. (Take a peak at the Cyan, Magenta, and Yellow channels and you'll see why.) This one fact alone is enough reason to a) never convert to CMYK right off the bat, and b) always store an archival version of your image in RGB mode to maintain your creative and conversion options.

Making Over Grayscale to Color

There are numerous ways to colorize grayscale images, and this particular makeover does its best to show you as many ways as possible.

Painting Grayscale from an Original RGB Image

Here you start with an RGB image, convert it to grayscale, and then paint *some* of the original RGB colors back in.

❶ Open the Gladiolus.tif image.

As always, you can download this image from the Web site associated with this book.

❷ Choose Image⇨Duplicate to make a duplicate copy.

After you have made a copy, save it to disk; having a saved image is required for this first section.

❸ Using the Channel Mix method from the previous section, convert this image to single-channel grayscale.

❹ Choose Windows⇨History to call up the History palette.

The History palette appears listing all the things you've done so far to this particular image: image duplication, channel mixing, and then conversion to a single-channel grayscale image.

❺ Choose Image⇨Mode⇨RGB.

Doing so adds two more channels to your image — so you end up with the requisite three (RGB) channels.

Keep in mind here that you are *not* returning to the original RGB image; rather, you've just added two other (identical) chan-

nels to your grayscale image — all three channels are alike as peas in a pod. This is a totally neutral RGB image, just waiting for you to add color.

⑥ Select the History Brush tool from the Toolbox.

Using the History Brush tool, you're free to paint in some image characteristics from a previous step. Here you use the History Brush tool to paint in color from the original image.

⑦ In the History palette (with the current RGB Color event selected), click the check box to the left of the original color image.

Doing so lets you borrow some color from your original RGB image so that you can then paint it on the RGB grayscale image.

Note: Be sure to click the check box to the left of the image in the History palette — NOT the actual Gladiolus RGB 300 entry in the palette.

⑧ Using the Options panel for the History Brush tool, set the Brush size to 60, the Mode to Normal, and both the Opacity and Flow to 100%.

You'll want to paint large sections at a time, so 60 is a good choice for the Brush size.

⑨ With your newly configured History Brush tool, paint in the gladiolus with the previous color.

Using long strokes, start out in the center of the gladiolus.

Note that the History palette records every stroke you make.

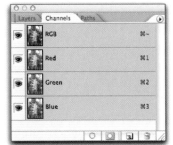

Making Over Grayscale to Color *(continued)*

⑩ Click and drag using your Spacebar and ⌘/Ctrl keys, zoom in on the image, and reduce the size of your brush to paint in the edges of the gladiolus.

Remember that you can use the [and] keys to change the size of your brush on the fly.

Keep painting until you have a fully colored gladiolus.

⑪ Using both the Magic Wand tool and the Lasso tool, select just the gladiolus part of the image.

For the Magic Wand tool, try Tolerances ranging from 50 to 10; for the Lasso tool, try a 1-pixel feather.

⑫ Choose Select⇨Feather.

The Feather Selection dialog box appears.

⑬ In the Feather Selection dialog box, set the Feather Radius on this selection to 2 pixels and then click OK.

Doing so should help create a smooth, gradated border on the gladiolus selection.

⑭ Choose Select⇨Save Selection.

The Save Selection dialog box appears.

⑮ In the Save Selection dialog box, name the selection Glad, select the New Channel radio button in the Operation section, and then click OK to save the selection as an Alpha channel.

You'll return to reload this selection in a few steps.

Keep this image open for the next Makeover technique.

Making Over by Painting with Color

Got the gladiolus image from the previous exercise handy? Good, because we're going to try something new with it. Clearly, you are free to add any color you've taken away from an image back into the image. But the point here is that you can also just paint with any color of your choice. You can select a color you'd like to use — from another image, for example — or you can mix one up yourself.

Start out by borrowing a color from another image. Here's the drill:

❶ With the gladiolus image you painted with the History Brush tool still open, open the Leaf_RGB.tif image.

As always, this image is available for download from the Web site associated with this book.

❷ Select the Eyedropper tool from the Toolbox, set its Average Sample size to 3 x 3, and then click the dark upper-right side of the middle lobe of the leaf to capture the dark green color as the foreground color.

This sampled green leaf color will show up in the Photoshop toolbox as the foreground color.

Note: If you have a Brush tool activated, you can simply hold down the Opt/Alt key to activate the Eyedropper tool.

❸ Click the gladiolus image to activate it.

The green leaf color (captured from the leaf image) is still the foreground color for the Eyedropper tool.

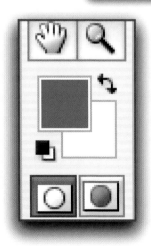

Making Over by Painting with Color *(continued)*

④ Select the Brush tool from the Toolbox and configure the tool's Options bar so the Mode is set to Color.

Using the Color mode (rather than Normal mode) maintains the original luminance values — and therefore the texture of the painted area.

⑤ Click and drag using the Spacebar and ⌘/Ctrl keys, to zoom in on the long grass stems in the lower-right area of the image.

The idea here is to substitute the green from the leaf for the greens you see in the original image.

⑥ In the Brush tool's Options bar, select an appropriate brush size (here it's 10 pixels), and begin painting the grass stems.

Note that the underlying texture is preserved as you paint.

⑦ Continue painting the grass until you are satisfied with your paint job.

Believe me, it's a lot easier than painting the bedroom.

⑧ Choose Select⇨Color Range.

Doing so calls up the Color Range dialog box.

⑨ Choose Sampled Colors from the dialog box's Select menu.

The idea here is that you want to select only the green from the leaf.

⑩ In the Preview window of the Color Range dialog box — and using the default Eyedropper tool — click the grass you just painted and set the Fuzziness to 200.

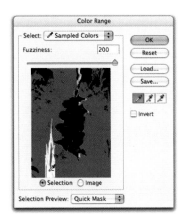

This Fuzziness value is a range of selection values similar to the Tolerance value of the Magic Wand tool.

⑪ Click the OK button to select the green grass.

⑫ With the Lasso tool from the Toolbox selected, press Opt/Alt to encircle and remove any extraneous selection areas.

⑬ Choose Select⇨Save Selection.

Doing so calls up the Save Selection dialog box.

⑭ In the Save Selection dialog box, name the selection Grass, select the New Channel radio button, and then click OK to save the selection as an Alpha channel.

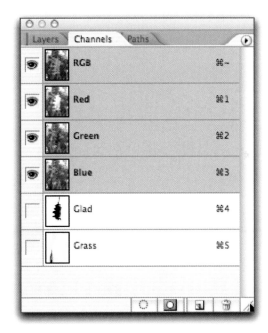

You use this grass (and the gladiolus selections you saved previously) in the next section.

Colorizing with Curves

In addition to painting, you can use curves to apply color to an image. In this section, you'll use the Curve tool to apply color to the remainder of the gladiolus image — the parts that have not yet been colorized.

Before you colorize the remainder of the image, though, you'll want to protect what you've already painted, so start off by doing that. . . .

❶ Choose Select⇨Load Selection.

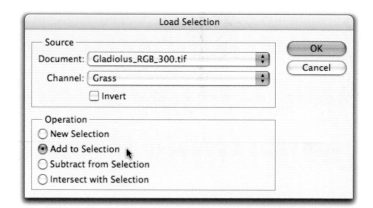

The Load Selection dialog box makes an appearance.

❷ In the Load Selection dialog box, select Glad from the Channel menu.

Doing so selects the painted glads.

❸ Choose Select⇨Load Selection again, but this time select Grass from the Channel menu and click the Add to Selection radio button.

Now both the glads and the grass are selected in the image.

❹ Choose Select⇨Inverse.

Doing so selects the remainder of the image, leaving the prepainted sections out in the cold. You're free to do some colorizing, using the Curves dialog box.

❺ Choose Window⇨Layers.

The Layers palette appears on-screen.

6 **Click the Adjustment Layer button (the half black/half white button located at the bottom of the Layers palette) and select Curves from the contextual menu that appears.**

A Curves layer appears above the Background layer in the Layers palette, and a Curves dialog box joins the palette on-screen.

7 **In the Curves dialog box, select Green from the Channel drop-down menu and then pull the middle of the Green curve down 10%.**

Doing so adds a slight magenta cast to the nonpainted portions of the image.

8 **Back in the Curves dialog box, select Blue from the Curves drop-down menu.**

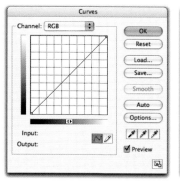

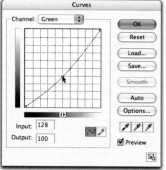

9 **Click the middle of the Blue curve to hold that point — a black control point will appear — and then pull the highlight end of the Blue curve all the way to the bottom.**

Doing so paints all background-highlight portions of the image yellow. (The blue is being removed from all the highlight areas.)

Note: Be sure to flatten and remove alpha channels from a COPY of your final image prior to use, while keeping a fully editable version for creating other color re-creations. This can be done quickly and easily by unchecking the Layers and Alpha channels check boxes in the Save As dialog box when saving the file.

Colorizing with Curves *(continued)*

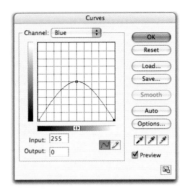

Before

After

Making Over Focus Attention by Desaturating

One very interesting, often subtle —
but always effective — attention-getting
makeover technique is to desaturate the
less important parts of an image. Here's an
example:

**1 Open the Whale_Tale.tif
image.**

As always, you can download this image
from the Web site associated with this book.

Now, this is a perfectly good picture of a
whale's tail, but — to be honest — some
of the impact gets lost simply because the
whole image has the same blue-green color
cast. Now you could go about adjusting colors . . . or, since the real focus of this image
is the tail, you can just desaturate the rest of
the image. (Which way sounds easier? Care
to guess?)

**2 Choose Image⇨Duplicate to
make a duplicate copy.**

Always, always work on a copy.

3 Choose Window⇨Channels.

Doing so activates the Channels palette.

**4 In the Channels palette,
select the Blue channel to work
with.**

The idea here is to make the process easier
by switching to one of the grayscale channels to make your selection. The Blue channel has the best contrast between the tail
and its surroundings.

**5 Select the Magnetic Lasso
tool from the Toolbox.**

Doing so automatically calls up the tool's
Options bar.

Making Over Focus Attention
by Desaturating *(continued)*

⑥ In the Options bar, set the Magnetic Lasso tool by checking the Anti-Alias check box and entering 1 pixel in the Feather field.

The Magnetic Lasso tool is a good choice here because it will do a good job of closely following and selecting the edge of the whale's tail.

⑦ Using your newly configured Magnetic Lasso tool, draw a path around the whale's tail.

⑧ When you have nearly completed your selection path, double-click with the Magnetic Lasso tool to complete the selection.

After your selection is made, save the selection so you can recall it and use it at any time.

⑨ Choose Select⇨Save Selection.

The Save Selection dialog box appears.

⑩ In the Save Selection dialog box, name your selection Whale Tale, click the New Selection radio button, and then click OK to save the selection.

The Whale Tale selection is now saved as an Alpha channel mask.

⑪ Choose Select⇨Inverse.

Doing so selects everything in the image outside the whale-tail selection.

⑫ Choose Window⇨Channels.

The Channels palette comes to attention again.

⑬ Select the RGB channel to activate the RGB view.

Note that the selection you made on the Blue channel is transferred just fine to the composite RGB display.

⑭ Choose Image⇨Adjustments⇨ Desaturate.

The entire image outside of the tail is now grayscale. Notice how the (colored) tail now pops out in contrast to the grayscale background.

Not bad at all, but we can tweak it a bit to make it look even better. We could, for example, increase the focus on the tail still further by sharpening the tail and/or blurring the background . . . heck, let's do both! Since the background is already selected, let's start there.

⑮ Choose Window⇨Layers.

Doing so activates the Layers palette.

⑯ Click the Layers palette menu and select Duplicate Layer from the menu that appears.

The Duplicate Layer dialog box appears on-screen.

⑰ In the Duplicate Layer dialog box, name this layer the Blur Layer and then click OK.

A new (duplicate) layer is created — and gets added to the Layers palette.

⑱ With the background still selected, choose Filter⇨Blur⇨ Gaussian Blur.

Doing so calls up the Gaussian Blur dialog box.

Making Over Focus Attention by Desaturating *(continued)*

⑲ In the Gaussian Blur dialog box, set the Radius to 1–2 pixels and then click OK.

Don't go overboard with the radius here. You can always bump it up later if you need to.

Note that the whole non-tail portion of the image is blurred. The blurred background looks good, but the blurred foreground looks a bit over the top. So let's modify the foreground blur with a layer mask to *gradually* increase the blurring toward the back of the image.

⑳ With the Blur layer selected in the Layers palette, click the Add Layer Mask button (located at the bottom of palette).

Doing so adds a layer mask to the Blur layer.

㉑ Select the Gradient tool from the Toolbox.

As is always the case, choosing the tool calls up its Options bar.

㉒ In the Options bar, select a default White to Black linear gradient, set the Mode to Normal, set the Opacity to 100%, and check both Dither and Transparency boxes.

㉓ With the layer mask selected in the Layers palette, click and drag the Gradient tool from about the middle of the image down to about 4 inches past the bottom edge.

Why extend beyond the bottom edge of the image? Because doing so grades the blur from a small amount in the foreground to maximum blur, starting about halfway up the image. This looks more natural and believable.

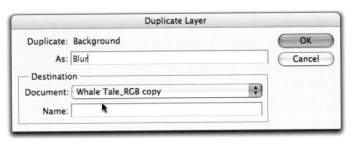

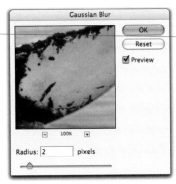

With the blurring out of the way, it's time to sharpen the tail. You probably lost your Whale Tale selection during the last layer-mask routine, though, so you'll have to retrieve it before you can do anything else.

24 Choose Select⇨Load Selection.

The Load Selection dialog box appears.

25 Choose Whale Tale from the Channel drop-down menu, select the New Selection radio button, and then click OK.

The chosen selection loads on-screen.

26 Choose Filter⇨Sharpen⇨ Unsharp Mask.

The Unsharp Mask dialog box appears.

27 In the Unsharp Mask dialog box, set the Amount between 50 and 100%, the Radius to 1 pixel, and the Threshold somewhere between 0 and 3.

I have chosen 3 here so I don't apply the sharpening to the smoothest areas of the tail.

Again, be sure not to overdo it here; a little sharpening goes a long way.

Now take a look at your final image and compare it to the initial image.

Note how the tail is really highlighted in the final version. Now if this is too much contrast for you, you can always fade the desaturation or partially desaturate the tail, or . . . well, you get the idea.

Prior to final output, be sure to flatten and remove your alpha channel from a COPY of this image, keeping at least one fully editable version for later modification.

Remember, this can be done quickly and easily by unchecking the Layers and Alpha channels check boxes in the Save As dialog box when you save.

Doing Duotone Makeovers

One really classy way to draw attention to your image is to create a *duotone* — an image created by adding/substituting an additional ink (or inks) to your image. Creating a duotone is really more about adding tonal richness than it is about adding color, but it is also a less expensive way (compared with printing in full color CMYK) to add color to an image while at the same time enhancing its tonality. Here is how to create a good-quality duotone:

❶ Open a good-quality grayscale image.

The Barn GS image, available for download from the Web site associated with this site, would be a good choice.

❷ Choose Image⇨Duplicate to make a duplicate of the image.

Always work on a copy.

❸ Choose Image⇨Mode⇨ Duotone.

The Duotone Options dialog box appears.

❹ In the Duotone Options dialog box, select Duotone from the Type drop-down menu.

Doing so activates a second ink field (Ink 2), complete with a curve and a color box. And this is where the uninitiated go astray: DO NOT click the color box just to the right of the Ink 2 curve. Instead, use a precreated duotone ink-curve set; Step 5 creates one.

Note: You have the option of creating tritones and quadtones as well, which utilize three and four inks, respectively.

❺ Click the Load button on the far-right side of the Duotone Options dialog box.

The Load window appears on-screen.

❻ In the Load window, navigate to the Pantone Duotone folder, select the Pantone 478 brown 100% bl 1 ink-curve set, then click the Load button.

Photoshop loads the brown ink (and its curve) as well as the black ink (and its curve).

Note that the Pantone Duotone folder is located in the Adobe Photoshop Preset folder. Note also that there are four ink-curve sets for each color; the number-1 sets have the largest addition/substitution of the Pantone color.

Taz's Take: If you have a specific color in mind for creating your duotone, but you don't see the color listed, try a similar color as a starting place.

❼ Back in the Duotone Options dialog box, click once on the black ink curve.

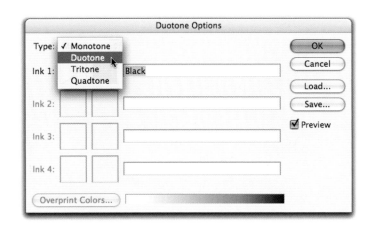

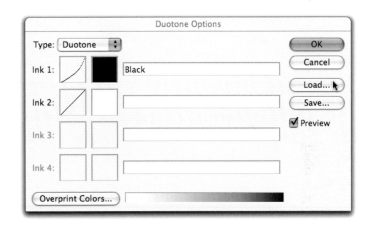

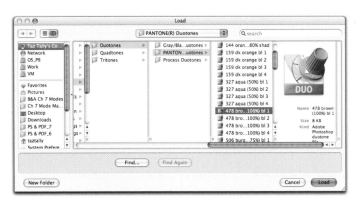

Doing Duotone Makeovers *(continued)*

The Duotone Curve dialog box for that color appears.

Note how the middle of the black curve has been significantly lowered (for instance, the 50% black is lowered to 30%).

8 Click OK to close the Duotone Curve dialog box for the black ink.

9 Back in the Duotone Options dialog box, click once on the brown ink curve.

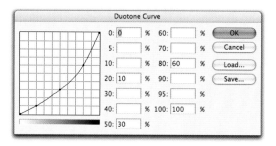

The Duotone Curve dialog box for brown appears.

Note how the brown ink curve is only slightly reduced — 50% lowered to 40% — but also how this ink stops at 90%. This sudden stop is to prevent your shadows from getting plugged up with too much black and brown ink.

You can use these starting curves to fine-tune where and how much of each ink to use in the creation of your duotone.

10 Click OK in the Duotone Curve dialog box to close the brown ink curve graph.

You are returned to the main Duotone Options dialog box.

11 Click OK in the Duotone Options dialog box to apply these black and brown ink curves to your new duotone image.

View your new duotone and compare it to your original grayscale image. Notice how much richer the duotone looks. And this difference will be even more evident in the actual printed versions of these images.

File-Format Note: Duotones must be saved in EPS file format so the ink-curve instructions can be properly included in the file.

Making Over Grayscale to B&W

One underutilized makeover adjustment involves converting multitonal grayscale images to bitonal black-and-white images. Being able to move from grayscale to black and white is a great skill to have, especially if you're creating fax images or reduced-tone images for the Web — or even if you just want a different "look." Of course, few folks even bother to convert images to black and white because the default conversion rarely yields even barely acceptable results. But who says you have to stick with the default? Here are some methods that can bring you some true B&W makeover success.

The Ugly Conversion

I call this the ugly conversion because of the less-than-beautiful results. This is the graphics version of reading a bad book so you can recognize a good one!

❶ Open the Denali_State_Park_ GS.tif image.

This image, like the other images featured in this book, is available for download from the Web site associated with this book.

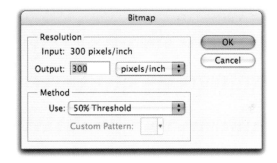

❷ Choose Image⇨Duplicate to make a working copy of the image.

Always, *always* work on a copy.

❸ Choose Image⇨Mode⇨ Bitmap.

Doing so opens the Bitmap dialog box.

Note: Bitmap is Adobe's name for a bitonal black-and-white image.

❹ In the Bitmap dialog box, select 50% Threshold from the Use drop-down menu.

The result of this default conversion is a nearly useless image. (Proof positive that machines have no imagination.)

Making Over Grayscale to B&W *(continued)*

The Separate-and-Threshold Makeover

One key to creating useful B&W images is to separate an image into segments and then control the conversion to B&W through setting thresholds for each segment. The following makeover walks you through the process.

❶ Open and duplicate the same Denali State Park GS.tif image used in the previous makeover.

You should separate this Denali State Park image into at least three segments: 1) the lower third of the image below the mountains, 2) the mountains and large left-side tree, and 3) the clouds and sky.

❷ Using the Rectangular Marquee tool from the Toolbox, select the lower third of the image.

Basically, select everything below the mountains.

❸ Choose Image⇨Adjustment⇨ Threshold.

Doing so calls up the Threshold dialog box.

❹ In the Threshold dialog box, move the Threshold slider to the left until the image has the "pop" you like, then click OK.

Here, 19 might be a good place to start. The position of the slider determines the grayscale level at which the black/white conversion takes place.

❺ Using the Lasso tool from the Toolbox, select the middle third of the image.

Make a jagged-edged selection around the large tree and mountains. (Don't worry about any overlap with the lower third of the image, which you converted in Step 4.)

Note: The jagged-edge nature of selection is important to prevent obviously-unnatural straight-line segments.

⑥ Choose Image⇨Adjustment⇨ Threshold.

The Threshold dialog box makes another appearance.

⑦ Move the Threshold slider to the left until the image has the amount of visual "pop" you like.

What the heck, 54 works for me. Remember, the position of the slider determines the grayscale level at which the black/white conversion takes place.

⑧ Using the Rectangular Marquee tool from the Toolbox, select the upper third of the image.

You'll want to get the remainder of the image — in this case, the sky and the clouds.

⑨ Choose Image⇨Adjustment⇨ Threshold.

The Threshold dialog box makes yet another appearance.

⑩ Move the Threshold slider to the left until the image has the amount of visual "pop" you like.

I'd try 120 here. The position of the slider determines the grayscale level at which the black/white conversion takes place.

Note: By using the Threshold tool, you've converted the image pixels to black-and-white-only values, but the image is still a grayscale image. So, to reap the full file-size-reduction benefits of the conversion, you must convert the whole image to 1-bit B&W.

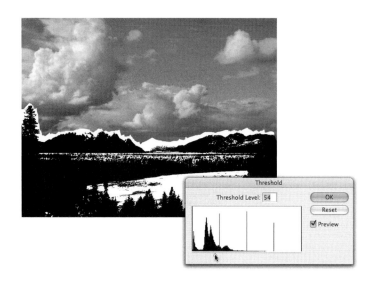

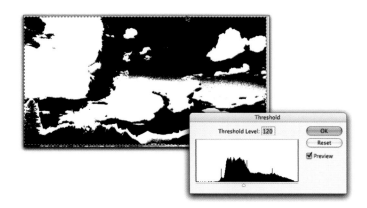

Making Over Grayscale to B&W *(continued)*

⑪ Choose Image⇨Mode⇨ Bitmap.

The Bitmap dialog box makes another appearance.

⑫ Click OK to close the dialog box and perform the Bitmap mode conversion.

You can use any Threshold value here, as the pixels have already been converted to black and white. All this step does is reduce the bit depth from 8 to 1.

Now take a look at your final composite B&W image, and compare it to the original (default) version.

The Dithering Makeover

Another very effective method for creating B&W images is to use a *dithering* technique. Instead of converting large areas of your image to either black or white, dithering creates varying densities of gray by mixing black and white pixels according to the original grayscale values in various areas of the image. Here's an example:

❶ Open and duplicate the same Denali State Park GS.tif image we've been using throughout this section.

❷ Choose Image⇨Mode⇨ Bitmap.

Doing so calls up the Bitmap dialog box.

❸ In the Bitmap dialog box, type 100 in the Output field and select Diffusion Dither from the Use drop-down menu.

Experiment with various resolutions to change the coarseness of the dithering. A 100ppi output is appropriate for use on the Web, but you might also choose a resolution

Before

After

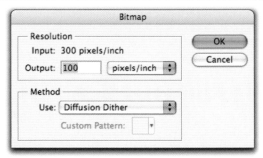

Bitmap

Resolution

Input: 300 pixels/inch

Output: 100 | pixels/inch

OK

Cancel

Method

Use: Diffusion Dither

Custom Pattern:

as low as this for printing if you wanted the dithering pattern to be more obvious.

④ Click OK to apply the diffusion dither to this image.

The diffusion dither creates a pattern of black pixels whose density depends upon (and is directly proportional to) the original grayscale values of the pixels.

The Halftone Pattern Makeover

Another very effective method for creating B&W images is to use a pattern of pixel-based halftone dots. Rather than converting large areas of your image to either black or white, you can halftone the image on-screen (as distinct from actual halftoning, which occurs during printing). The idea is (as with dithering, mentioned earlier) to use grayscale values from various areas of the image to create pixel patterns (that resemble halftone dots) of various size — in this case, to create halftones. Here's an example:

① Open and duplicate the same Denali State Park GS.tif image used in the previous makeover.

It's been working pretty well for us so far, so why change?

② Choose Image⇨Mode⇨ Bitmap.

The Bitmap dialog box makes another appearance.

③ In the Bitmap dialog box, select Halftone Screen from the Use drop-down menu and then click OK.

Doing so brings up the Halftone Screen dialog box.

Using the Halftone Screen dialog box, you can control both the frequency and angle of the dot pattern, as well as the shape of the dots.

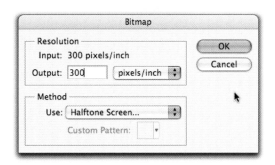

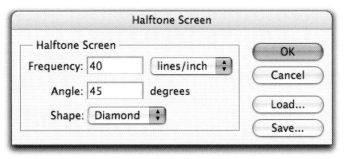

Making Over Grayscale to B&W *(continued)*

④ In the Halftone Screen dialog box, try a frequency of 40, an angle of 45°, and a Diamond pattern, and then click OK.

The selected halftone characteristics are applied to this image.

Experiment with various combinations of frequency, angle, and pattern to create different looks.

The Posterize Makeover

While posterization may not be strictly a conversion to B&W, it does represent an interesting and useful design alternative — plus it's easy to do.

① Open and duplicate the same Denali State Park GS.tif image we've been using throughout this section.

② Choose Image⇨Adjustment⇨ Posterize.

Doing so calls up the Posterize dialog box.

③ In the Posterize dialog box, select the number of shades of gray you want used in the posterization of your image, then click OK.

I'd start out with 10 levels, but experiment with various values to test the effects of fewer (or more) shades of gray. Posterization can be a great way to capture a viewer's attention.

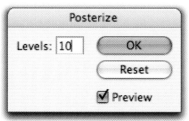

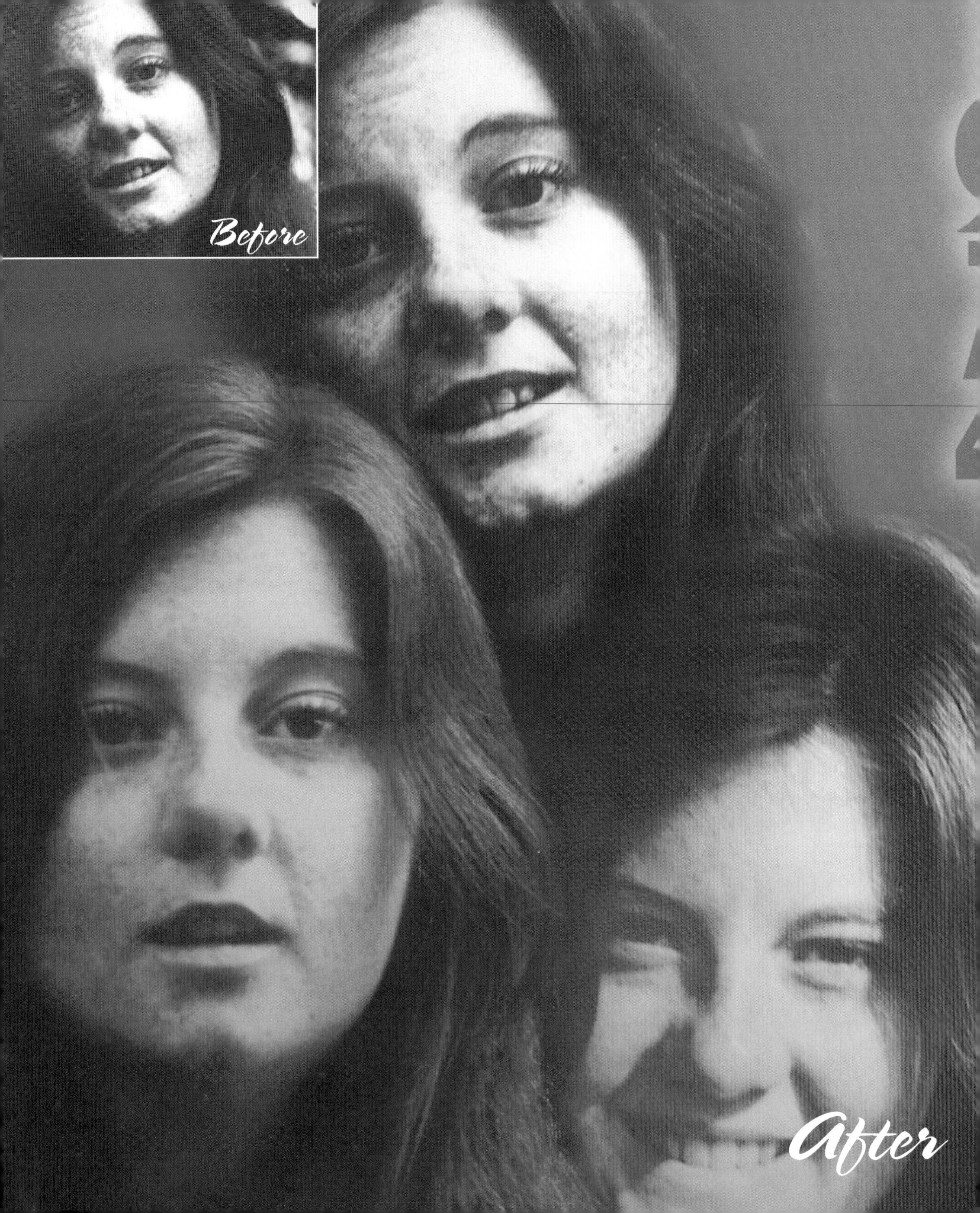
Before
After

8

ADDING ELEMENTS AS A MAKEOVER

The first seven chapters focus primarily on adjusting what is already in the image. Here you zero in on *adding* elements as a way to enhance — or make over — your image. Something as simple as adding a white border (for example) can dramatically alter the appearance of an image. In other cases, adding major image elements — even dragging in whole other images — may be the order of the day. Here are some element-addition examples to consider.

Often one of your key challenges when adding elements to an image is making sure that the added elements fit in seamlessly with the image you already have. A seamless addition is largely controlled at the edges of the added element. In natural, pixel-based images, nearly all edges are gradational. Even the edges of the sharpest pixel-based objects, such as type or rasterized vectors, have gradational or gradual edges. It is the very gradational nature of an edge that allows the human eye to fit or merge objects together seamlessly.

You get gradational edges by creating semi-transparent pixels — and Photoshop has three primary tools for creating such edges: anti-aliasing, feathering, and blurring. Anti-aliasing is the simplest of the three — you typically either just turn it off or on or vary it in discreet steps, such as Sharp, Crisp, Strong, and Smooth. Anti-aliasing is commonly used when creating type or converting vector objects to pixel-based objects.

As for the other two tools, feathering offers pixel-width steps of edge smoothing, whereas blurring of edges (often applied as the blurring of a selection stored as a mask in an alpha channel) offers the finest edge control, allowing 0.1 pixels steps in smoothing. The edge-smoothing tool you choose will depend upon the objects you are fitting together, but controlling your edges should always be a top priority.

A 3D Transparent-Frame Makeover

We're going to create a 3D frame out of the image itself, using the image pixels that are already present rather than going out and creating something that then gets added to the image. The idea here is to foster the illusion that the image is somehow framing itself. (Pretty neat, huh?)

① Open and duplicate an image suitable for framing.

The Arches_Juniper.tif image, available for download from the Web site associated with this book, would be a good choice. This desert image (with its light edges) would look really spiffy with a 3D border. (The idea here is not to detract from your image by heaping graphic elements along the border; rather, you use the image itself as *part* of the border.)

② Choose Select⇨All from the main menu (or just press ⌘/Ctrl+A).

Doing so selects the entire image.

③ To convert this image selection into a border, choose Select⇨Modify⇨Border.

The Border Selection dialog box appears on-screen.

④ In the Border Selection dialog box, enter 100 (pixels) in the Width field.

To see how your entry translates into inches, divide your border width by your linear resolution. For example, 100 pixels (border width) ÷ 300 ppi (linear resolution) = 0.333333 inches.

⑤ Press the Q key to activate the QuickMask view.

Note that the border is already feathered. If you want to feather this edge a bit more, be sure to complete Steps 7 and 8; if the feathering looks fine to you, don't bother with those steps at all.

6 Press Q again to return to Normal view.

7 (Optional) If you'd like to expand the feathering here, first choose Select⇨Feather.

Doing so calls up the Feather Selection dialog box.

8 (Optional) In the Feather Selection dialog box, enter 5 (pixels) in the Feather Radius field.

I call Steps 7 and 8 optional because the Border command already feathers the edge to some extent. After some practice with this technique, you'll know whether you want to add more feathering.

With feathering out of the way, it's time to set up your new border selection as a layer.

9 Choose Layer⇨New⇨Layer Via Copy.

Creating a new layer allows you to control it as a separate element.

10 Label this layer 100 Pixel Border + Lighten.

You'll lighten this layer in the steps that follow.

Note: If you hold down your Opt/Alt key as you create the new layer, that will allow you to name the layer as you create it, otherwise click on the layer name in the Layers palette to rename the layer.

11 Create another border layer.

In the Layers palette, click the original image (Background) layer, and then create another border layer (as described earlier in

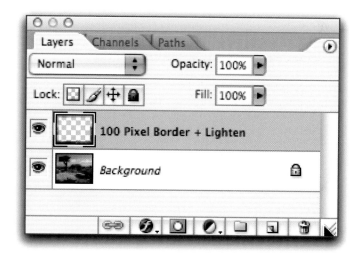

A 3D Transparent-Frame Makeover *(continued)*

Steps 1 through 10), but make this one 50 pixels wide — and be sure not to add any more feathering. Label this layer **50 Pixel Border + Multiply.**

⓬ In the Layers palette, click the 100 Pixel Border + Lighten layer to activate it.

Time for some lightening.

⓭ Choose Layer⇨New Adjustment Layer⇨Curves.

Doing so opens the Curve dialog box.

⓮ In the Curves dialog box, drag the midpoint of the curve up 30% and then click OK.

Your 100 Pixel Border + Lighten layer is noticeably lighter (and an Adjustment Curve layer is added to the Layers palette).

You'll notice that this lightening seems to be affecting the background layer as well as the border — a turn of events you don't necessarily want. So you're going to want to tie this Curve Adjustment layer exclusively to the 100 Pixel Border + Lighten layer — which you do by creating a Clipping Mask.

⓯ With the Curves Adjustment layer selected in the Layers palette, choose Layer⇨Create Clipping Mask.

Doing so physically moves the Curves Adjustment layer slightly to the right in the Layers palette, which indicates that this Curve Adjustment Layer is now applied only to the layer immediately beneath it (the 100 Pixel Border + Lighten layer).

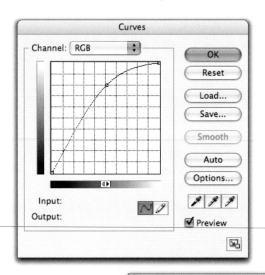

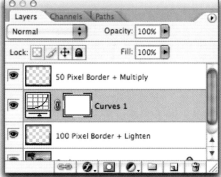

⓰ Back in the Layers palette, click the 50 Pixel Border + Multiply layer.

You want to make sure the layer is active.

⓱ Select Multiply from the Layer Blending pull-down menu.

This pull-down menu is located in the upper-left corner of the Layers palette.

Selecting Multiply here adds the luminance values of the 50 Pixel Border + Multiply layer and the underlying layer together, thereby darkening the layer.

⓲ With the 50 Pixel Border + Multiply layer still active, select Duplicate Layer from the Layer palette menu.

Doing so makes a duplicate copy of the multiplied 50 Pixel Border + Multiply Layer — and doubles its effect.

Note: You access the Layers Palette menu by clicking the right-pointing arrow in the top-right part of the Layers palette.

⓳ *(Optional)* Moderate the effect of the second 50 Pixel Border + Multiply layer.

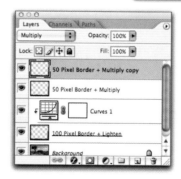

Photoshop Confidential

Curve Alone versus Curve Adjustment Layer

It would, of course, be faster to just apply a Curves correction to this layer (without the hassle of creating a Clipping Group Adjustment layer), but the result would lack the editability of the Clipping Group Adjustment layer. So — provided you know exactly what you want to apply as a layer adjustment — you can just use the Curves tool without the Adjustment layer . . . with one heads-up: Each time I've gotten lazy and have taken this shortcut, I've usually regretted it; typically I end up wanting to tweak the results — and wishing I had taken the time to set up an Adjustment layer so I could. (Sometimes an image you can't tweak is like an itch you can't scratch.)

A 3D Transparent-Frame Makeover *(continued)*

If you like the overall effect of the second 50 Pixel Border + Multiply layer, but think it's just a bit strong, you can reduce its impact by adjusting the percentage in the Fill field (located in the upper-right corner of the Layers palette).

Either click and drag the Fill slider, or just type **75** in the Fill field.

Note: The three layers — the 100 Pixel Border + Lighten layer and the two 50 Pixel Border + Multiply copies — combine to create a nice 3D frame. All you need now is a bit of white to set it off.

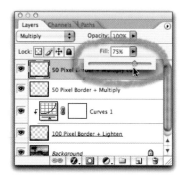

⑳ In the Photoshop toolbox, set your background color to white.

Simply press the D key to return your foreground/background colors to their default values of black and white, respectively.

㉑ Choose Image⇨Canvas Size.

The Canvas Size dialog box makes an appearance.

㉒ Enter 120 in both the Width and Height fields, and then select Percent as your unit of measurement.

Make sure you've set the Canvas Extension Color to Background.

㉓ Click OK to add the 20% white border.

Now view your finished image with a 3D border and a white frame.

Note: Prior to final output, make a copy of this image and flatten it. (Leave the original PSD file intact for later editing.) Flattening can be accomplished quickly and easily by performing a Save As and unchecking the Layers and Alpha Channels check boxes in the Save As dialog box — this forces you to save a simplified copy.

When you feel you have the hang of it, go for it — create your own variations!

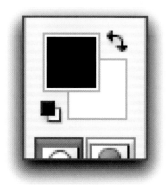

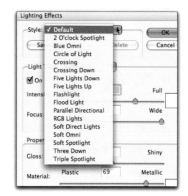

Making Over How You Present Your Image

Having a terrific image is a good start — but it's only a start. What you really want to do is then present your image in as attractive a way as possible.

You have countless ways to present an image (limited, in fact, only by your imagination), but here are a couple of good starting points: adding depth and borders and adding some text — headings, captions, whatever. Here's one makeover I hope you can keep mining for ideas for years to come.

❶ Open the Alaska_Light_RGB.tif image.

You can download a copy of this image from the Web site associated with this book.

To present this image in a better light, you're going to create a white border, add a full-image drop shadow, and add some type to the side of the image.

Note: With some images, you may want to add type on top of the image itself. This image, however, works best if you add your type to one of the sides. (Frankly, adding type to the body would distract too much in this case.) Here the image carries its own message all by itself; you're better off just adding a tasteful title.

❷ Choose Image⇨Duplicate to make a duplicate copy.

Always work using a copy.

To get started — before you even think of adding a white canvas frame — you'll want to create an exact mask of the original image. This step makes the image a snap to select later!

❸ Choose Edit⇨Select All (or press ⌘/Ctrl+A).

Doing so selects your entire image.

Making Over How You Present Your Image *(continued)*

④ Choose Select⇨Save Selection.

The Save Selection dialog box appears.

⑤ In the Save Selection dialog box, name this selection Image Mask, check the New Channel radio button, and then click OK.

Your selection of the entire image is saved as Alpha channel #4 in the Channels palette.

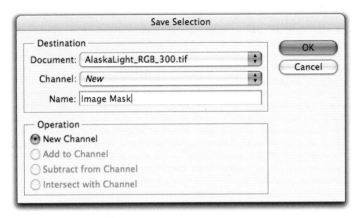

⑥ Choose Layer⇨New⇨Layer Via Copy.

Note: If you hold down your Opt/Alt key as you create the new layer, you'll be able to name the layer as you create it; otherwise, just click on the layer name in the Layers palette to rename the layer.

⑦ In the Layers palette, double-click the Layer name and then rename the layer *Image*.

⑧ In the Layers palette, click the Background layer to activate it.

Time to set the stage for that white canvas.

⑨ Choose Edit⇨Fill.

The Fill dialog box makes an appearance.

⑩ In the Fill dialog box, select White from the Use drop-down menu, and then click OK.

The Background gets its requisite fill of White. Now all you have to do is enlarge the canvas a bit.

⑪ Choose Image⇨Canvas Size.

The Canvas Size dialog box makes an appearance.

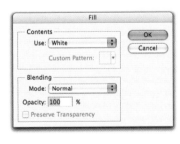

⑫ **In the Canvas Size dialog box, enter 3 in the Width field and 2 in the Height field, and then set your unit of measurement to inches.**

Doing so enlarges the white background canvas and surrounds the Image layer with transparent space — no pixel gets added to the layer, only space.

Note: Make sure that the middle Anchor square is selected (darkened) — this instructs Photoshop to add canvas all the way around the image.

⑬ **Click the Create a New Layer button located near the lower-right corner of the Layers palette.**

Your image gains a new transparent layer (which duly shows up in the Layers palette).

⑭ **In the Layers palette, double-click the new layer and rename it Image Shadow.**

The name is appropriate, because we're going to use it for the drop shadow.

⑮ **With the Image Shadow layer selected in the Layers palette, choose Select⇨Load Selection.**

The Load Selection dialog box makes an appearance.

⑯ **In the Load Selection dialog box, select Image Mask from the Channel drop-down menu, check the New Selection radio button, and then click OK.**

Doing so loads the original Image Mask layer onto the Image Shadow layer.

You'll notice that the selection appears as if it's surrounding the image, but it's really

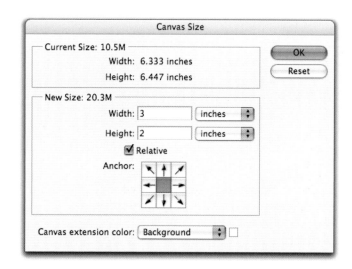

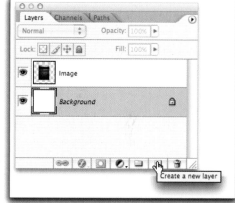

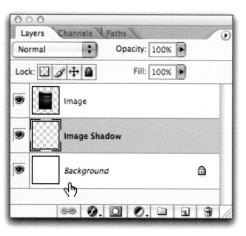

Making Over How You Present Your Image *(continued)*

on top of the Image Shadow layer — the layer currently selected.

Time to add some shadows.

⑰ Choose Edit⇨Fill.

The Fill dialog box reappears.

⑱ In the Fill dialog box, select Black from the Use drop-down menu and then click OK.

Doing so fills the selection on the Image Shadow layer with black.

⑲ In the Layers palette, click on the eye to the left of the Image layer to view just the black-filled selection.

You get a peek at some nice black "shadows."

⑳ Press ⌘/Ctrl+D to deselect the selection on the Image Shadow layer.

㉑ Click (again) the eye to the left of the Image layer to toggle the image back into visibility.

Note: At this point, I'd click the Image Shadow layer to make sure it's selected.

㉒ Press Spacebar+⌘/Ctrl to zoom in on the lower-right corner of your image.

You'll want to clearly see the offset of the shadow.

㉓ Select the Move tool from the Toolbox and use the Arrow keys to move the shadow down and to the right until it suits you.

I'd say moving the shadow approximately 5 pixels down and to the right would do nicely.

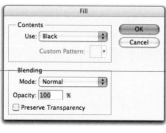

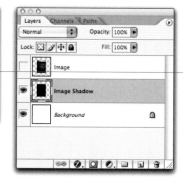

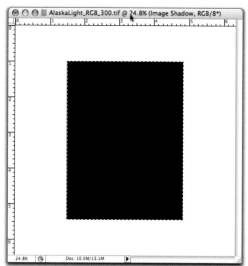

Note: Make sure that your Image Shadow layer is still selected as you go on to the next step.

㉔ Choose Filter⇨Blur⇨ Gaussian Blur.

The Gaussian Blur dialog box makes an appearance.

㉕ In the Gaussian Blur dialog box, select a blur radius that suits your fancy.

Try a 20-pixel blur to start out with — just remember that you can always add more later.

Note: You can build your drop shadow in several layers and offsets, with the inner shadows having less blur than the outer shadows . . . the possibilities are endless.

Now, when you create a drop shadow by applying a large Blur radius to an entire black mask, often a bit of the shadow spills over the shadow edges (here it happens at the top and left edges). While it's not absolutely necessary to remove this shadow spill, you get a cleaner look if you do.

Note: You can quickly tell whether you have any shadow spillover by measuring the

---

Photoshop Confidential

Building Shadows

Here, you're building the full image shadow the old-fashioned way — manually, with layers. You could easily create shadows using a Layer style — which is what happens when we add type to the image, later in this makeover — but it's always good to know how to create a shadow the manual way, in case you cannot achieve the results or look you want with the Layer style.

In this makeover, you'll be creating very clean upper and left edges with no shadow showing at all. Cleaning up these edges and fine-tuning the upper-right and lower-left corners of the shadow is much easier when the shadow exists on its own layer. Plus, if you want to create compound shadows with two or more shadow layers, you'll find that the old-fashioned way is the better way to go.

Making Over How You Present Your Image *(continued)*

proximal edge areas with your Info tool. Here, a value of 228 (instead of a pure white 255) indicates that there is indeed some shadow spillover.

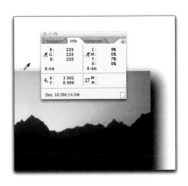

㉖ Select the Eraser tool from the Toolbox.

As always, calling up the tool calls up the tool's Options bar as well.

㉗ In the Eraser tool's Options bar, set both the Opacity and Flow to 100% and select a large enough brush to completely span the spillover area.

A setting of 70 pixels is probably big enough here.

㉘ Place the lower edge of the Eraser tool so it overlaps the image *and* the remainder of the tool extends over the spillover edge.

㉙ Click and drag the Eraser tool along the edge to remove the shadow-spillover pixels.

You should be able to see a noticeable difference as you slide the Eraser tool along the edge.

Note: When working near the corners of the image, switch to a smaller and softer (0% to 20% Hardness) Eraser brush with lower Opacity (about 50%) to fine-tune the transition between the two edges.

With everything nice and tidy now, it's time to bevel the edge.

㉚ In the Layers palette, click the Image layer to select it, and then double-click the right side of the layer — to the right of the word *Image* — to activate the Layer style for that layer.

Doing so opens the Layer Style dialog box.

㉛ In the Layer Style dialog box, check the Bevel and Emboss check box in the Styles listing on the left.

The Bevel and Emboss options appear on the right side of the Layer Styles dialog box.

㉜ Set your options for the Bevel and Emboss layer style.

I'd recommend the following:

Style: Inner Bevel
Technique: Smooth
Depth: 200
Direction: Up
Size: 13
Soften: 0

Use the remainder of the default settings as shown here.

㉝ Still in the Layer Style dialog box, click the Contour check box in the Styles listing.

Doing so adds a nicely embossed, beveled, and contoured edge to the image.

Note: As you can see, there are tons of different settings to play around with here, so feel free to experiment.

Add title type

To finish up the presentation makeover of your image, add some title type.

Since several key aspects of this image are vertical — including the portrait orientation and the eye line from foreground to background — I'd recommend orienting our type vertically as well.

㉞ Click and hold the Type tool in the Toolbox until the hidden Type tool fly-out menu appears, and then select the Vertical Type tool.

As expected, selecting the tool calls up the tool's Options bar.

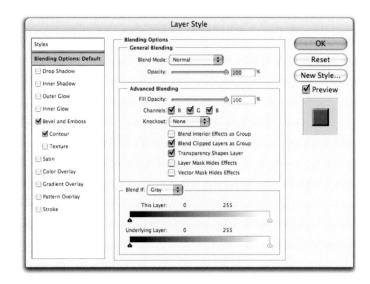

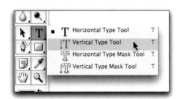

Making Over How You Present Your Image *(continued)*

③⑤ In the Vertical Type tool's Options bar, set the font type to Anna, font size to 25, and Anti-Alias to Smooth.

I like the Anna look, but you can try something else if you like.

We're going to need a color for the text, so we might as well choose a complementary color from the image itself.

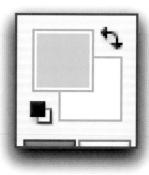

③⑥ Select the Eyedropper tool from the Toolbox.

③⑦ Using the Eyedropper tool, click the gold sky.

Doing so sets the gold color as the foreground color, which (in turn) will be the color applied to the type when we set it.

③⑧ Reselect the Vertical Type tool from the Toolbox and then click the white background just to the left of the upper-left corner of the image.

Okay, I guess you *could* pick the right side, but I think it looks better here on the left.

③⑨ Type in the word *Alaska* and then press the Enter key.

As expected — given your use of the Vertical Text tool — the word *Alaska* appears vertically next to your image.

Note: You'll also see *Alaska* appear as the name of a new Type layer in the Layers palette.

④⓪ Still using the Vertical Type tool, click just below the word *Alaska*, type in the word *Light*, and press the Enter key.

This text also appears vertically and as a new layer in the Layers palette.

Note: In circumstances like this, it's usually easier to set each word as a separate layer, so the positioning is easier.

④ (Optional) In the Layers palette, click and drag the Light layer so it's below the Alaska layer, so both appear in the Layers palette as they do on-screen.

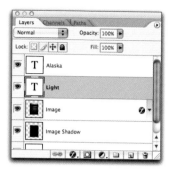

The only reason to do this is to make it a bit easier to keep straight how the two layers relate to one another.

You now have your text basically in place, but "basically" can be improved upon with a little fine-tuned tweaking.

④ On the right side of the Vertical Type tool's Options bar, click the Character and Paragraph Page icon.

Doing so displays the Character tab of the Character/Paragraph palette.

④ Back in the Layers palette, double-click the "T" icon for the Alaska Type layer.

Double-clicking here quickly selects all the type in the Alaska Type layer.

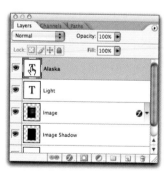

④ In the Character tab of the Character/Paragraph palette, adjust the point size to 28 and the tracking to –50, and then click OK.

④ Apply this same formatting to the Light Type layer.

You want the type to match up, so be sure to be consistent in your formatting.

④ Press ⌘/Ctrl+R to activate the Ruler.

Making Over How You Present Your Image *(continued)*

47 **Click the Vertical Ruler scale, drag a guideline out, and place it where you'd like to line up the type.**

48 **Select the Move tool from the Toolbox, click the Alaska Type layer (in the Layers palette) to activate it, and then use the Move tool to drag the ALASKA type over to where you want it.**

You'll want to move it until it snaps into place on the vertical guideline.

49 **Using the same Move tool, drag the ALASKA type up until the "A" is even with the top of the left image edge.**

Time now for the LIGHT text.

50 **In the Layers palette, click the Light Type layer to activate it and then use the Move tool to drag the LIGHT type over.**

Again, you'll want to drag the type over until it snaps into place on the vertical guide.

51 **Still using the Move tool, drag the LIGHT type up until the "T" is even with the bottom of the left image edge.**

With the type in place, you can press ⌘/Ctrl+H to hide the vertical guide if you want, lest it drive you crazy trying to look through it!

So, everything is lined up correctly, just waiting for a bit of drop shadow and bevel.

52 **Double-click the right side of the Alaska Type layer in the Layers palette.**

Doing so activates the Layer Style dialog box.

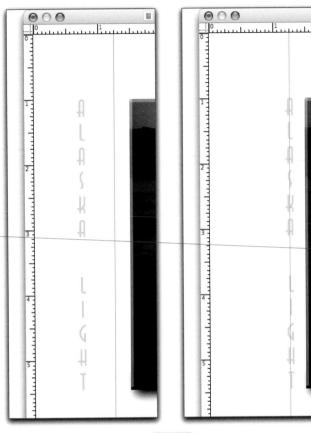

⑤③ Click the Drop Shadow option (in the Styles list to the left) to activate it.

The options specific for the Drop Shadow feature appear on the right in the Layer Style dialog box.

⑤④ Configure the Drop Shadow options as shown here, with Opacity at 50%, Distance at 10px, Spread at 15%, and Size at 14 px.

Treat these settings as a good starting point, not as absolutes.

⑤⑤ Now click the Bevel and Emboss check box (in the Styles list) to activate it. Use the default setting to start, and then edit as you see fit.

Here's a chance to express your own creative vision.

⑤⑥ Click OK to apply both styles to the Alaska Type layer.

The type is styled according to your wishes.

⑤⑦ Press Opt/Alt and then, in the Layers palette, click and drag the "f" symbol from the Alaska Type layer to the Light Type layer.

Doing so applies the same Layer Style formatting to the Light Type layer — in the process, adding the Layer Style "f" symbol to the Light Type layer as well.

Now take a look at the finished Layers palette. Each element that contributes to this presentation piece is on its own layer — including the white background — and is fully editable at any time.

Compare and contrast the original and final images, and see what a nice image presentation you've created.

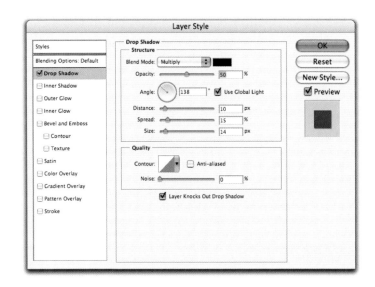

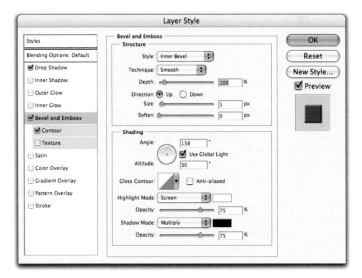

Making Over How You Present Your Image *(continued)*

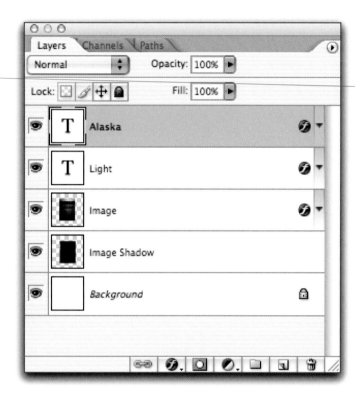

Before

After

Making Over Your Boring Space

Sometimes, otherwise-good-looking images are diminished by a really boring image element — a dull (whether overcast or uninteresting) sky, for example. One possible solution — actually implemented earlier in this book — is to crop the image. Another approach is to add something with a bit more flair to liven up that boring space.

❶ Open the Tutka_Bay.tif image.

You can snag this image from the Web site associated with this book.

This is a photo of beautiful Tutka Bay, taken from one of my favorite hikes, Grace Ridge, near my home in Homer, Alaska. The bay is certainly pretty enough, but the sky is boring, boring, boring (on that day, anyway). Rather than crop out the sky, I thought it would be nice to add some title type over the sky.

❷ Choose Image⇨Duplicate to make a duplicate copy.

Always, always work with a copy.

❸ Select the Eyedropper tool from the Toolbox and click the blue of the water near the mouth of Tutka Bay.

Doing so assigns this blue color to Photoshop's foreground color, which you will then use to create the title type. By using this blue color, you get to match the look of the type to the image.

Note: Be sure the Eyedropper Sampling is set to 3 by 3 in the Eyedropper Options bar.

❹ Select the Horizontal Type tool from the Toolbox.

You use this tool to configure the type.

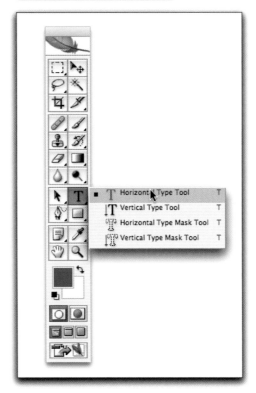

Making Over Your Boring Space *(continued)*

⑤ Using the Horizontal Type tool's Options bar, set the font to Gill Sans, Bold Condensed, and 22 pt with a Smooth Anti-Alias.

Gill Sans is one of my personal favorites, but feel free to try something different.

⑥ With the Horizontal Type tool selected, click the left side of the sky and then type Tutka Bay from Grace Ridge.

The text duly appears at the top of the image; a separate type layer that corresponds to this text also appears in the Layers palette.

Photoshop Confidential

Type Edges

When most of us think about type, typically we think about hard edges. Normally this is an appropriate thought — after all, you want the words to be legible — but when you're working in Photoshop, your perspective should change a bit to consider the type not as words, but as a visual part of the image. Type set in Photoshop should typically have a gradational — also-known-as *anti-aliased* — edge. An anti-aliased edge displays semitransparent pixels along the edges of the type, rather than going with 100% opaque — which would give you an abrupt edge and a blocky, pixelized/rasterized appearance that shows the obvious, apparent edges of the type — usually not too attractive. An anti-aliased edge, with its gradational semitransparent nature, provides a smoother transition between the type and the surrounding image. To the human eye, this allows the type to fit in with the image; the result is usually far more appealing. Now, if (for some design-inspired reason) you're going for the hard, pixelized look, you always have that option as well. In Photoshop, you can control the hardness of type edges through the Anti-alias control menu in the Type tool's Options bar or in the Character tab of the Character/Paragraph palette.

Let me close with a few general thoughts about anti-aliasing in Photoshop:

It seems counter-intuitive to most people, but the fact is that to make type look "crisp" in a pixel-based image, it needs to have a soft edge.

The four anti-alias options do *not* provide different degrees of anti-aliasing. They are four different algorithms (or methods of figuring the math) for doing anti-aliasing. In all cases, the anti-aliasing is completely on (or off) — there's no such thing as partially anti-aliased type.

There are some typefaces that are specifically designed not to be anti-aliased. These are intended for use on Web pages, and only at specific (small) pixel sizes. If you use these fonts (sometimes called "pixel fonts") at any sizes other than the specific size intended, or with anti-aliasing turned on, they will almost always look just awful. But they're the only way to get good, crisp type at small sizes (typically smaller than 12 point) — with anti-aliasing turned off.

⑦ Double-click the right side of the type layer in the Layers palette. (Be sure to click to the right of the type itself.)

Doing so activates the Layer Style dialog box.

Note: Layers that have a long name (this Type layer is a good example) can make it hard to get to the Layer Style dialog box — when you double-click, you often end up renaming the layer because you double-click into the name. If this happens, you can always choose Blending Options from the Layer palette's Options menu (it takes you to the same place).

⑧ In the Styles listing, select the Drop Shadow check box as well as the Bevel and Emboss check box.

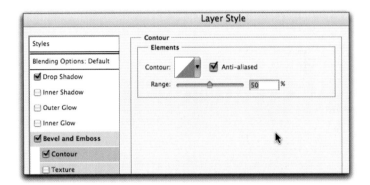

⑨ Under the Bevel and Emboss option, select the Contour and Satin check boxes then click OK.

Doing so applies the desired Layer Style set.

Taz's Take: You can control each of the above Layer styles by simply clicking the desired effect and adjusting the options for that effect. For each effect, you might want to activate (check-on) the anti-alias feature to create smooth transitions between effects, as seen here in the Contour options settings.

If the image you're making over is a commercial one, you may want to add a corporate logo to the image. If so, check out the next series of optional steps. If not, you're free to enjoy your creation as is.

Now, it's true that the logo can be added in a page-layout application (such as InDesign), but if you add the logo in Photoshop, you have the advantage of making the logo an actual part of the image, so it will always be there. In addition, this approach also gives you much more control over how the logo fits in with the rest of the image.

Making Over Your Boring Space *(continued)*

Adding an optional logo

Options make the world go 'round, right? If you want to add a corporate-type logo to the image, do the following:

❶ Choose File⇨Place.

The Place dialog box makes an appearance.

❷ Locate (and double-click) the file containing the logo you want to place.

The logo (in this case, the Mako Water Taxi logo) gets placed as a transformable object on-screen.

❸ Press the Shift key and click and drag a corner of the Transform box to resize the logo.

Pressing the Shift key keeps the resizing proportional.

❹ Drag the scaled image to where you want it.

The lower-right corner works for me.

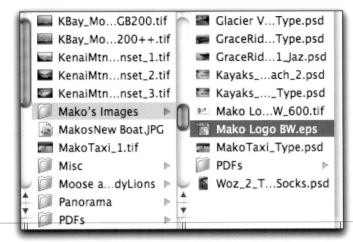

Photoshop Confidential

Working with Vector Logos

A vector object is a graphic constructed from continuous lines, known as *vectors*, rather than from discrete pixels. Vector objects are typically created and edited in drawing programs like Illustrator. When it comes to bringing such a vector object (a vector logo, for example) into Photoshop, you actually have several methods. You can place a logo (File⇨Place), you can open it (File⇨Open) and move it from one image to another, or you can copy the logo from Illustrator and paste it into Photoshop. The first two methods, Place and Open, result in *rasterization* of the logo: Photoshop converts the vector paths to pixels. The third method — copying and pasting from Illustrator — allows you the option of not only retaining the vector nature of the logo in Photoshop but also placing *and* editing the vector path in Photoshop (and, for that matter, outputting the vector path from Photoshop as a vector path). Unless you're sure you want to rasterize the logo and keep it that way forever, you might want to use the Copy and Paste from Illustrator method so you can keep your options open.

➎ Fine-tune the scaling and then press the Enter key (or double-click the Transform box).

Doing so applies the Scaling transformation.

➏ Choose Window➪Layers.

The Layers palette makes an appearance.

Note that the Mako's Water Taxi logo is placed on its own layer in the Layers palette. In Photoshop CS2, the logo is automatically placed as a *Smart Object*, which means that it's linked back to the original vector logo. Double-clicking the layer's thumbnail image transports you instantly to the original vector image in Illustrator so you can edit.

➐ In the Layers palette, click the logo layer to activate it. and then choose Layer➪Rasterize➪ Smart Object.

The logo is converted to pixels and the Smart Object icon disappears form the layer. (Rasterization of the layer is required for any pixel-based editing to occur.)

Note: If you want to retain a Smart-Object-editable copy of the vector logo, simply make a copy of this logo layer *before* you rasterize it. Then just turn off that view in the Layers palette to keep it out of your way while working (as I have done here).

As you can see, the black logo gets kind of lost in the corner — especially against the darker grassy area. So let's make it shine a bit.

➑ Double-click the right side of the Mako Logo BW layer in the Layers palette (to the right of the text).

Doing so activates the Layer Style dialog box.

Making Over Your Boring Space *(continued)*

9 Click the Drop Shadow effect in the Styles listing to activate it.

The options particular to the Drop Shadow effect appear on the right in the Layer Style dialog box.

10 Double-click the Color swatch, located just to the right of the Blend Mode menu.

The idea here is to choose a shadow color appropriate for the image.

11 In the Color Picker that appears, select White, and then click the OK button to apply the white color.

12 Back in the Layer Style dialog box, set the Blend Mode to Normal, Opacity to 75, Distance to 0, Spread to 20, Size to 40, Noise to 10, and then click the OK button to apply the Layer Style characteristics you've chosen.

Using these settings creates a symmetrical, semitransparent, slightly grainy, white glow behind the logo.

Feel free to experiment with your own setting to create your own look.

Now compare the original Tutka Bay image with the new version.

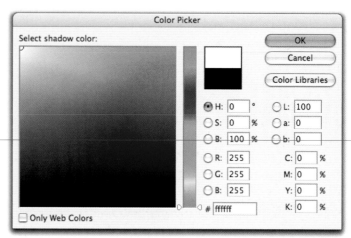

Doing a Collage/Montage Makeover

Hey, sometimes pictures just look better when you put them together.

Technically, because you're going to use related images in this makeover, you're going to end up with a montage, but many folks use the term "collage" as a catchall term for all multipart images . . . I say call it what you like!

Combining images to make a multipart image can yield some very satisfying results. People and other animals provide good fodder for montages; you often have a range of expressions and/or postures to provide interesting image components. Here is an example.

❶ Open and duplicate the images you want to use in your montage.

If you like, you can grab three photos of Nancy (Nancy_1, Nancy_2, and Nancy_3) from the Web site associated with this book.

You can either use one of the images as a *base* image — using it as the ground onto which you will place the other images — or you can start from scratch and bring in whole images or sections of all the images as you see fit. The latter method gives you the most flexibility for image arrangement; you'll be starting with a separate, blank image, onto which you can place all three images — each with its own separate layer.

Since I'm a fan of flexibility, lets go with the Blank Canvas approach.

❷ With one of the images active, choose Image⇨Image Size.

The Image Size dialog box appears, displaying information about the image's dimensions and linear resolution.

The linear resolution for the image I chose is 200 ppi and the dimensions are approximately 4"x5.3". Given that information, I'm going to create a somewhat larger blank canvas at the same (200ppi) resolution.

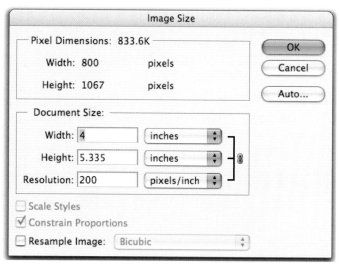

Doing a Collage/Montage Makeover *(continued)*

③ Choose File⇨New.

The New dialog box comes to attention.

④ In the New dialog box, create a new 5"x6" 200ppi grayscale image with a white background and name it Nancy Montage.

Here you'll want grayscale to match the color mode of the images you're using.

⑤ Choose Window⇨Layers to call up the Layers palette.

Note that you now have one layer with a completely white background.

With your canvas set, now is the time to start thinking about how you want to arrange your images. Start out by selecting an image around which you'd like to arrange the other images. (For my money, I'd go with Nancy_3 as the reference image around which to arrange the others.)

⑥ Choose the Lasso tool from the Toolbox and use its Options bar to set it up with a 40-pixel feather.

Using a feather on your initial selection gets the isolation-and-blending process started right away.

⑦ Draw a Lasso selection around the portion of Nancy_3 that you want to include.

You can use my selection as a guide, if you like.

8 **Choose QuickMask mode from the Toolbox to check the selection and the feather.**

Doing so gives you a sense of how the selection will look.

9 **Click and drag the Nancy_3 selection onto the Nancy Montage (blank) canvas.**

The feathered transferred selection appears as a separate layer in the Nancy_Montage image.

10 **Double-click the layer's name in the Layers palette and change the name to Nancy_3.**

Okay, I know this may seem kind of anal . . . but you'll be pleased to have this whole layer-naming thing as an established habit when you start creating images with dozens of layers. (Spurn me now . . . thank me later!)

11 **With the Nancy_3 layer active, choose the Move tool from the Toolbox and drag the Nancy_3 image up to the top and middle of the page.**

Note: Pressing ⌘/Ctrl key calls up the Move tool as well.

12 **Using the feathered Lasso tool and the Move tool, select and move Nancy_1 and Nancy_2 into the Nancy Montage.**

Use lower Feather values of approximately 15 for selecting the second and third images, so the image edges are less gradational.

Note: With some practice, you'll get the hang of which feather values to use in which circumstances. Just remember: When in doubt, *lower* the feather; you can always take more off later.

Doing a Collage/Montage Makeover *(continued)*

⑬ Position each image roughly where you think you want it. (This can be changed at any time, of course.) And yes, name the respective layers . . . Nancy_2 and Nancy_3.

Notice that each image is on its own layer.

⑭ In the Layers palette, arrange the images vertically the way you'd like them, with the top image at the top of the palette.

Nothing is set in stone yet — you can still move things around later.

⑮ Select the Nancy_3 layer in the Layers palette and then press ⌘/Ctrl+T.

Doing so places a Free Transform control box around the selection.

⑯ Press the Shift key while you drag the lower-right corner of the control box to resize the Nancy_ 3 image proportionally.

Handy, yes?

⑰ Click and drag the middle of the Free Transform control box to adjust the placement of the image, and then press Enter to apply the resize transformation.

One down, two to go.

⑱ Using the same Free Transform tool, resize the Nancy_1 and Nancy_2 images.

Looking pretty good, but the edges could use some touching up.

⑲ Select the Lasso tool from the Toolbox (again).

Calling up the tool automatically calls up the tool's Options bar as well.

⚫20 In the tool's Options bar, set the feather to 15–25 pixels, then draw a selection around Nancy_3's most obvious image edges (and other areas you would like to delete).

Repeat this step (with appropriate feathers) with the Nancy_1 and Nancy_2 images.

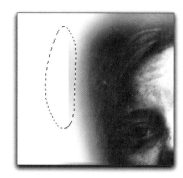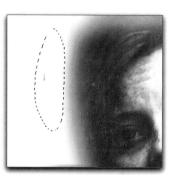

⚫21 Select the Eraser tool and, using the tool's Options bar, set the Mode to a soft-edged brush and the Opacity to 50%.

⚫22 Using your newly configured Eraser tool, fine-tune the edges of your image vignettes.

To achieve more subtle removal results, try just pointing and clicking rather than dragging the tool.

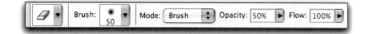

The edges are looking much better, but it's time to move beyond the boring white background.

⚫23 In the Layers palette, click the Background layer to activate it.

⚫24 Select the Eyedropper tool from the Toolbox.

⚫25 Choose Window⇨Colors.

Doing so calls up the Color palette.

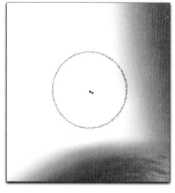

⚫26 Using the Eyedropper tool, sample the grayscale values around the hair values, select one you would like to use as a background, and then click this to make it the foreground color.

I'd go for approximately 65%K.

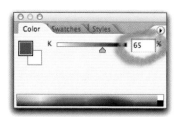

Doing a Collage/Montage Makeover *(continued)*

㉗ Choose Edit⇨Fill to call up the Fill dialog box.

Make sure that Foreground Color is selected in the Use drop-down menu.

㉘ Click OK to fill the background color with the 65% gray.

The gray sets off the images nicely, but a caption of some type wouldn't hurt.

㉙ Select the Vertical Type tool from the Toolbox.

As usual, calling up the tool calls up the tool's Options bar as well.

㉚ Using the tool's Options bar, first format the type to your liking and then type in a caption. (Here "1974.")

I'd go for a Gill Sans font with Ultra Bolding at 56 pt.

Note: As you'd expect, when you add type to the image, a Type layer shows up automatically in the Layers palette.

㉛ Choose Window⇨Character.

Doing so calls up the Character tab of the Character/Paragraph palette.

㉜ In the Character tab, decrease the tracking until the characters are just barely separated (here it's –210).

Note that the type here is barely visible; it's assigned the same value as the image background color of 65%K — the color we assigned back in Step 26. To get that text to stand out, we'll have to tweak it a bit.

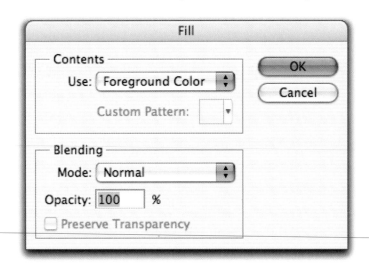

㉝ In the Layers palette, double-click the right side of the Type layer entry (to the right of the layer name) to activate the Layer Style dialog box.

The Layer Style dialog box always comes when called.

㉞ In the Styles listing on the left, click on the Drop Shadow option.

The settings for this particular option appear on the right in the Layer Style dialog box.

㉟ For your Drop Shadow settings, set the Blend Mode to Normal, the Color to White, the Opacity to 35%, the Distance to 0, the Spread to 22, the Size to 32, and the Noise to 10; then click OK to apply the Layer style.

Note that the type now has a soft glow around it — and that your Type layer now has a Layer Style symbol (the small *f*) assigned to it as well.

We're so close to being done now, but we can't let the opportunity to colorize an old photo pass us by.

㊱ Choose Image⇨Duplicate to make a duplicate copy of your Nancy Montage image.

Go ahead and name the duplicate copy Nancy Montage_Colorize.

㊲ In the new Nancy Montage_Colorize image, choose Layer⇨Flatten Image to collapse all the layers into one.

Doing so will simplify — and reduce the file size of — the image.

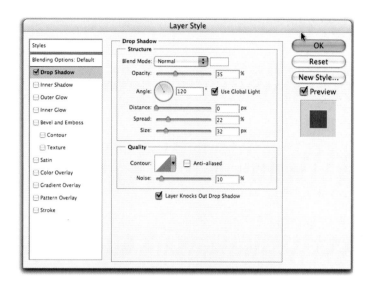

Doing a Collage/Montage Makeover *(continued)*

③⑧ Choose Image⇨Mode⇨RGB.

Doing so converts the Nancy Montage_ Colorize image into an RGB image. With the additional channels that come with RGB images, you are now free to colorize to your heart's content.

③⑨ Choose Image⇨Adjustment⇨ Curves to call up the Curves dialog box.

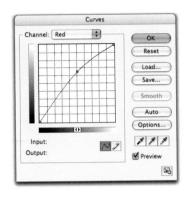

Make sure that the highlight end of the horizontal gradient is on the right. (If it's on the left, click the appropriate arrow in the center of the gradient to change it.)

④⓪ In the Curves dialog box, choose Red from the Channel drop-down menu.

The Red curve is displayed in the Curves dialog box.

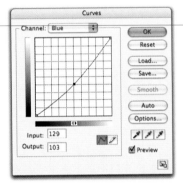

④① Drag the middle of the Red curve up 15%.

④② In the Curves dialog box, choose Blue from the Channel drop-down menu and then drag the middle of the Blue curve down 10%.

④③ Click OK to apply and view the color change.

Now you can enjoy your new (colorized) Nancy montage!

Applying an optional lighting effect

If you're feeling adventurous, you might consider adding a lighting effect to your montage. Lighting effects can be applied to individual layers at any point as you construct the image — or you can simply add them to a completed image (which is what's going on here). Lighting effects can be used

for a variety of purposes, including creating moods or highlighting a particular part of an image.

If you take a quick look at all the Lighting Effects choices — first choose Filter⇨ Render⇨Lighting Effects to call up the Light Effects dialog box and then make your way through the Style drop-down menu for a peek — you'll see that you have quite a few different options and variations you could apply. Here are two that should serve as good introductions to the whole lighting-effects process.

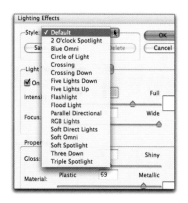

The Omni lighting effect

The Omni lighting effect — along with its myriad variations — is a good effect for focusing a viewer's attention on a specific area of an image. Here's how you can put it to work for you:

❶ In the Lighting Effects dialog box, choose Soft Omni from the Style drop-down menu.

The Lighting Effects dialog box updates to show the default settings for the Soft Omni lighting effect.

❷ Set the Intensity at 50–60.

Note (in the Preview window) how this lighting effect focuses attention on the middle of the image.

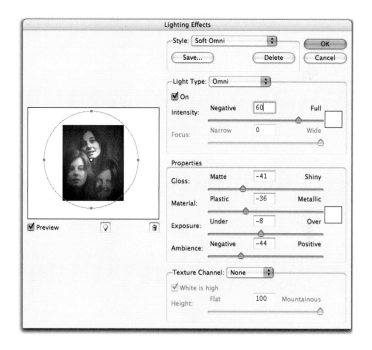

❸ Click and drag the circle in the Preview window to spread the effect out a bit, then click OK.

The overall effect here is to focus attention on the middle of the image — and draw attention away from the background and periphery.

The 2 O'Clock Spotlight lighting effect

The 2 O'Clock Spotlight focuses even more of the attention on a particular part of the image. Here's how you can put this effect to use for you.

Doing a Collage/Montage Makeover *(continued)*

① In the Lighting Effects dialog box, choose 2 O'Clock Spotlight from the Style drop-down menu.

The Lighting Effects dialog box updates to show the default settings for the 2 O'Clock Spotlight lighting effect.

② In the (updated) Lighting Effects dialog box, choose Spotlight from the Light Type drop-down menu and set the Intensity to 15–20.

③ In the Preview window, adjust the shape and position of the Spotlight control circle to suit you.

The idea here is to "spotlight" one particular point in the image. (I decided to concentrate on the 1974 date.)

④ Click OK to apply the lighting effect.

Note how the date really pops out with the help of this lighting effect.

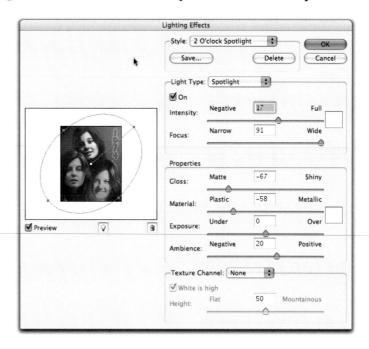

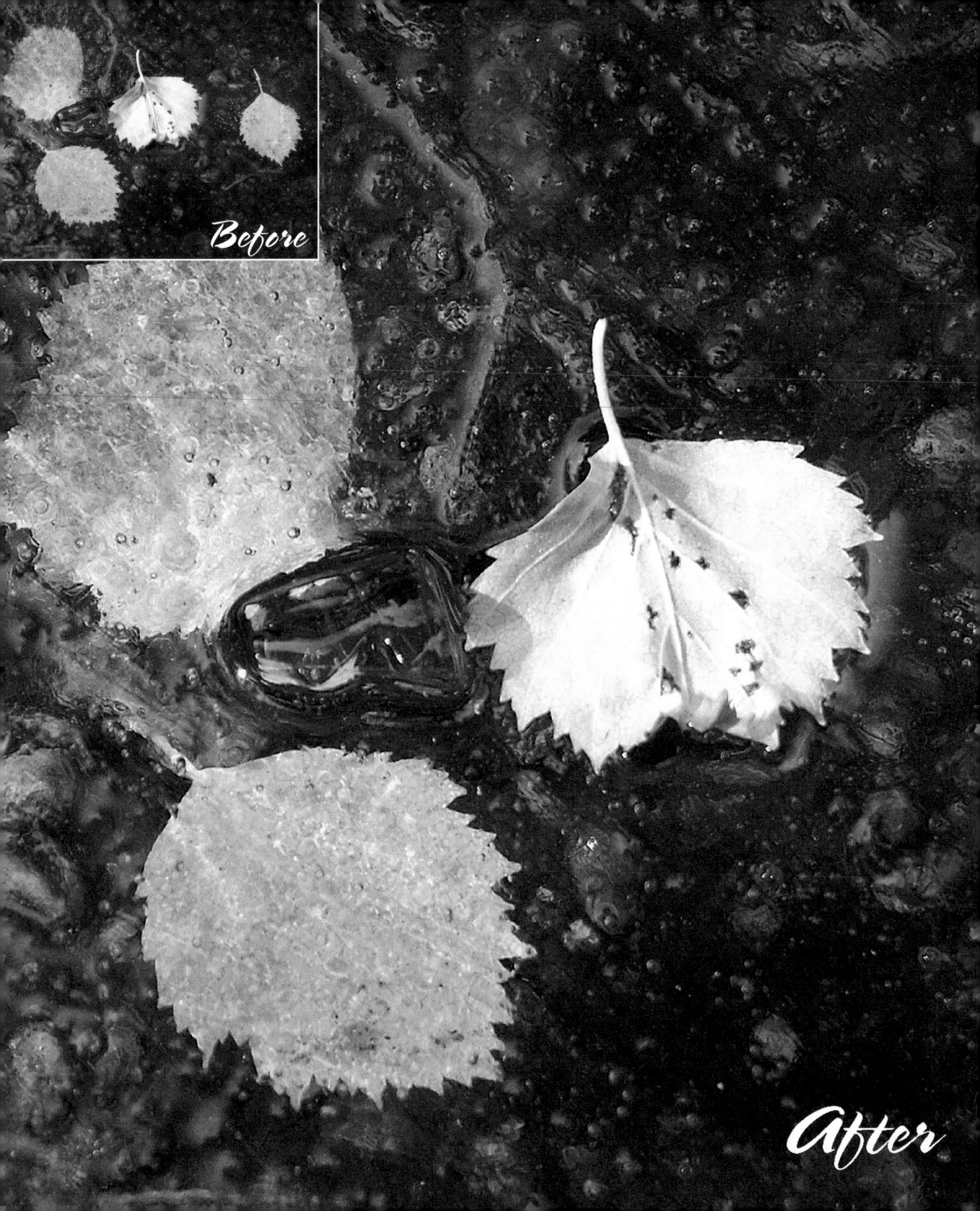
Before
After

9 SHARPENING MAKEOVERS

One of the more interesting collections of makeover tools you can find in Photoshop is the Sharpening tool set, the topic of this very chapter. Now, you may ask yourself why sharpening warrants its own chapter. My answer is simple: Sharpening is so flexible that you'll find yourself using it in a dozen or more (quite creative) ways. In addition, the vast majority of original digital images can benefit from sharpening, because the very act of capturing a digital image (whether you use a scanner or a digital camera) softens it. Most originals beg to be sharpened!

All sharpening tools accomplish their basic task — they increase the contrast between adjacent pixels. Or, stated another way, they increase the difference in grayscale value between two side-by-side pixels. But some sharpening tools are more sophisticated (provide more controls) than others. The better sharpening tools, such as Photoshop's Unsharp Mask and Smart Sharpen tools, allow you to control *how* much sharpening (contrast enhancement) is applied as well as *where* it is applied.

Small to moderate amounts of sharpening can be applied to provide the traditional sharpening functions, i.e., improving the visual focus of an image. But when applied in large amounts over large areas or widths, a sharpening tool can be used as an *image transformation* tool — not just sharpening the focus of an image, but in fact changing its entire look. And, like most tools, when applied in excess, you can sometimes create unexpected problems, such as high-edge contrast color shifts. So, understanding how a sharpening tool works will provide you with the creative control you want to achieve the look you want, as well as the ability to mitigate any problems you might inadvertently create.

Making Over Your Focus

Having the right amount of focus (sharpening) in the right places can make the difference between a good image and a stunning image. Here is just such an example:

① Open the Leaves_in_Ice.tif image.

Remember that you can grab this particular image from the Web site associated with this book.

I captured the aspen leaves you see here after an early autumn freeze in a High Sierra lake in John Muir Wilderness Area. Because it was the first freeze, the ice was clear and the leaves were still fresh. This image is all about

Photoshop Confidential

Capturing, Softening, and Sharpening

It turns out that the very act of capturing an image with a digital camera or scanner softens — defocuses — an image or scene. If you stop to think about what actually happens during this *digitizing* process (converting an image into pixels), you can understand why softening or defocusing occurs. The digital-capture process involves converting a scene (in digital photography) or image (in the case of scanning) from a very high-resolution image into a relatively low resolution. How high a resolution? Well, image scanning resolves at the level of film grain — really small — but digital photography resolves at the angstrom level — really, *really* small. That leaves the digital image with a lot of pixels to fill in via *interpolation* (averaging of data) — and this approximation softens the image. A typical transformation from high resolution to relatively low gives you pixels that measure about 1/300" square — 300 pixels per inch — and that involves a *lot* of interpolation, which means a big loss of focus. The softening is most pronounced along high-contrast edges (such as the edges of the leaves in the Leaves_in_Ice image). This makes sense, too; high-contrast edges have more difference in grayscale value than do low-contrast areas — and averaging those values mutes the contrast. No wonder high-contrast edges are softened more than low-contrast areas.

As a rule, whenever you evaluate an image for possible sharpening, watch for the presence of both high- and low-contrast edges. To represent the original focus or sharpness in the image, its high-contrast edges need more sharpening (because their contrast has been averaged); a low-contrast area needs less. Luckily, the handy Sharpening tools allow you to control not only how much to sharpen the edges (by contrast enhancement) but also where to apply the sharpening — more around the edges and less in low-contrast areas. Sophisticated tools such as Photoshop's Unsharp Mask and Smart Sharpen assist with this control, and so are most used.

One final word of caution about sharpening: A little bit goes a long way. Too much sharpening — especially in highlight areas or along very high-contrast edges — can lead to sharpening artifacts known affectionately as "blooming" (about which more in a minute) where light pixels are blown out to pure white. These obvious white ("bloomed") edges are tricky and tedious to fix; better to avoid them in the first place.

crispness in the leaves and the ice . . . but just capturing this image reduced the very crispness that was so compelling about the scene. So, if this image is to regain that crisp look, you'll want to push the sharpening pretty hard to hone the focus much as possible.

② Choose Image⇨Duplicate to make a duplicate copy.

It would be a shame to lose such a nice original image, so be sure to work on a copy.

③ Using your Spacebar and ⌘/Ctrl keys, zoom in on a portion of the image you suspect may need sharpening.

High-contrast edges are good candidates. Here, zoom in on the edge of the central, lighter-colored leaf so you can see part of the interior of the leaf, its edge, and some of the surrounding water.

Taz's Take: When applying critical sharpening adjustments, it's always a good idea to zoom in to see the pixel-level impact of the effect, and then zoom out to 100% every once in a while to see the Normal View results.

The view you see here is at about 250%.

④ Choose Filter⇨Sharpen⇨ Unsharp Mask.

Doing so calls up the Unsharp Mask dialog box.

⑤ In the Unsharp Mask dialog box, set the Amount to 100%, the Radius to 1 pixel, and the Threshold to 0 pixels.

Be sure to check the Preview check box so you can see what the sharpening results will look like before you apply them. (It's a good habit to develop.)

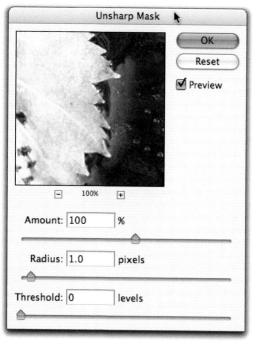

Making Over Your Focus *(continued)*

Note how the edge of the leaf pops out of the water, the small veins in the leaf stand out, and the water actually looks clearer.

If 100% does such a good job, why not try something a bit higher?

⑥ Choose Filter⇨Sharpen⇨ Unsharp Mask.

The Unsharp Mask dialog box makes another appearance.

⑦ In the Unsharp Mask dialog box, set the Amount to 200%, the Radius to 1 pixel, and the Threshold to 0 pixels.

Again, be sure to check the Preview check box so you can preview the sharpening results.

Note how the edge of the leaf noticeably pops out more, and the small veins in the leaf are even more obvious, and the bubbles in water really pop out.

In the midst of all this crispness, however, you'll also notice that there is an obvious light edge starting to form around the border of the leaf. This is the early onset of the sharpening artifact known as *blooming or haloing*, and it's definitely a danger sign.

Now, this sharpening and incipient blooming is more obvious at the current 250% magnification — so you may want to view this image at the standard 100% magnification; the effects of sharpening may be easier to evaluate at a more normal viewing size.

It turns out that at 100% you can still see the incipient blooming on the light-colored leaf edge. (Okay, some folks might not notice it, but you now know what to look for.) But notice that the incipient blooming is not apparent along the darker-colored leaf edges. That's because the pixels along the

edge of the lighter leaf are close to white —
and are in higher contrast to the surrounding dark water — so the sharpened contrast
is visually more obvious.

In circumstances like these, you may
want to actually measure the grayscale value
of the edge pixels to make sure they're not
blowing out (showing up as pure white).
Here's how that's done. . . .

8 **After returning to 250%
magnification, choose Window⇨
Info.**

Doing so calls up the Info palette.

9 **Select the Eyedropper tool
from the Toolbox and then move
the Eyedropper over the edge
pixels of the light leaf.**

You'll want to set your Eyedropper Sample
Average (in the Eyedropper Options bar) to
3 by 3. Avoid 5 by 5, as that will sample too
large an area to just sample the edge pixels.

Start your sampling here with no
Unsharp Mask filter applied.

Note that the RGB values here are 243,
251, and 243. Our target diffuse highlight
value is 5% or 242, 242, 242 (on the 0–255
scale); at 242, you don't get the loss of
detail or "blow-outs" in the highlight.

10 **Now choose Filter⇨Sharpen⇨
Unsharp Mask to call up the
Unsharp Mask dialog box, set
the Amount to 100%, the Radius
to 1 pixel, and the Threshold to
0 pixels and then remeasure the
RGB values.**

You'll see that the values are now 246, 252,
and 246, which means that the RGB values
have in fact increased but are not blown out
(yet).

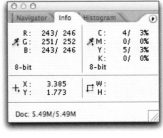

Making Over Your Focus (continued)

⓫ Using the Unsharp Mask dialog box, increase the Amount to 200% and then remeasure the RGB values.

Notice the RGB values are now 249, 252, and 248 — the RGB values have definitely increased even more and are getting close to blowout stage. (In fact, they may not print if RGB values drop much below 5% (242)).

Okay, time for one more adjustment.

⓬ Using the Unsharp Mask dialog box, keep the Amount at 200% but increase the Radius to 1.5 pixels, and then remeasure the RGB values.

This time we went over the line. The RGB values are all in the 250's (253, 255, 252), which means these values will likely blow out when printed. In any event, they'll probably *bloom* visually (display artifacts that were left by the sharpening process).

All of which goes to show that, if you want to use the Unsharp Mask filter on an image like this one, you're going to need to keep the Amount under 200% and the Radius at 1 pixel.

Taz's Take: The best radius for an image usually varies with the image resolution. High-resolution images typically require a higher radius to achieve the same amount of sharpening; that's because the radius is based on the number of pixels, not on percentages.

Now, *before* you click that OK button to apply your final sharpening values, cancel out of the Unsharp Mask dialog box and try Step 13.

⓭ Choose Filter➪Sharpen➪ Smart Sharpen.

Doing so calls up the Smart Sharpen dialog box.

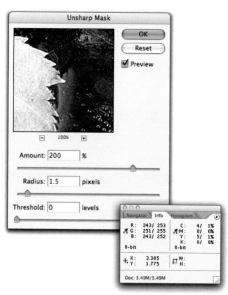

14 In the Smart Sharpen dialog box, check the Preview check-box, click the Advanced option, and then set the amount to 200% and the Radius to 1 pixel in the Sharpen tab.

You'll recognize these as the same values you used in the Unsharp Mask dialog box.

Note: Since we're dealing with a digital camera image here, be sure to choose Lens Blur from the Remove drop-down menu in the Smart Sharpen dialog box.

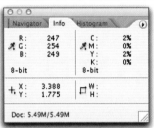

Now, the Smart Sharpen filter (only available in CS2) allows you to control the sharpening in the Highlight and Shadow areas separately. Here's how to regulate that feature.

15 Click on the Highlight tab in the Smart Sharpen dialog box.

The Smart Sharpen dialog box updates to show the new tab.

16 In the Highlight tab, set the Fade Amount to 5%, set the Tonal Width to 5% as well, and then remeasure your RGB values.

You'll see that the RGB values are now at 247, 254, and 249 — which means the RGB values in the highlight area are less likely to bloom visually or in print.

17 Click OK to apply the Smart Sharpen.

Compare and contrast the starting and sharpened versions of the Leaf in Ice images.

Notice how, in the sharpened image, the leaves really jump out at you and the ice seems to sparkle a bit more in the light?

Doing a Portrait-Sharpening Makeover

Whenever you sharpen portraits and other images that have both high-contrast edges and low-contrast areas, it's really important to avoid oversharpening the low-contrast areas so they don't become grainy. When you're working in the Unsharp Mask dialog box, you want to use the high-contrast edges to set your Amount and Radius values; use the image's low-contrast areas to set your Threshold values. (If you have different needs in your highlight and shadow areas, then I'd recommend using the Smart Sharpen tool.)

① Open the Woman_with_Wine. tif image.

You can download this image from the Web site associated with this book. (You might recognize it as the image color-corrected in Chapter 4.)

② Choose Image⇨Duplicate to make a duplicate copy.

Be sure to work on a copy here.

③ Using your Spacebar and ⌘/Ctrl keys, zoom in close on the area containing her eyes, cheek, hair, and lips.

You want crispness in the facial features, since the eye is naturally drawn to the face.

④ Choose Filter⇨Sharpen⇨ Unsharp Mask.

The Unsharp Mask dialog box makes an appearance.

⑤ In the Unsharp Mask dialog box, set the Amount to 100%, the Radius to 1 pixel, and the Threshold to 0 levels.

Notice that the high-contrast edges here are now nicely sharpened — but the skin is over-sharpened and has a mottled appearance.

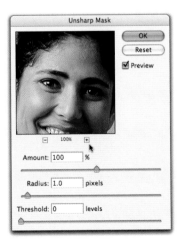

The Unsharp Mask values of 100/1/0 used here are the ones most often recommended for general sharpening, but you can see that such generalizations don't always work. With this image, using these "standard" values oversharpens the lower-contrast skin areas.

Taz's Take: There are as many opinions about how much sharpening to apply as there are images and people who sharpen them. I have two colleagues (both well respected and knowledgeable) who offer quite different recommendations for the same image: One suggested 35–50 and the other argued for 150–200. The main point is: If you understand how your sharpening tool works and you zoom in and view and measure your images and their edges, you will make your own well-informed decisions . . . and to heck with what anybody else says!

Note: Such oversharpening is a common occurrence with portrait images, especially those created with a digital camera, where some sharpening has already been applied.

6 **Back in the Unsharp Mask dialog box, leave the Amount at 100% and the Radius at 1 pixel, but change the Threshold to 3 levels.**

Note how much smoother the low-contrast skin-tone areas are now, while the high-contrast edges (such as hair, eyes, and teeth) are still well sharpened.

Note: You should experiment with Threshold values ranging from 3 to 5, depending on the image.

7 **Click OK to apply these Unsharp Mask values.**

Looking pretty good, but because your RGB image has *three* channels — each with its own contrast — sharpening tends to be applied unevenly on the three channels. This can sometimes cause color shifts to occur

along high-contrast edges. These shifts are most apparent when white is present along one side of the edge.

To make sure that the sharpening is applied equally, you'll need to do two more steps after each sharpening event.

⑧ Choose Edit⇨Fade Unsharp Mask.

The Fade dialog box duly appears.

⑨ In the Fade dialog box, choose Luminosity from the Mode drop-down menu, and then click OK.

Now look at your high-resolution finished image.

Because you're applying the Unsharp Mask to just the Luminance values, you redistribute the Unsharp Mask effect evenly on all three channels — ensuring that no color shifts occur.

Note: You can accomplish the same effect by converting your image to Lab mode (Choose Image⇨Mode⇨Lab) and applying your sharpening to only the Lightness channel.

Before

After

Making Over Line Art

Sharpening tools are most commonly used to improve the focus or sharpness of photographic images — which is precisely what you've used sharpening for up to this point in this chapter. Sharpening tools, however, can also be used creatively to alter line-art images to great effect. Here is a dandy example:

1 Open a line-art image that was captured or created in either Grayscale or RGB mode.

The Doggie_GS image, available for download from the Web site associated with this book, would be a good choice. You'll notice that this particular image has light lined edges that are soft and not very well defined — and its background is a tad dingy.

Note: Having your line art captured in grayscale or RGB mode is critical if you want to creatively adjust your image; a 1-bit mode will not provide enough editable image data for you to work with.

2 Choose Image⇨Duplicate to make a duplicate copy.

Always, always work on a copy.

With copy in hand, start out by taking care of the dingy background.

3 Choose Image⇨Adjustments⇨ Levels.

Doing so calls up the Levels dialog box.

Notice the tall data peak at the highlight end of the histogram. The dingy paper is the root cause of that spike.

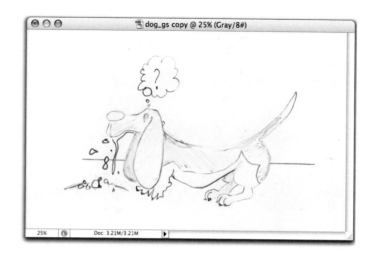

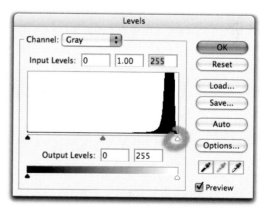

Making Over Line Art *(continued)*

④ In the Levels dialog box, move the Highlight slider to the left until it is in the middle of the space where the tall data peak bumps (massively) upward.

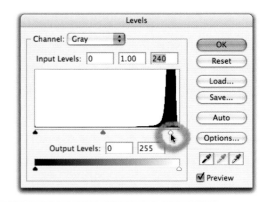

Doing so scrubs away a lot of the dinginess in the background.

Note: You can use the Info palette here (Window⇨Info) to measure the background; make sure that it measures 255 — the value for pure white.

⑤ Click OK to close the Levels dialog box.

Doing so applies the specified levels adjustment.

With the background set, it's time to sharpen the line art itself. To see what kind of flexibility you have, I'm going to suggest coming up with several (competing) sharpened versions.

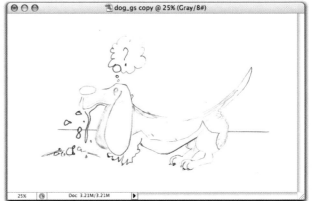

⑥ Choose Image⇨Duplicate four times to make four duplicate copies of this levels-adjusted image.

The four, the merrier.

⑦ Activate one of the four copies and then choose Filter⇨Sharpen⇨Unsharp Mask.

Doing so calls up the Unsharp Mask dialog box.

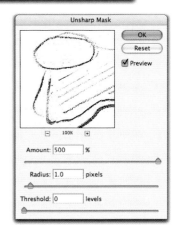

⑧ In the Unsharp Mask dialog box, set the Amount to 500%, the Radius to 1 pixel, and the Threshold to 0 levels.

You'll notice right away that the line-art lines are much better defined. The large amount of Unsharp Mask pushes your pixel values strongly toward either black or white.

9 Choose File⇨Save As and then use the Save As dialog box to save the file as Doggie_500_1_0.

One down, three to go.

10 Activate the second of the four copies and then choose Filter⇨Sharpen⇨Unsharp Mask.

The Unsharp Mask dialog box makes another appearance.

11 In the Unsharp Mask dialog box, set the Amount to 500%, the Radius to 5 pixels, and the Threshold to 0 levels.

The line-art lines are now much better defined. That's because the large amount of Unsharp Mask is pushing the pixel values strongly toward either black or white. (Yep, there's a theme developing here.)

Note: Assigning a larger radius applies the amount of the sharpening (edge contrast enhancement) to a wider swath of pixels, thereby making thicker edges.

12 Choose File⇨Save As and then use the Save As dialog box to save the file as doggie_55_5_0.

That's two in the bag.

13 Activate the third of the four copies and then choose Filter⇨Sharpen⇨Unsharp Mask.

The Sharp Unmask dialog box appears yet again.

14 In the Sharp Unmask dialog box, set the Amount to 500%, the Radius to 20 pixels, and the Threshold to 0 levels.

Increasing the Radius here to 20 creates even thicker, darker appearing edges.

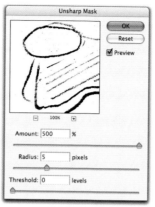

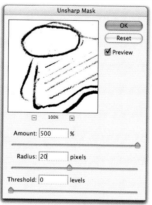

Making Over Line Art (continued)

15 Choose File⇨Save As and then use the Save As dialog box to save the file as doggie_500_ 20_0.

One more to go.

16 Activate the last of the four copies and then choose Filter⇨ Sharpen⇨Unsharp Mask.

The Unsharp Mask dialog box makes yet another appearance.

17 In the Unsharp Mask dialog box, set the Amount to 500%, the Radius to 100 pixels, and the Threshold to 0 levels.

Note how much better defined the line-art lines are now. Applying a large amount of Unsharp Mask pushes the pixel values strongly toward either black or white, while thickening the edges at the same time, creating another variation. (Same approach, different look.)

18 Choose File⇨Save As and then use the Save As dialog box to save the file as doggie_100_0.

You now have all four versions safely stowed on your hard drive.

19 Compare and contrast all versions of the adjusted image.

Look at these five variations on the original line-art image.

Each one has different adjustments applied to it, from a levels-only adjustment through four different Unsharp Mask adjustments. Add to that a nearly-infinite variety of settings you can apply and you get a huge range of creative makeover possibilities.

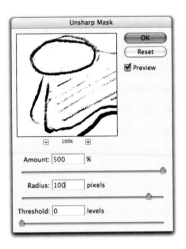

Doing a Wood-Grain Makeover

The previous makeover demonstrated that the creative uses of sharpening tools can give you some pretty dramatic makeover alterations of line-art images. You can use a similar range of sharpening-based creative makeover possibilities to jazz up photographic images as well. Here's an especially cool one.

① Open the Wood_Grain_RGB. tif image.

You can download this image from the Web site associated with this book.

Let's try a little role-playing exercise here. Imagine that some clients have approached you and want you to take this initial image as a starting point to create a variety of background textures for them to look at. Here's what you'd do. . . .

② Choose Image⇨Duplicate to make a duplicate copy.

Keep the original safe and sound by working on a copy.

③ Choose Window⇨Layers.

Doing so calls up the Layers palette.

④ With the original Background layer active in the Layers palette, choose Layer⇨Duplicate Layer.

Doing so calls up the Duplicate Layer dialog box.

⑤ In the Duplicate Layer dialog box, name the duplicate layer Wood Grain_Source and click OK.

The duplicate layer joins its twin in the Layers palette.

Doing a Wood-Grain Makeover *(continued)*

⑥ In the Layers palette, click on the Background layer to select it.

We'll want to use the white background to set off the wood grain.

⑦ Choose Edit⇨Fill.

The Fill dialog box makes an appearance.

⑧ In the Fill dialog box, choose White from the Use drop-down menu, set the Blending Mode to Normal, and set the Opacity to 100%.

With these settings, your Background layer will be completely filled with white.

⑨ With Wood Grain_Source active in the Layers palette, first choose Layer⇨Duplicate Layer and then use the Duplicate Layer dialog box that appears to name the new layer Wood Grain_500_1.

⑩ In the Layers palette, click on the Eye icon to the left of Wood Grain_Source layer to make the layer invisible.

With the Wood Grain layer's visibility turned off, you'll only be able see and edit the Wood Grain_500_1 layer.

⑪ With the Wood Grain_500_1 layer selected in the Layers palette, choose Filter⇨Sharpen⇨ Unsharp Mask.

The Unsharp Mask dialog box appears on-screen.

⑫ In the Unsharp Mask dialog box, set the Amount to 500%, the Radius to 5 pixels, and the Threshold to 0 levels.

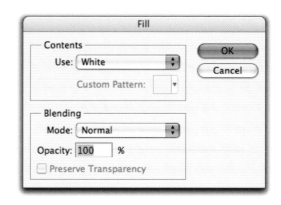

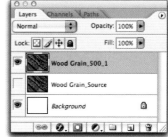

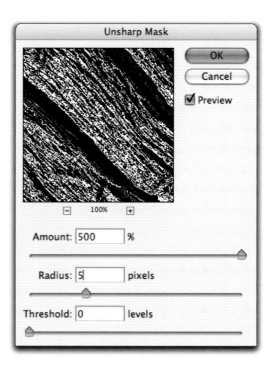

Note the fine-grained texture created in the wood.

⓭ With the Wood_Grain_Source layer active in the Layers palette, choose Layer⇨Duplicate Layer.

The Duplicate Layer dialog box appears.

⓮ In the Duplicate Layer dialog box, rename the layer Wood_ Grain_500_5 and click OK.

The Wood_Grain_500_5 layer is added to the Layers palette.

⓯ Drag the Wood_Grain_500_5 layer to the top of the Layers palette and then choose Filter⇨ Sharpen⇨Unsharp Mask.

The Unsharp Mask dialog box appears yet again.

⓰ In the Unsharp Mask dialog box, set the Amount to 500, the Radius to 10, and the Threshold to 0.

This is a coarser-grained texture than the texture created in Step 12.

⓱ Duplicate the Wood_Grain_ Source layer and rename the duplicate layer Wood_Grain_ 500_100.

The Layers palette is getting a tad crowded by now.

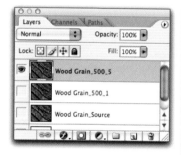

Doing a Wood-Grain Makeover *(continued)*

⑱ Drag the Wood_Grain_500_100 layer to the top of the Layers palette and then choose Filter⇨Sharpen⇨Unsharp Mask.

Yes, it's the Unsharp Mask dialog box again.

⑲ In the Unsharp Mask dialog box, set the Amount to 500%, the Radius to 100 pixels, and the Threshold to 0 levels.

You'll notice that things are getting coarser and coarser around here.

Note: Remember that the whole purpose of this exercise was to create a useful background texture. And, by inverting at this point, you are adding to the texture effect.

⑳ Duplicate the Wood_Grain_500_100 layer and rename the duplicate layer Wood_Grain_500_100_Invert.

Here's a perfect example of why it's such a good idea to completely label your layers with info about how you created them. (You can't tell the players without a scorecard.)

㉑ With the Wood_Grain_500_100_Invert layer selected in the Layers palette, choose Image⇨Adjustments⇨Invert.

Note that the Invert command creates a negative image by swapping black for white and white for black, and swapping other grayscale values for their opposite values at the other end of the tonal range.

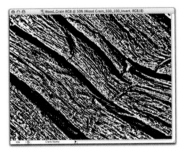

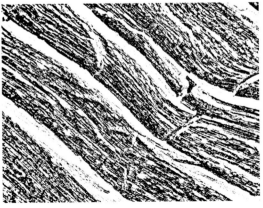

㉒ With the Wood_Grain_500_100_Invert layer still selected in the Layers palette, choose Filter⇨Sharpen⇨Unsharp Mask.

Doing so calls up the Unsharp Mask dialog box.

㉓ In the Unsharp Mask dialog box, set the Amount to 500%, the Radius to 5 pixels, and the Threshold to 0 levels.

Notice here how the light and dark layers spread farther apart.

We're close to having a workable background texture here, but we'll have to reduce the opacity a bit.

㉔ In the Layers palette, select the Wood_Grain_500_100_Invert layer and toggle off the visibility of all other layers except the Background layer.

㉕ Using the Opacity drop-down menu in the upper-right corner of the Layers palette, reduce the opacity to 5%.

The reduction in opacity here sends the texture to the background.

㉖ To save a specific layer or combination of layers as your final result, simply turn off the views of all the unwanted layers and then choose Layer⇨Flatten.

A single image emerges from your layer and/or layers.

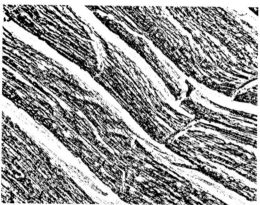

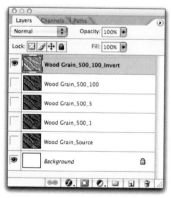

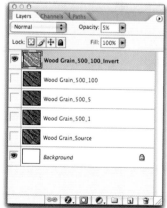

10

SHADOW MAKEOVERS

Adding shadows to images can provide a variety of effects to your images — and give your images a finished look to boot. Some shadows, such as naturally cast shadows, can help added image elements fit in with their surroundings. In other circumstances (product shots on flat backgrounds comes to mind), you can use shadows to help an object stand out from its surroundings.

Shadows can be made either manually or, for a more automatic touch, by using Layer styles. In either case, you want to be able to control the placement, width, color, and transparency of your shadow, as well as its interaction with objects beneath the shadow. The makeovers in this chapter walk you through how to deal with such contingencies.

Making Over the Shadows for Your Objects

People generally expect objects to have shadows. If an object in one of your images doesn't have a natural shadow (for whatever reason), you can give nature a helping hand by using any of several techniques to create your object's shadows. Here are three useful methods.

Knocking Out Shadows

Got your boxing gloves ready? Time to do some "shadow boxing"!

❶ Open an image you feel could use a shadow.

If you like, you could go with the Lens.tif image here, available for download from the Web site associated with this book. The idea here is to find an image on a white background — the white makes it fairly easy to select (and work with) the image.

❷ Choose Image⇨Duplicate to make a duplicate copy.

Always work on a copy. Always.

Now, most methods of creating shadows require that you make a selection of the image so the image can be handled separately from the shadow. Time to do that now.

❸ Select the Magic Wand tool from the Toolbox.

As always, selecting the tool calls up the tool's Options bar as well.

❹ In the tool's Options bar, leave the Tolerance at 32 (the default setting) and check both the Anti-Alias and Contiguous check boxes.

A Tolerance of 32 should work fine, but be prepared to raise or lower that tolerance

depending upon how your initial selection looks.

⑤ Using the Magic Wand tool, click on the white background.

Doing so should select just the white background. If it doesn't, then you'll want to tweak the Tolerance setting and reselect the background.

⑥ Choose Select⇨Inverse to select the lens instead of the background.

A neat trick, don't you think?

⑦ Using your Spacebar and ⌘/Ctrl keys, zoom in on the edge of your selection and check the position of the selection.

If, after inversion, the selection is several pixels inside the edge of the object, you may want to use the Magic Wand's Options bar to reduce the initial Tolerance setting and then make another selection. If the selection border is too far outside the selection, then you may want to increase the Tolerance setting.

Note: The marching-ant selection should be within 1 pixel of the edge of the image.

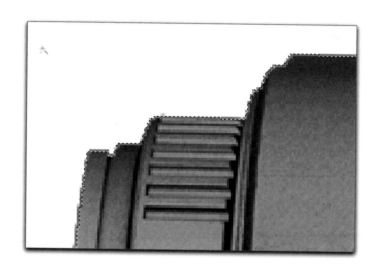

Photoshop Confidential

Silhouette-Oriented Image Capture

You can make your shadows far easier to create if you think about *future* shadow-creation challenges when you capture your image. If you can control the image capture of objects that you intend to shadow, consider capturing your object against a red, green, or blue background. Select the background color to provide the greatest contrast with the image. If one of those colors is in high contrast with the image, then make the silhouette selection of the image on that color's channel — it's a lot easier than making the selection on the composite RGB channel. Images with chrome are usually best captured on white or another neutral color, to prevent the reflection of the color being captured and reproduced in the reflection of the chrome.

Making Over the Shadows for Your Objects *(continued)*

❽ (Optional) Click the Edit in QuickMask Mode button in the Toolbox to provide you with a more complete view of your selection.

The QuickMask color should extend to the edge of the selection, fading right at the edge.

Taz's Take: If you are creating and using shadows on white backgrounds, the precision of your silhouette and the cleanliness of your selection edge is a lot less critical than if you end up placing your image and shadow on a color background. For some tips on fine-tuning and cleaning up your selection edges, see the next makeover on testing and fine-tuning your silhouette.

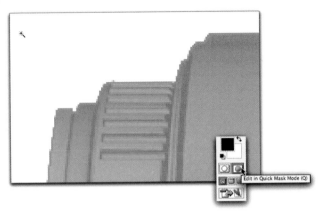

❾ Choose Select⇨Save Selection.

Doing so calls up the Save Selection dialog box.

❿ In the Save Selection dialog box, name your selection Lens Mask, and click OK.

Doing so saves your selection and adds it to the Channels palette.

Now its time to get the Shadow layer ready.

⓫ Choose Layer⇨New⇨Layer.

A new layer is created. Go ahead and name this layer Shadow.

Note: If you hold down the Opt/Alt key as you create your new layer, you can name this layer as you create it. Otherwise you'll want to select the layer's name in the Layers palette and rename it there.

⓬ With the Shadow layer selected in the Layers palette, choose Select⇨Load Selection.

The Load Selection dialog box appears.

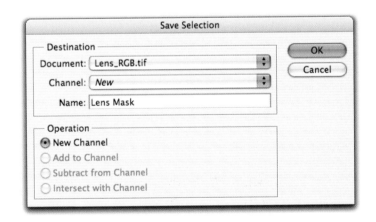

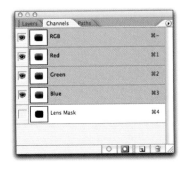

⓭ In the Load Selection dialog box, choose Lens Mask from the Channel drop-down menu and select the New Selection radio button.

Your selection is duly loaded into the Shadow channel.

⓮ Choose Edit⇨Fill.

Doing so calls up the Fill dialog box.

⓯ In the Fill dialog box, choose Black from the Use drop-down menu, choose Multiply from the Mode drop-down menu, set the Opacity to 100%, and uncheck the Preserve Transparency check box.

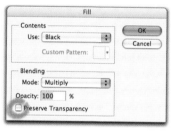
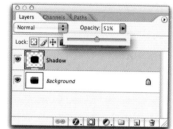

It is *really* important that you uncheck the Preserve Transparency check box; otherwise, you will not be able to effectively make transparency-dependent adjustments such as blurs and opacity changes.

⓰ In the Layers palette, reduce the opacity of the Shadow layer to approximately 50%.

The idea here is to see the lens through the shadow.

⓱ With the Shadow layer still active in the Layers palette, select the Move tool from the Toolbox and use your arrow keys to move the shadow down and to the right.

I'd try moving the shadow 5 pixels in each direction.

⓲ Deselect your selection by pressing ⌘/Ctrl+D.

Making Over the Shadows for Your Objects (continued)

You have your shadow in position, but it could use a little blurring to make it look a bit more natural.

⓳ Choose Filter⇨Blur⇨ Gaussian Blur.

Doing so calls up the Gaussian Blur dialog box.

⓴ In the Gaussian Blur dialog box, set the Radius to 5.0 pixels.

You now have a nice blur added to the Shadow layer.

Note: Be sure to deselect your shadow beforehand: otherwise the blur will not be applied completely.

　　Okay, now comes the *knockout* part.

㉑ With the Shadow layer still active in the Layers palette, choose Select⇨Load Selection.

The Load Selection dialog box duly appears.

㉒ In the Load Selection dialog box, choose Lens Mask from the Channel drop-down menu.

The Lens Mask selection is loaded in the original shadow position, directly on top of the lens image.

㉓ Press the Delete key to knock out the section of the shadow that is directly over the lens.

The idea here is to create the impression of a drop shadow, even though the Shadow layer is on top in the Layers palette.

㉔ Deselect your selection to see the finished (shadowed) product.

Note: You can adjust the opacity of the Shadow layer to change the strength of the shadow appearance.

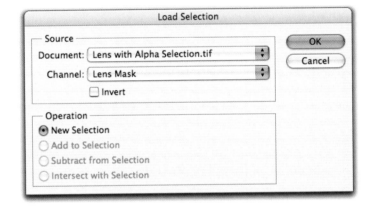

Also try duplicating the Shadow layer and adjusting the opacity of both shadow layers to achieve various shadow effects.

Keep the Lens.tif image open for the next makeover.

Layer Style Object Shadow

It used to be that you had to create all your shadows — and many other effects — manually in Photoshop. But since Photoshop added the Layer Styles feature, applying many of these effects has become easier. You can now choose from a wide variety of special effects to add to any layer by simply activating the Layer Style dialog box for that layer: Here's how:

❶ Open an image with an Alpha channel selection.

If you want, you can use the Lens.tif image from the previous makeover, as long as it has an Alpha-channel selection. (If you haven't completed the previous Knockout makeover, you'll need to complete at least Steps 1 through 10 of that makeover to create an image with an Alpha-channel selection.)

❷ Choose Select⇨Load Selection.

The Load Selection dialog box duly appears.

❸ In the Load Selection dialog box, choose Lens Mask from the Channel drop-down menu.

The Lens Mask selection is loaded directly on top of the lens image.

❹ Choose Layer⇨New⇨Layer via Cut.

Doing so moves the lens to a new layer surrounded by transparency (clear checkerboard area) and fills the original background layer with white. Name this layer Lens.

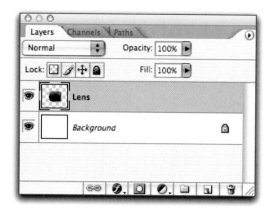

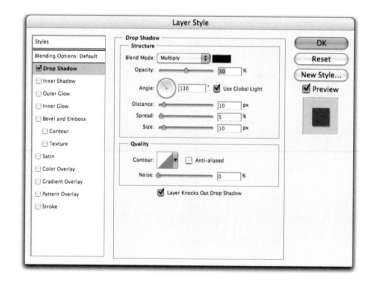

Making Over the Shadows for Your Objects *(continued)*

⑤ In the Layers palette, double-click the blank space in the Lens entry to the right of the name.

The Layer Style dialog box makes an appearance.

⑥ In the Layer Style dialog box, click on the Drop Shadow option in the Styles list to activate it.

The options in the main section of the dialog box update themselves to reflect your choice.

⑦ Click the Preview check box, choose Multiply from the Blend Mode drop-down menu, set the Opacity to 50%, the Angle to 130°, the distance to 10 pixels, the spread to 5%, the size to 10 pixels, and then click OK to apply the Drop Shadow Layer Style.

Your Lens now sports a nice new drop shadow.

Note: Whenever you add a layer style, a small *f* appears in the Layers palette next to the affected layer.

One really nice aspect of creating a drop shadow this way is that if you change your mind about the look of your drop shadow, all you need to do is double-click the right side of the Lens layer to reactivate and edit the Layer Style dialog box.

As is the case with any adjustment layer, a Layer effects adjustment is temporary, completely changeable, and nondestructive until you flatten your layers. This provides you with Editing-Without-Fear confidence!

Note: Be sure to flatten and remove the Alpha channel from a *copy* of this image before you use it for final output. This can be done by choosing File➪Save As and then unchecking the Layers and Alpha Channel

check boxes in the Save As dialog box when you save a copy of your image.

Spot-Shadow Creation

Here is an interesting and useful drop-shadow variation that may come in handy when you need to make a few drop shadows quickly.

① Open an image that has an Alpha-channel selection.

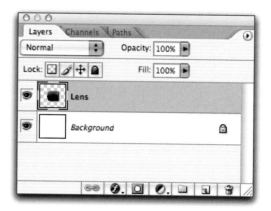

Again, feel free to use the Lens.tif image from the previous makeover, as long as it has an Alpha-channel selection. (If you have not yet completed the previous Knockout makeover, you'll need to complete at least Steps 1 through 10 of that makeover to create an image with an Alpha-channel selection.)

② Choose Select⇨Load Selection.

The Load Selection dialog box duly appears.

③ In the Load Selection dialog box, choose Lens Mask from the Channel drop-down menu.

The Lens Mask selection is loaded directly on top of the lens image.

④ Choose Layer⇨New⇨Layer via Cut.

Doing so moves the lens to a new layer surrounded by transparency (clear checker-board area) and fills the original background layer with white. Name this layer Lens.

⑤ In the Layers palette, click the Background layer.

The white Background layer is now active.

⑥ Choose the Elliptical Marquee tool from the Toolbox.

As always, calling up the tool calls up the tool's Options bar as well.

Making Over the Shadows for Your Objects *(continued)*

❼ In the tool's Options bar, set the Feather to 15 pixels.

You can tweak this setting later if you want.

❽ Using the Elliptical Marquee tool, draw a selection under the lens.

Your ellipse should be slightly smaller than the lens itself.

With our ellipse in place, it's time to fill it with something appropriately dark and shadowlike.

❾ Choose Edit⇨Fill.

Doing so calls up the Fill dialog box.

❿ In the Fill dialog box, choose Black from the Use drop-down menu, choose Multiply from the Blending Mode drop-down menu, set the Opacity to 100%, be sure to *uncheck* the Preserve Transparency check box, and then click OK.

Our elliptical selection is now black as (feathered) night.

⓫ Choose Layer⇨Layer New⇨Layer via Cut.

This moves the feathered elliptical selection to its own layer in the Layers palette. Name this layer Spot Shadow.

⓬ Using the Opacity drop-down menu in the Layers palette, lower the opacity of this layer to 75%.

Doing so creates a nifty little spot drop shadow beneath your object.

Before

After

Testing and Fine-Tuning Your Silhouette

If you're unlucky enough to have to place your image and its drop shadow on a colored background, even small imperfections in the edge of your silhouette will be obvious. Here is a little silhouette-testing method and fine-tuning technique you may find useful.

❶ Open the Lens.tif image.

Might as well stick with something familiar.

❷ Choose Image⇨Duplicate to make a duplicate copy.

Always work on a copy. Always.

Most shadow-creation methods require that you make a selection of the image so the image can be handled separately from the shadow. Let's do that right now.

❸ Select the Magic Wand tool from the Toolbox.

As expected, choosing the tool calls up its Options bar as well.

❹ In the tool's Options bar, keep the initial Tolerance setting at 15 (the default level) and check both the Anti-Alias and Contiguous check boxes.

The default setting should work fine, but be prepared to raise or lower the Tolerance setting, depending upon how your initial selection looks.

❺ Using the Magic Wand tool, click the white background.

Doing so selects just the white background.

❻ Choose Select⇨Inverse to select the lens instead of the background.

I love how that works.

Now it's time to make a silhouette layer.

Testing and Fine-Tuning Your Silhouette *(continued)*

⑦ Choose Layer⇨New⇨Layer via Cut.

Doing so moves the lens to a new layer surrounded by transparency (clear checkerboard area) and fills the original background layer with white. Name this layer **Lens**.

One layer down, one more to go.

⑧ Choose Layer⇨New⇨Layer.

A brand-spanking-new layer appears in the Layers palette. Name this layer Black and move it below the Lens layer.

⑨ In the Layers palette, select the new layer and then choose Edit⇨Fill.

The Fill dialog box appears on-screen.

⑩ In the Fill dialog box, choose Black from the Use drop-down menu, choose Normal from the Blending Mode drop-down menu, set the Opacity to 100%, uncheck the Preserve Transparency check box, and click OK.

Doing all this places a completely black layer below the Lens layer — a layer that you can then use for examining your silhouette edge.

⑪ Click the Lens layer in the Layers palette, and then (using your Spacebar and ⌘/Ctrl keys) zoom in on the edge of the lens.

Note that there is a row of lighter-colored pixels along the edge. They aren't obvious when this selection is placed on a white background, but they may become glaringly obvious when placed on a darker background.

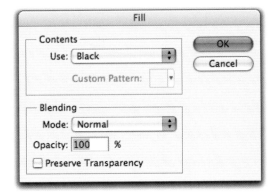

To remove these subtle-but-problematic pixels, we're going to do something Photoshop calls *defringing*.

⑫ Choose Layer⇨Matting⇨ Defringe.

Doing so calls up the Defringe dialog box.

⑬ In the Defringe dialog box, set the Width to 1 pixel, and then click OK.

All those lighter pixels are surgically removed, creating a very clean edge.

Your silhouetted image can then be placed on any background with confidence.

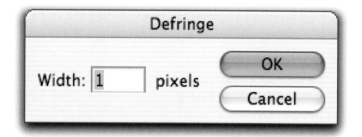

Doing a Full-Image Drop-Shadow Makeover

Creating a drop shadow under the entire image can enhance many images — and it isn't even that hard to do!

❶ Open an image you would like to shadow.

The Kbay_Gradient Sky.tif image, available for download from the Web site associated with this book, would do nicely.

❷ Choose Image⇨Duplicate to make a duplicate copy.

Always, always work with a copy.

❸ Press ⌘/Ctrl+A to select the entire image, and then choose Select⇨Save Selection.

The Save Selection dialog box appears.

❹ Using the Save Selection dialog box, name the selection Shadow Mask.

We're going to need a bit more room if we want our shadow to show, so let's add some canvas.

❺ Choose Image⇨Canvas Size.

The Canvas Size dialog box appears on-screen.

❻ In the Canvas Size dialog box, set the increase in both the Width and the Height fields to 20%, check the Relative check box, and then click OK.

The original image now appears in the middle of an extended white canvas, ready for its new shadow.

⑦ Choose Layer⇨New⇨Layer.

A new layer appears in the Layers palette. Name this layer Shadow.

⑧ With the Shadow layer selected in the Layers palette, choose Select⇨Load Selection.

The Load Selection dialog box makes an appearance.

⑨ In the Load Selection dialog box, choose Shadow Mask from the Channel menu and click OK.

Doing so loads the original full-image selection, but this time on the Shadow channel.

⑩ Choose Edit⇨Fill.

The Fill dialog box appears on-screen.

⑪ In the Fill dialog box, choose Black from the Use drop-down menu, Multiply from the Blending Mode drop-down menu, set the Opacity to 100%, uncheck the Preserve Transparency check box, and then click OK.

The specified fill is applied.

⑫ In the Layers palette, set the Opacity drop-down menu for the Shadow layer to approximately 50%.

The idea here is to see the position of the shadow in relationship to the underlying image.

⑬ Using your Spacebar and ⌘/Ctrl keys, zoom in on the lower-right corner of the image.

It's always important to see (in detail) what you're about to do.

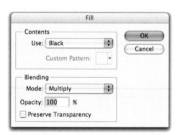

Doing a Full-Image Drop-Shadow Makeover (continued)

⑭ **With the Shadow layer active, select the Move tool from the Toolbox and move the shadow 6 pixels down and 6 pixels to the right.**

You definitely have a shadow now, but it could use some blurring.

⑮ **Choose Filter⇨Blur⇨ Gaussian Blur.**

Doing so calls up the Gaussian Blur dialog box.

⑯ **In the Gaussian Blur dialog box, set the Radius to 5 pixels.**

You can tweak this setting later, if you like.

⑰ **Back in the Layers palette, select Multiply from the Layers Blending menu.**

Selecting Multiply here creates a darker, denser, more apparent shadow.

This is starting to look pretty good, but the shadow looks a bit excessive.

⑱ **Choose Select⇨Load Selection.**

The Load Selection dialog box appears yet again.

⑲ **In the Load Selection dialog box, choose Shadow Mask from the Channel drop-down menu.**

This loads the original full-image selection once again onto the Shadow layer in its original position.

⑳ **Press the Delete key to remove the excess shadow.**

Your image is now blessed with a beautiful full-image drop shadow.

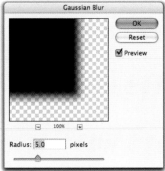

Making Over Cast Shadows

Creating a *cast shadow* — where one object "casts a shadow" on another object — is an effective way to create the impression of light shining from a particular direction. Here is one way to add your own cast shadows to an image.

❶ Open two images where you would like to create a cast shadow of one on top of the other.

The Leaf.tif and and Rust.tif images, available for download from the Web site associated with this book, would be good choices.

❷ Choose Image⇨Duplicate twice to make a duplicate copy of each image.

When in doubt — or when not in doubt — make a copy.

❸ With the Leaf.tif image active, select the Magic Wand tool from the Toolbox.

The tool becomes active and the tool's Options bar appears on-screen.

❹ In the tool's Options bar, set the Tolerance to 30, and check both the Anti-Alias and the Contiguous check boxes.

A tolerance of 30 should work, but be prepared to tweak this setting if the selection doesn't come out as you expect.

❺ Using the Magic Wand tool, click the white background in the Leaf.tif image.

Just the background is selected.

❻ Choose Select⇨Inverse to select the leaf.

In a flash, just the leaf is selected.

Making Over Cast Shadows *(continued)*

❼ Choose Layer➪New➪Layer via Cut.

Doing so moves the leaf to its own layer in the Layers palette.

❽ Choose Layer➪Matting➪ Defringe.

The Defringe dialog box makes an appearance.

❾ In the Defringe dialog box, set the Width to 1 pixel and click OK.

Doing so removes any white spillover originating from the white background.

❿ Select the Move Tool from the Toolbox, and then click and drag the Leaf layer onto the Rust image.

The Leaf image is placed on its own layer over the Rust image (as can be seen in the Layers palette). Name the new layer Leaf.

⓫ With the Leaf layer active, press ⌘/Ctrl+T to activate the Free Transform tool.

Doing so adds a Free Transform Control box around the selection.

⓬ Press the Shift key and click and drag one of the corner points of the Free Transform Control box to scale down the leaf image.

You will want to scale down the leaf at least enough so that there's room to cast a shadow across the background.

⓭ Press the Enter key to apply the transformation.

Then, using the Move tool (V), move the leaf over toward the lower-right corner of

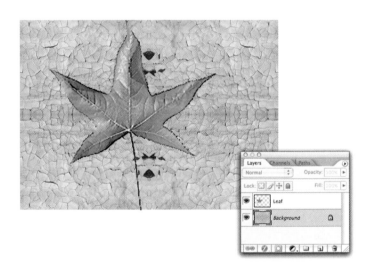

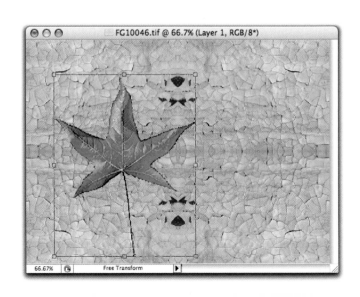

the image. (You can either manually drag the leaf or use your arrows keys.)

Now that all your ducks are in a row, it's time to add the shadow.

⓮ With the Leaf Layer active in the Layers palette, choose Layer⇨Duplicate Layer.

Name this layer Cast Shadow.

⓯ In the Layers palette, click and drag this Cast Shadow Layer so it is located under the Leaf layer.

Shadows appear beneath objects, right?

⓰ With the Cast Shadow layer selected, press ⌘/Ctrl+T to activate the Free Transform tool.

A Free Transform Control box appears around the leaf on the Cast Shadow layer.

⓱ Press the ⌘/Ctrl key while clicking and dragging first one then the other top corner points on the Free Transform Control box so the Cast Shadow layer is skewed off to the right.

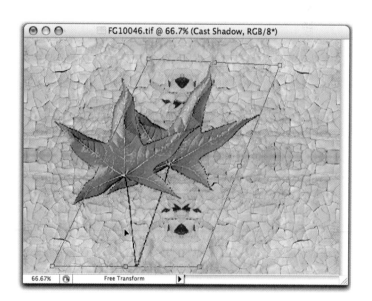

Note: You can also drag the top center point to transform both corner points simultaneously.

Using the ⌘/Ctrl key here provides you with the ability to freely move your control points, as compared with using the Shift key earlier that allowed us to scale proportionally.

⓲ Click the Enter key to apply the transformation.

Your Shadow layer is now appropriately skewed, just like cast shadows in the real world.

Making Over Cast Shadows *(continued)*

⑲ Select the Gradient tool from the Toolbox and, in the Options bar that appears, select a standard black-to-white gradient, choose Normal from the Mode drop-down menu, and set the Opacity to 100%.

The idea here is to give some character to your shadow, rather than keeping it a uniform black.

⑳ With the Cast Shadow layer active, click the Lock Transparent Pixels button at the top of the Layers palette.

Locking the transparency of this layer protects the transparency of the cast-shadow part of the layer (the Leaf Shadow part) so that, when you apply the Gradient tool to the entire layer, it will be applied only to the leaf's shadow. The current transparent area (surrounding the leaf shadow) of the image remains transparent; no gradient is applied to it.

Note: As a sign that the button has been engaged, a Lock icon appears next to the layer in the Layers palette.

㉑ Using the Gradient tool, click at the base of the leaf's cast shadow in the Cast Shadow layer, and then drag well past the end of the leaf tip.

The idea here is that the end of the leaf should still have some grayscale value applied to it.

㉒ Select Multiply from the Blending drop-down menu located at the top left of the Layers palette.

Doing so blends the gradient cast shadow into the underlying rust surface, creating a cast-shadow effect.

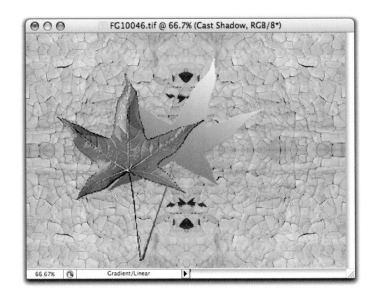

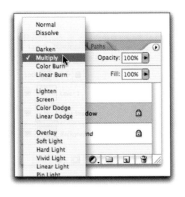

㉓ Back in the Layers palette, toggle off the Lock Transparent Pixels button for the Cast Shadow layer.

This will now allow you to use a Gaussian blur on the semi-transparent edge of the leaf in the following step.

㉔ Using your Spacebar and ⌘/Ctrl keys, zoom in on the long tip of the leaf.

You'll notice that the shadow edge is anti-aliased, but it may still be a bit abrupt for a cast shadow. A slight blur should smooth this out nicely.

㉕ Choose Filter⇨Blur⇨ Gaussian Blur.

The Gaussian Blur dialog box appears on-screen.

㉖ In the Gaussian Blur dialog box, set the Radius to between .2 and .4.

Doing so adds just a bit of smoothness, so the shadow looks even more realistic.

Now view your final cast-shadow makeover.

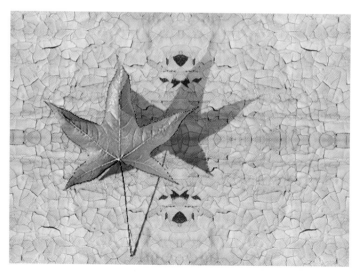

Iliamn

Before

After

11

EFFECTS MAKEOVERS

Photoshop offers a wide variety of effects — mostly in the form of filters — that you can use to alter captured images or painted images, or even to create images from scratch. Sometimes the impact of these effects is subtle, and sometimes it's dramatic — it all depends on the spin you put on what's in the picture. Here is a sampling of some of the effects and some ways to use these effects to create various makeover results.

One wonderful advantage of digital imaging is that you can try out a wide range of options easily, in very little time, for no extra money. Snags that used to mean starting over — such as adjusting the size or shape of your image — can be handled with just a few mouse clicks or keystrokes. And tools such as the Layer Style dialog box provide more options than you can try out in a lifetime! What you can do is truly limited only by your imagination.

Of course, the special effects in Photoshop can (and do) take up whole books by themselves, so this chapter mainly hits the high points of the more practical effects — such as painting, glowing, and metal-surface effects. It also gives you a taste of what is possible; from there you can launch your own search to discover and develop your own favorite image effects.

In addition, the last makeover in this chapter ("The Creating-a-Background-from-Nothing Makeover") demonstrates how you can use simple tools and techniques to create some very interesting and useful images. Cool stuff doesn't have to be difficult.

Doing Photo-Effects Makeovers

Photoshop's Clouds filter is handy for those situations where you need to add some clouds where none exist — or when you just need to create a consistent, fluffy cloud backdrop for any foreground elements (such as type) that your image might have.

❶ Open the Illiamna.tif image.

This image is available for download from the Web site associated with this book.

Note that the sky here is pretty nondescript, making it a good candidate for the Clouds filter, particularly if you want to use this area as a backdrop for adding some type.

❷ Choose Image⇨Duplicate to make a duplicate copy.

Always work on a copy.

❸ Using your selection tool(s) of choice, select the sky.

I went with the Magic Wand tool with a Tolerance of 10 and then cleaned up with the Lasso tool with a Feather of 2.

❹ Choose Select⇨Feather.

Doing so calls up the Feather dialog box, appropriately enough.

❺ In the Feather dialog box, set the Feather to 2 pixels.

This will give you a nice transitional edge between your sky and the mountains.

❻ Press the (Q) key to activate your QuickMask, and then use your Spacebar and ⌘/Ctrl keys to zoom in on the Mountain-Sky boundary.

If you needed any proof of how smooth your transition is, here it is.

❼ Choose Select⇨Save Selection.

Doing so calls up the Save Selection dialog box.

8 **In the Save Selection dialog box, select the New Channel radio button and then name this new channel Sky Mask.**

You can now reload this selection at any time by choosing Select⇨Load Selection and then navigating to this selection in the Load Selection dialog box that appears.

9 **Select the Eyedropper tool, with a sampling average of 3 x 3 from the Toolbox, and then click the blue-green background sky in the image.**

Doing so places this color as the foreground color in Photoshop so you can then use it to generate your sky pattern.

Note: To try out variations on your results, you can try sampling other colors in the image as well. Typically it's best to sample colors from within your image to create a sky that complements the rest of your image.

10 **With the sky selected, choose Filter⇨Render⇨Clouds.**

Your selected Sky area immediately fills with a pattern of clouds, with an overall color scheme that matches that of the original sky.

Note: The Clouds filter also uses your current background color — and if you chose white, that usually works well (especially if you chose a blue foreground color). But if you chose something else as the background color during your last bit of tweaking (say, bright green), you can end up with clouds that look pretty weird (or cool, if you like an otherworldly look).

Not bad at all, but we can work a bit on the contrast.

Doing Photo-Effects Makeovers *(continued)*

⑪ With the sky selection still active, choose Layer⇨New⇨ Layer via Copy.

Doing so makes a copy of your new sky and places it on its own layer. (You'll notice that it appears as a new line in the Layers palette.)

⑫ In the Layers palette, name the new layer Sky, click to select the new layer, and then choose Multiply from the Blending Mode drop-down menu in the top-left part of the Layers palette.

Doing so doubles the density of the sky and dramatically increases the contrast in the whole image.

Note: By placing this (multiplied) sky on its own layer, you can change the opacity of the layer in the Layers palette to control and fine-tune the Multiple effect.

We've got some impressive, cirrus-looking clouds now, but wait . . . there's more!

⑬ Select the Eyedropper tool from the Toolbox and then click the water in the foreground.

Doing so samples this color and places it as Photoshop's Foreground color. The Toolbox will remain as configured earlier.

Photoshop Confidential

Hiding Selection Borders

If you're at all like me, you'll agree that the selection border that pops up whenever you select something just serves to block one's view and (ahem) drive one crazy. And yet, normally I don't want to deselect just so I can have a clear view of my image. Being able to hide the selection without deselecting is a bonus. Here's how: Press ⌘/Ctrl + H to hide the active selection boundary. Then press ⌘/Ctrl + H again to show the selection border again. (By the way, you can press ⌘/Ctrl + D to deselect.)

14 **Select the Type tool from the Toolbox.**

Activating the tool calls up the tool's Options bar as well.

15 **In the tool's Options bar, set the type to 60 pt, make it a Bold or Wide typeface (Felt Marker Wide here), and set the Anti-Alias to smooth.**

Your water Foreground color (which will be used as your text color as well) shows up on the right side of the Options bar.

16 **Using the Type tool, type the word Illiamna — the name of this particular mountain — and press the Enter key to apply the type.**

Your type is placed in the image, occupying its own layer.

17 **Using the Move tool from the Toolbox, position your type in the center of the sky.**

Setting the type close to the topmost edge works for me, but I'll leave the exact placement up to you.

18 **Back in the Layers palette, double-click the right side of the Type layer entry to activate the Layer Style for that layer.**

The Layer Style dialog box makes an appearance.

Note: When double-clicking, be sure to double-click a blank area of the line, not the layer's title itself.

19 **In the Layer Style dialog box, click the Drop Shadow option in the Styles list to add a drop shadow.**

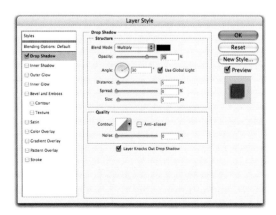

Doing Photo-Effects Makeovers *(continued)*

Start with the default Drop Shadow settings and then fine-tune them to your liking.

㉕ With the Type layer active in the Layers palette and the Type tool selected, click the Warp Type button on the right side of the Type tool's Options bar.

The Warp Text dialog box appears on-screen.

 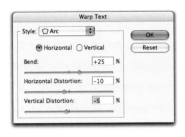

㉑ In the Warp Text dialog box, choose Arc from the Style drop-down menu, select the Horizontal radio button, and move the Bend slider to the right to create a bend that pleases you.

A bend of +25 works for me.

㉒ Still in the Warp Text dialog box, set the Horizontal distortion to –10 and the Vertical Distortion to –5.

Or just use your own settings!

㉓ Click OK to apply the distortion — and then view your finished image.

You'll of course want to flatten and remove the Alpha channel from a *copy* of this image prior to final output — keeping the original image (with its layers and Alpha channel) intact for future editing. The easiest way to accomplish this is to perform a Save As (File⇨Save As) and uncheck the Layers and Alpha Channels check boxes in the Save As dialog box.

Doing a Glow-Effects Makeover

In the old days (before Layer Styles), we used to create Metal effects with the Gradient tool and Glow effects by blurring multiple feathered selections. And although that was fun — if we had time, I'd love to show you how we did it in the Good Old Days — Layer Styles are simply easier and faster. (Okay, I admit that every now and then I still use the old ways . . . but so much for the history lesson.) Now to create some effects the modern way. Let's start by creating some type to work with.

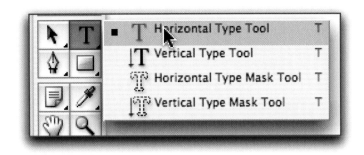

❶ **Select the Horizontal Type Tool from the Toolbox.**

Doing so calls up the tool's Options bar, which we'll set in a moment.

❷ **Press X (for Exchange) to swap the foreground and background colors.**

The idea here is to set white as the foreground color and black as the background color.

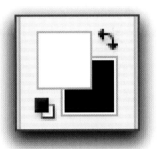

❸ **Choose File⇨New.**

The (appropriately named) New dialog box appears on-screen.

❹ **In the New dialog box, format a new 4" x 2" 300ppi RGB document with Black as the Background color, and then name it Metal.**

Now we're set with a White foreground and a Black background.

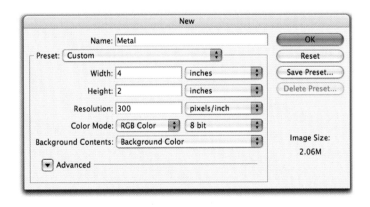

❺ **Using the Horizontal Type tool's Options bar, set the font type to Gills Sans, Ultra Bold, at 52 pts; specify a Smooth Anti-Alias and Centered alignment.**

If you don't have Gill Sans loaded on your machine, try some other sans-serif typeface with an Ultra Bold style.

Doing a Glow-Effects Makeover *(continued)*

⑥ Click in the middle of the black sheet with the Horizontal Type tool and type METAL (using all caps).

⑦ In the Layers palette, double-click the right side of the Type layer entry to activate the Layer Style for that layer.

Note: When double-clicking, be sure to double-click a blank area of the line, not on the layer's title itself.

The Layer Style dialog box makes an appearance.

⑧ In the Layer Style dialog box, click the Outer Glow option in the Styles listing.

The Layer Style dialog box updates to show the Outer Glow options.

⑨ To assign the glow color, single-click the color swatch.

Doing so calls up the Color Picker dialog box.

⑩ In the Color Picker dialog box, select a red color and then click OK.

I say red here, but feel free to try another color if you'd like.

⑪ Back in the Layer Style dialog box, choose Normal from the Blend Mode drop-down menu, choose Softer from the Technique drop-down menu, set the Spread field to 15 and the Size field to 35, choose Half Round from the Quality Contour drop-down menu, and then click OK.

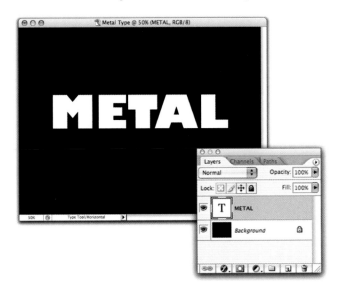

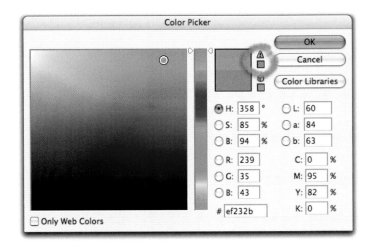

Take a break to check out how things are going before moving on to the Inner Glow part.

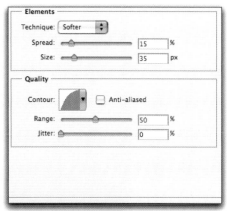

⑫ With the Type Layer Style still active, click the Inner Glow option in the Styles listing of the Layer Style dialog box.

The Layer Style dialog box updates to show the Inner Glow options.

⑬ Single-click the color swatch, select a blue color from the Color Picker that appears, and then click OK.

Blue's my choice, but don't let me dictate colors to you.

⑭ Back in the Layer Style dialog box, choose Normal from the Blend Mode drop-down menu, choose Precise from the Technique drop-down menu, set the Choke field to 10 and the Size field to 20, choose Normal from the Quality Contour drop-down menu, and then click OK.

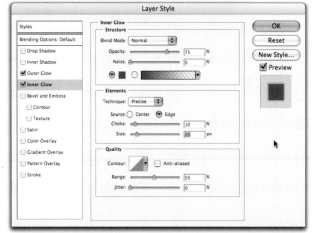

Doing a Glow-Effects Makeover *(continued)*

Take another break to admire your handiwork.

We are definitely on a roll, but something tells me a bit more glow would be more effective here.

⓯ With the Type layer selected in the Layers palette, choose Layer⇨Duplicate Layer.

A new, identically formatted layer (named METAL Copy) is created. And the outer glow doubles in intensity.

⓰ With the METAL Copy layer selected in the Layers palette, choose Multiply from the Blending Mode drop-down menu in the upper-left corner of the palette.

The inner glow now has a bit more oomph to it.

Note: You can also go back to the Layer Style dialog box and choose Multiply from the Blend Mode drop-down menu for the Inner Glow style to further intensify the inner glow.

⓱ In the Layers palette, double-click the right side of the Metal Copy layer entry to activate the Layer Style for that layer.

The Layer Style dialog box again graces the screen.

⓲ In the Layer Style dialog box, select the Outer Glow option and then set the noise level to 25%.

Doing so adds some sizzle to the outer glow.

Note: You can adjust all these settings to suit your fancy!

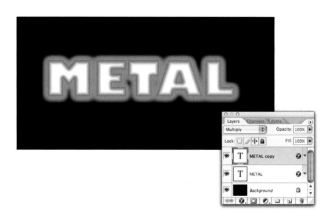

Before

After

Doing a Metal-Effects Makeover

Creating a metal effect will produce a surface that looks like (well, yeah) metal. Near-infinite varieties of metal effects can be created. This exercise will get you started, and then it's off into the cool variations.

1 **Create the same 4" x 2" RGB 300ppi White type on Black background created in Steps 1–4 of the Glow Effects makeover.**

2 **In the Layers palette, click to toggle off the visibility of the black Background layer.**

Note: The checkerboard pattern indicates areas on the layer that are occupied by transparent space.

3 **Double-click the right side of the Metal type layer to activate the Layer Style for that layer.**

The Layer Style dialog box makes an appearance.

Note: When double-clicking, be sure to double-click a blank area of the line, but don't click the layer's title itself.

4 **In the Layer Style dialog box, click the Gradient Overlay option in the Styles listing.**

The Layer Style dialog box updates to show the Gradient Overlay options.

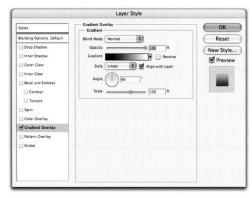

5 **Choose the Black-to-White gradient from the Gradient drop-down menu.**

The Gradient Editor dialog box appears on-screen.

6 **In the Gradient Editor dialog box, click under the middle of the gradient to add a gradient stop.**

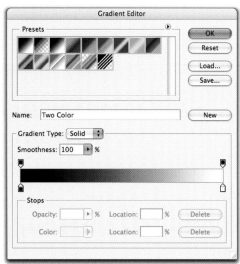

Chapter 11: Effects Makeovers **307**

Doing a Metal-Effects Makeover *(continued)*

I'd put the stop near the 50% point. (The Location field pinpoints where the slider ends up.)

❼ Double-click the color stop in the bottom-right corner of the gradient.

Doing so calls up the Color Picker dialog box.

❽ In the Color Picker dialog box, select a black color and then click OK to apply it.

The bottom gradient stop points should now be black-white-black.

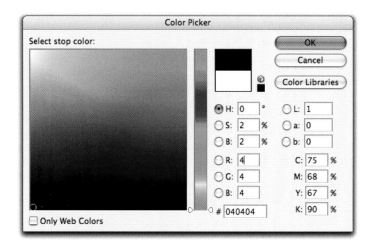

❾ Click the OK button in the Gradient Editor to apply this gradient to the Metal layer.

Note that your type now has that touch-of-metal look to it . . . but it's only a touch. We're going to improve on that now.

❿ Back in the Gradient Editor dialog box, first click and drag the small, clear, diamond-shaped gradient midpoint sliders closer to the central gradient stop (added in Step 6) and then click OK.

Your new gradient is applied to the Metal type layer.

⓫ Back in the Layers palette, toggle the visibility on to put the black Background layer back on-screen.

This creates a cool metal-type-fading-into-black look. But let's bring that type out of the background just a bit.

⓬ Return to the Gradient Editor dialog box; click the black color stops in the lower-left and lower-right corners.

Doing so calls up their respective Color Pickers.

⑬ In the Lab section of their Color Picker dialog boxes, set the L field to 10 for both end points.

The idea here is to assign a slightly lighter shade of gray to the Metal type layer.

⑭ Click OK.

Note how the type emerges more forcefully from the black background.

⑮ Back in the Layer Style dialog box, click the Bevel and Emboss option in the Styles listing.

The Layer Style dialog box updates to display the Bevel and Emboss options.

There's lots of neat stuff here, but we're going to start with one of the Bevel and Emboss secondary features.

⑯ Under Bevel and Emboss in the Styles listing, click the Contour check box to activate it.

The Layer Style dialog box duly updates.

⑰ In the Contour section of the Layer Style dialog box, set the Range to 10%.

Doing so lightens and widens the beveled edge.

⑱ Click the Bevel and Emboss option again in the Styles listing.

The Layer Style dialog box updates yet again.

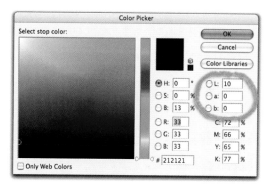

Doing a Metal-Effects Makeover *(continued)*

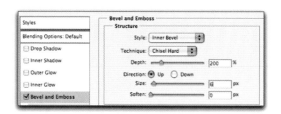

⑲ In the Structure section of the updated dialog box, choose Chisel Hard from the Technique drop-down menu, set the Depth to 200%, and set the Size to 6.

See the difference already?

⑳ In the Shading section of the updated dialog box, choose Linear Dodge from the Highlight Mode drop-down menu, and then choose Color Burn from the Shadow Mode drop-down menu.

Doing so both expands and lightens the highlight areas of the bevels while narrowing their shadow areas.

Okay, one more recommended alteration before you're off on your own.

㉑ Under Bevel and Emboss in the Styles listing, click the Texture check box to activate it.

As expected, the Layer Style dialog box updates.

㉒ In the updated dialog box, click on the Pattern swatch, and select the Herringbone 2 Pattern from the dialog box that appears; then set the Scale to 200% and the Depth to 100% and toggle the Invert option On.

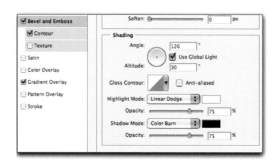

Note how this adds a rough metal texture to the surface of the type.

Now here's an idea . . . why not have the Glow Effects and the Metal Effects join forces? You might end up with something that looks a bit like what you see on the next page.

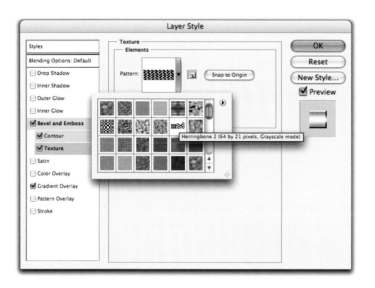

Before

After

Doing Painting-Effects Makeovers

Another gallery of Photoshop effects can be not only attractive but useful: the artistic effects. If you're one of those folks who are already comfortable with real-world canvases and oils and brushes, these artistic effects are a great way to quickly try out a style or combination of styles. And for those of us who are challenged if we have to paint a door with a single color . . . the Filter Gallery is a Technique Library godsend!

Note: It really helps that (a) all the creative filters are accessible in one place — the aforementioned Filter Gallery — and (b) you can combine any number of filter effects to achieve a customized look.

❶ Open an image you would like to paint.

Not sure where to start? Why not paint a volcano? Try the Sadie_Volcano.tif image, available for download from the Web site associated with this book.

❷ Choose Image⇨Duplicate to make a duplicate copy.

Always work on a copy. Always.

❸ Choose Filter⇨Filter Gallery.

Doing so launches the Filter Gallery, with its six categories of filters on the left (Artistic, Brush Strokes, Distort, Sketch, Stylize, and Texture) and its Options area on the right.

For our purposes, let's try out two different filters for painting our volcano.

❹ Using your Spacebar and ⌘/Ctrl keys, zoom in on your image.

The idea here is zoom in to the level you're comfortable with.

❺ In the Filter Gallery, click the Brush Strokes folder.

The folder opens to display the various Brush Strokes offerings.

⑥ Click the Sprayed Strokes option.

The Options area updates to show the default settings for the Sprayed Strokes option.

⑦ In the Options area of the Filter Gallery, set the Stroke Length to 7 and the Spray Radius to 10, and then choose Right Diagonal from the Stroke Direction drop-down menu.

Feel free to experiment with various Stroke Lengths and Spray Radii if the spirit moves you.

⑧ Click the OK button to apply this Brush Stroke filter to your image, and then view the results.

Definitely subtle here.

⑨ Using the Save dialog box (File⇨Save), save a copy of this image as Sadie_Sprayed Strokes.

We came up with a nice "painted" version of the image, but why stop with just one?

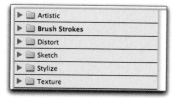

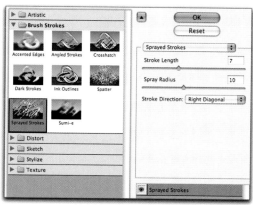

Photoshop Confidential

Different Strokes for Different Images

When you are applying the various stroke options offered with the different filter styles, consider the composition of your image. For instance, the Right Diagonal stroke directions fit this Sadie Peak image well; the Right Diagonal strokes are perpendicular to the direction of the major ridgeline, which allows for maximum visual impact. When you select a filter effect you like, experiment with the various stroke options and how they work — and consider how you'd like those stroke options to interact with your image elements.

Doing Painting-Effects Makeovers *(continued)*

⑩ Open another copy of the original Sadie_Volcano image, choose Filter⇨Filter Gallery, then click the Texture folder.

The Texture offerings (including the neat-sounding Craquelure) are displayed.

⑪ Click the Grain filter.

The Options area updates to show the default settings for the Grain filter.

⑫ In the (updated) Options area, set the Intensity to 50 and the Contrast to 60, and then choose Regular from the Grain Type drop-down menu.

I like these particular settings, but feel free to try something different.

⑬ Click the OK button to apply this Grain Texture filter to your image, and then view the results.

A bit more dramatic than our earlier version, wouldn't you say?

⑭ Using the Save dialog box (File⇨Save), save a copy of this image as Sadie_Grain Texture.

Okay, now that we have two versions, why not combine the two to come up with a whole new version?

⑮ Open yet another copy of the original Sadie_Volcano image, choose Filter⇨Filter Gallery, and then click the Texture folder.

The Texture offerings are again displayed.

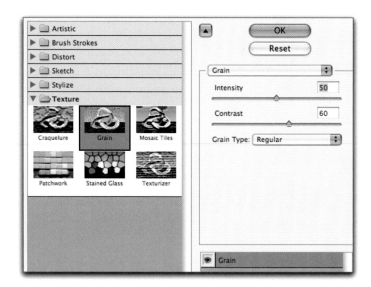

⑯ Click the Grain filter.

The Options area updates to show the default settings for the Grain filter.

⑰ In the (updated) Options area, set the Intensity to 50 and the Contrast to 60, and then choose Regular from the Grain Type drop-down menu.

These settings worked for me before, so I'm sticking with them.

⑱ Click the New Effect Layer button, located in the lower-right corner of the Filter Gallery window.

Doing so creates (and selects) a duplicate of the Grain Texture filter in the Filter Effects list of the Filter Gallery.

⑲ Click the Brush Strokes folder in the Filter Gallery.

The Brush Strokes offerings duly reappear.

⑳ Click the Sprayed Strokes filter.

The Options area updates to show the default settings for the Sprayed Strokes filter.

㉑ In the (updated) Options area, set the Stroke Length to 7 and the Spray Radius to 10, and then choose Right Diagonal from the Stroke Direction drop-down menu.

Yes, I know, these are the same settings I used before, but using them in combination with the Grain Texture filter gives us different results.

㉒ Click the OK button to apply the combined Brush Stroke and Grain Texture filters to your image.

And then . . . view the results.

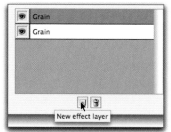

Doing Painting-Effects Makeovers *(continued)*

Note: An alternative way to control the interaction between the two versions of the Sadie Volcano images takes just two general steps: First, place the two images on separate layers; then use the Layer interaction tools to create a combination image. Here's how that's done.

㉓ Open the saved copies (File⇨ Open) of both the Sprayed Stroked and Grain Texture Sadie images.

You did save them, didn't you?

㉔ Press ⌘/Ctrl+Shift and drag the Sprayed Stroked version onto the Grain texture image.

Using the Shift key when you move one image onto another will center the image directly on top of its companion, creating perfect image registration between the two Sadie images.

Note: The Sprayed Stroke image will be placed on its own layer in the Layers palette — right above the Grain image.

㉕ In the Layers palette, double-click each layer name and rename it; rename the layers Sprayed and Grain, respectively.

Keeping names short and to the point (and informational) is always a good idea.

㉖ With the Sprayed layer selected in the Layers palette, set the Opacity to 75% and choose Screen from the Blending Mode drop-down menu.

Now view the results of all your hard work!

Before

After

The Creating-a-Background-from-Nothing Makeover

Here is a fun and interesting approach to creating backgrounds — one that requires nothing more than Photoshop and a healthy dollop of your own creativity.

First off, let's assume that you're creating a background for an on-screen presentation that will be projected at 1024 x 768 resolution.

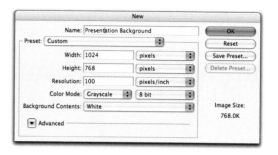

① Choose File⇨New.

Doing so calls up the New dialog box.

② In the New dialog box, set up a new image at 1024 x 768, 100ppi resolution, with a White background in grayscale mode; name it Presentation Background.

Here's a blank slate, as it were, ready for your creative efforts.

③ Choose Filter⇨Noise⇨Add Noise.

The Add Noise dialog box appears on-screen.

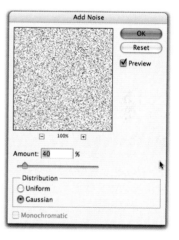

④ In the Add Noise dialog box, set the Amount to 40%, and check the Gaussian Distribution radio button.

Doing so adds noise to the background layer, but it may seem a bit harsh. To soften any potential harshness, you may want to add some grayscale fill between the noise grains.

⑤ Choose Layer⇨New⇨Layer.

A new blank layer appears in the Layers palette.

Name this layer 30% Gray.

The Creating-a-Background-from-Nothing Makeover *(continued)*

6 **Choose Window⇨Color.**

Doing so calls up the Color palette.

7 **In the Color palette, set your color to 30% Gray.**

You're going to use this gray to fill in the spaces between your noise grains.

8 **Choose Edit Fill⇨Foreground.**

The Fill dialog box appears.

9 **Check to make sure that Foreground Color is selected in the Use drop-down menu, and then click OK.**

Doing so fills the layer with 30% gray.

10 **Back in the Layers palette, select Multiply from the Blending Mode drop-down menu.**

The 30%-gray pixels can now fill in between the Noise pixels.

I like the look here, but I'd like it even more if it had separate left- and right-side gradients.

11 **Press ⌘/Ctrl+R to activate the Ruler, and then click and drag a guide from the vertical ruler to the 2.5-inch horizontal position.**

The idea here is to create a contrast area that starts 2.5 inches in from the left.

12 **Choose Layer⇨New⇨Layer to create a new blank layer.**

Name this layer **Left Gradient**.

13 **Select the Rectangular Marquee tool from the Toolbox.**

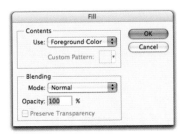

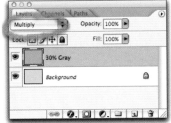

Selecting the tool calls up the tool's Options bar as well.

⑭ In the tool's Options bar, set the Feather to 0 pixels.

Setting the Feather to "0" ensures that the whole area with the marquee will be 100% selected. There will be no partially selected pixels along the edge.

⑮ With the Left Gradient layer active in the Layers palette, drag the Rectangular Marquee tool from the lower end of the Ruler guide to the upper-left corner.

You now have a nice rectangular selection, ready for some gradient work.

⑯ Select the Gradient tool from the Toolbox and configure its Options bar with a standard black-to-white gradient, in Dissolve mode.

We don't need anything fancy here; a standard black-to-white gradient should work just fine.

⑰ Drag the Gradient tool from top to bottom across the selection rectangle on the left side of the image.

Holding down the Shift key here, as you drag your gradient, keeps it in a vertical line.

⑱ With the Left Gradient layer active in the Layers palette, select Multiply from the Blending Mode drop-down menu, and then set the Opacity for the layer to 60%.

The Multiply Blending Mode allows the gradient to be added to the background; the 60% opacity allows the entire gradient to be visible against the background.

The Creating-a-Background-from-Nothing Makeover *(continued)*

Leave the left-side gradient selected for the next step, and stay in the Gradient tool.

⑲ Choose Layer⇨New⇨Layer to create a new blank layer.

Name this layer Right Gradient.

⑳ Choose Select⇨Inverse to select the right side of the image.

That's why I asked you to keep the Left Gradient selected earlier. Neat, huh?

㉑ Drag the Gradient tool from bottom to top across the Rectangular Marquee selection on the right.

㉒ With the Right Gradient layer active in the Layers palette, select Multiply from the Blending Mode drop-down menu, and then set the Opacity to 60%.

The Multiply Blending Mode allows the gradient to be added to the background; the 60% opacity allows the entire right gradient to be visible against the background.

All you have to do now to finish your presentation background is place your logo.

㉓ Choose File⇨Place.

Doing so calls up the Place dialog box.

㉔ Navigate through the Place dialog box to find the logo you want to place (here it's the Taz Tally Seminars logo), and then click the Place button.

The logo is placed as a transformable object on your background.

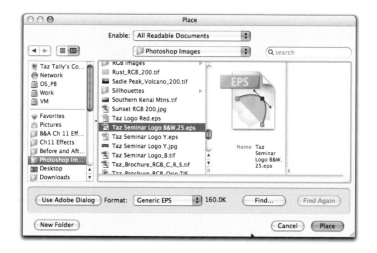

25 **Proportionally resize the logo: Click the middle of the logo, drag it to the lower-left corner, press the Shift key, and then drag the upper-right control point of the logo Transform Control box border.**

The idea here is to reduce the width of the logo until it's just slightly smaller than the left gradient area.

Your background is now complete.

When you create each background element on a separate layer, each element is completely editable.

Be sure to flatten a *copy* (by selecting Save As and unchecking the Layers check box in the Save As dialog box) of this image before you use it for final placement as a background in your presentation program or Web page. Leave the original image fully editable with all its layers.

Neutral Backgrounds' Blessings

You'll notice that you created a background constructed from all neutral components. Neutral backgrounds come with a number of inherent benefits. From a design standpoint, neutral backgrounds are very flexible; they can accommodate any color scheme. From a technical standpoint, neutral backgrounds can be constructed in grayscale mode — which gives you smaller file sizes (1/3 the size of an RGB background). This reduced file size is a huge bonus in terms of display speed; it's better for on-screen presentations, Web pages, and for printing. And finally, neutrals are least likely to be negatively affected by proprietary quirks and the vicissitudes of various display environments.

SeaSid

Before

After

12

EXTREME MAKEOVERS

Throughout this book, you've been working to improve or enhance basic image characteristics while staying pretty much within normal image-editing behavior. This chapter gets a bit more unruly — and that can be even more fun. Okay, what's extreme (even what's effective) is subject to individual taste . . . but pushing the envelope can give you new techniques and develop new ideas.

Here you use many of the same tools used in other makeovers — Selection tools, levels, curves, Unsharp Masks, Layer masks, Clone tools, Repair tools, the Transform function, blended layers, and more. Even if these tools are familiar, they're capable of changing your images even more dramatically. If you reach the cool conclusion that just about any Photoshop tool can be used in many ways (some wild) to create some unexpected effects, you're on to something.

Here you will also see proof positive that some fairly straightforward Photoshop techniques can produce unusually striking images: Australian artist Neil Fraser shares with us the thoughts, tools, and techniques he used to create an award-winning entry in a juried competition held by NAPP (the National Association of Photoshop Professionals).

Extreme Landscape Makeover

This adventure starts with a landscape photo I took in the Yukon. The image composition is okay, but the exposure range of the original scene is so wide that no part of the image is well exposed. The sky is way overexposed; the foreground flowers are way underexposed — so making a standard highlight and shadow adjustment won't do much good. Something a bit more dramatic is in order!

Getting a Handle on the Challenge

Before venturing into the deep end of the Photoshop pool, take a minute to find out what kind of work you have cut out for you.

❶ Open the Yukon.tif image.

You can download the image from the Web site associated with this book. Note how the background is blown out and the foreground is too dark and flat.

❷ Choose Image⇨Duplicate to make a duplicate copy.

Even with such a problematic image, you'll still want to work on a copy.

❸ Choose Image⇨Adjustments⇨ Levels.

The Levels dialog box appears on-screen.

There's almost no room on the RGB histogram for any adjustment here. If you look through the individual channels, you'll see the same full histogram. The challenge is that in terms of the image data, there are really two separate images here: the low-key (dark) foreground and the high-key (light) background. You have to handle each image area separately.

Isolating and Improving the Background

Time to start carving up this image into more manageable pieces.

❶ Choose Window⇨Channels to activate the Channels palette.

The idea here is to use the Channels palette to find the best contrast between the mountains and foreground.

In the Channels palette, look at the composite image as well as all individual channels; select the view that offers the greatest contrast between mountains and foreground. Here the Blue channel offers the best contrast; activate the Blue channel.

❷ Select the Magic Wand tool from the Toolbox.

As always, selecting the tool calls up the tool's Options bar.

❸ In the tool's Options bar, set the Tolerance to 50 and check the Anti-Alias and Contiguous check boxes.

Using these settings expands the range of the tool a tad, ensures a gradational edge to the selection, and restricts the selection to just those pixels that are actually touching.

Photoshop Confidential

Hidden Histograms

Images with vastly different highlight and shadow regions and few (or no) midtone regions — such as our Yukon image — are best approached and edited as two separate images. Doing so requires that you carefully select and isolate each portion of the image. Then you can adjust levels and curves to tweak the image data for *each portion of the image.* Isolating image portions also means isolating the histogram data for those specific portions — in effect, each one has a *hidden histogram* that you make visible and workable. This makeover illustrates how to access that "hidden" histogram data for the foreground and background areas separately, and contrast these isolated area histograms with the initial full-image histogram.

Extreme Landscape Makeover *(continued)*

④ With your newly configured Magic Wand tool, click the mountains or the sky.

Doing so selects a large portion of the mountain and sky.

⑤ Press the Shift key and click the unselected portion of the sky or mountain to add the remainder of the sky and mountain to the initial selection.

The idea here is to keep adding until the entire mountain/sky region is selected.

⑥ Back in the Channels palette, select RGB from the Channel drop-down menu so the color image is visible on-screen.

Note that the selection you made on the Blue channel is active in the composite RGB view as well.

After selecting the major portion of the sky and mountain, add the "peek-through" areas (where the lower sections of the mountains peek through the tops of the vegetation).

⑦ Using your Spacebar and ⌘/ Ctrl keys, zoom in on any "peek-through" areas.

⑧ Choose Select⇨Similar.

Your "peek-through" areas are added to your initial selection. Now deselect any stray areas selected by mistake.

⑨ Again using your Spacebar and ⌘/Ctrl keys, zoom out to view the entire image.

Oops — Step 8 left some of the lighter foreground pixels selected (that's a no-no).

⑩ Select the Marquee tool from the Toolbox.

⓫ In the tool's Options bar, set the Feather to 0 pixels.

Assigning a 0 feather here ensures that the de-selection area created in Step 12 will be 100% deselected.

⓬ Press Opt/Alt and then click and drag the Marquee tool across the portion of foreground that contains the selected pixels you want to deselect.

This completely deselects any stray pixels you don't want included in your selection.

With everything cleaned up and (relatively) tidy, the next step is to do some final smoothing of your selection, and then save it.

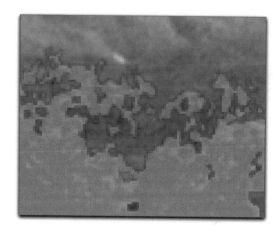

⓭ Using your Spacebar and ⌘/Ctrl keys, first zoom in on the "peek-through" area and then press the Q key to activate the QuickMask.

The QuickMask makes the fairly abrupt edges of the selection show up clearly.

You could smooth these selected edges by using the Feather feature (choose Select⇨Feather), but you'll have greater control if you first save this selection as an Alpha-channel mask and then apply a blur — which is what I'll do now.

⓮ Press the Q Key to deactivate the QuickMask and then zoom out to view the entire image.

Nothing wrong with getting some perspective here.

⓯ With the Channels palette visible, choose Select⇨Save Selection.

The Save Selection dialog box appears on-screen.

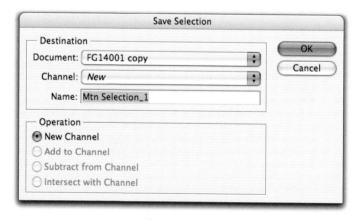

Chapter 12: Extreme Makeovers

Extreme Landscape Makeover *(continued)*

⑯ In the Name field of the Save Selection dialog box, type Mtn Selection_1.

Check out the upcoming sidebar for my take on naming stuff.

⑰ Still in the Save Selection dialog box, make sure the New Channel radio button is selected and then click OK.

Doing so creates a new Alpha channel from your selection.

⑱ In the Channels palette, click your new Mtn Selection_1 Alpha channel to activate it.

Note: Press ⌘/Ctrl+D to make sure there are no active selections.

⑲ Using your Spacebar and ⌘/Ctrl keys, zoom in on the (black-and-white) edge of the selection mask.

The white area represents the selection, the black areas the non-selected areas, and the intermediate gray values the transition between them.

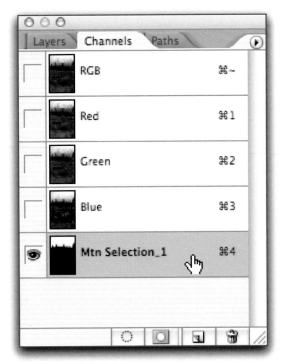

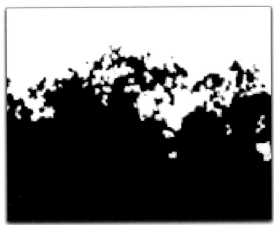

Photoshop Confidential

Naming Channels and Layers

✓ strongly recommend allowing yourself to get a little obsessive when it comes to naming the layers or channels you create. After you create your thirteenth layer and seventh channel for your umpteenth project, you'll find it's not that easy to remember what's what and why (or how) you created something in the first place. Using explicit names can help. You may even want to get in the habit of modifying the names of your layers and channels as you apply changes to them, to remind yourself of what you did to create and/or modify the layer or channel. For instance, I often add a "GB" to the name of a layer or channel to indicate that I've applied a Gaussian Blur to it.

The abrupt B&W edge here is what we want to smooth.

⓴ Choose Filter⇨Blur⇨ Gaussian Blur.

The Gaussian Blur dialog box appears on-screen.

㉑ In the Gaussian Blur dialog box, first type 1.5 pixels in the Gaussian Blur Radius field, and then click OK to apply the blur.

Note how the B&W edge in the alpha channel is now much smoother, with a wider band of intermediate grayscale values, indicating a smoother, less abrupt transition between the selection mask and the unselected area outside of that mask.

㉒ Back in the Channels palette, double-click the Mtn Selection_1 channel to activate it and then rename the channel by adding GB1.5 to its name.

Taz's Take: You may want to make a copy of the original mask before you modify it, so you can always return to the original selection — and its associated Alpha channel mask.

Okay, you've got a (nicely renamed) selection that you've cleaned up quite a bit — time to load it into your original image.

Note: One of the many nice features of saving selections as Alpha-channel masks is that you can modify them at will and then recall them to the screen at any time. And they can be duplicated and moved from one image to another. What's not to like?

㉓ Using your Spacebar and ⌘/Ctrl keys, zoom out to view your whole image.

Zooming in and out should be second nature by now.

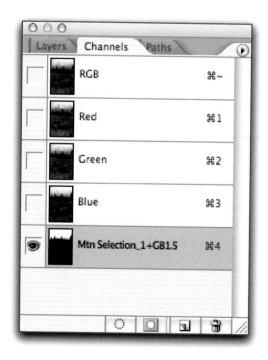

Extreme Landscape Makeover *(continued)*

㉔ In the Channels palette, double-click the RGB channel to make it active.

㉕ Choose Select⇨Load Selection.

The Load Selection dialog box makes an appearance.

㉖ In the Load Selection dialog box, choose Mtn Selection_1+ GB1.5 from the Channel drop-down menu and then click OK.

Your newly smoothed selection is loaded into your image.

㉗ Choose Image⇨Adjustments⇨ Levels to active the Levels dialog box, and then view the histogram data for the mountain/ sky portion of the image.

You should compare and contrast this histogram with the initial whole image histogram. Note that here you see only the high-key portion of the data — which makes sense because you've isolated just the highlight end of the image data.

Now note the flat end of the histogram data on the left side (or shadow end) of the graph.

㉘ Drag the histogram's Shadow slider to the right until it's directly below the initial up-tick in the histogram data.

Note how the overall exposure and contrast of the mountains improves as you darken the shadow values by moving the shadow slider to the right.

Wait a minute: This shadow adjustment really destroys the nice contrast between the light mountains and the dark spruce trees.

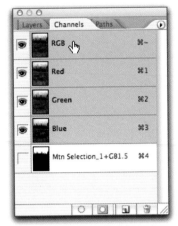

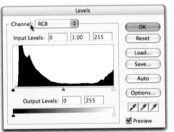

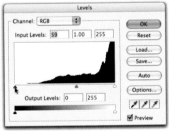

At this point, you may still want to make this shadow adjustment anyway — and you could — but there's another approach that allows you to have your image-editing cake and eat it too. (Hey, why not?) For now, click the Cancel button to leave the image unaffected.

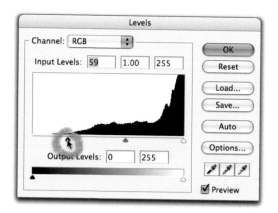

㉙ Choose Window⇨Layers.

The Layers palette appears on-screen.

㉚ With the Mtn Selection_1 +GB1.5 selection still loaded and active, choose Layers⇨ New⇨Layer via Copy.

Doing so adds a new copy of the Mtn Selection_1+GB1.5 layer to the palette.

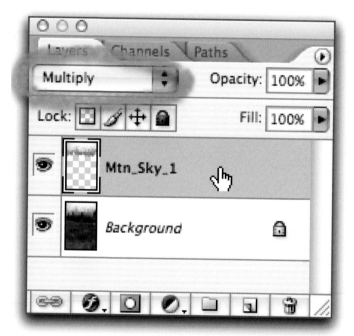

㉛ Double click your new layer and rename it Mtn_Sky_1.

㉜ In the Layers palette, choose Multiply from the Blending Mode drop-down menu.

Note how the exposure and contrast of the mountains improves. But once again, the

---

Photoshop Confidential

Hiding Active Selections

When you're evaluating potential adjustments — as you're doing here — it's often helpful if you can momentarily hide the selection (while keeping it active) so you can get a clearer view of what's going on. (Selections can be quite distracting.) This bit of magic is easy to do, but also potentially frustrating. To hide an active selection while keeping it active, simply press ⌘/Ctrl+H.

Sounds simple enough. But frustration rears its ugly head when, after a few minutes of blissful viewing without the selection visible, you might forget that you have in fact hidden your selection . . . which might prompt you to unwittingly apply an adjustment when you still have an active (hidden) selection. Then, when you try to use another tool on some other portion of the image, the tool may not respond properly. If that happens, spare your vocabulary; just get in the habit of pressing ⌘/Ctrl+H to bring any hidden selection out of hiding. Then you can deselect it and move on.

Extreme Landscape Makeover *(continued)*

contrast between the dark spruce trees in the foreground and the once-lighter mountains has degraded. But fret not — you made this adjustment using a new layer (instead of adjusting the original image layer), so you have more flexibility. Set this mountain/spruce tree transition aside for a few steps.

㉝ Click the Mtn_Sky_1 layer to make sure it's active, then choose Layer⇨New⇨Layer via copy.

Doing so creates a second (multiplied) Mtn_Sky_Layer.

Note how the mountains are even darker now . . . perhaps even a shade too dark.

㉞ Double-click the Opacity field in the upper-right corner of the Layers palette and then type 50 (%).

Doing so cuts the effect of the addition of the second, multiplied Mtn_Sky_1_copy layer by 50% . . . which leaves us with a pretty nice-looking mountain/sky section for our image. Time to shift focus and work on the foreground.

Isolating and Improving the Foreground

The foreground in this image is notably darker, requiring a somewhat different approach.

❶ Back in the Layers palette, click the Background layer.

Doing so makes it the active layer.

❷ Choose Select⇨Load Selection.

The Load Selection dialog box makes an appearance.

3 **In the Load Selection dialog box, choose Mtn Selection_1+ GB1.5 from the Channel drop-down menu and then click OK.**

Doing so loads the mountain/sky selection (the one you so lovingly adjusted in the previous steps) into your image.

4 **Choose Select⇨Inverse.**

Doing so selects the foreground portion of the image — basically, everything outside the mountain/sky selection.

5 **Choose Layer⇨New⇨Layer via Copy.**

Doing so creates a new Foreground layer, which is duly added to the Layers palette.

6 **Back in the Layers palette, double-click this layer and rename it Foreground.**

Sensible names make sense when something just is what it is. So to speak.

7 **With the Foreground layer selected, choose Image⇨ Adjustments⇨Levels to call up the Levels dialog box.**

Note the long flat area on the highlight end of the histogram. (You'll also recognize this as the other half of the initial whole-image histogram.)

8 **In the Levels dialog box, drag the Highlight slider until it's directly underneath the first up-tick in the histogram data.**

Notice the dramatic improvement in both the brightness and contrast of the foreground image area. The color really jumps out as well.

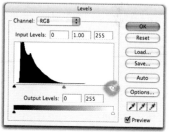

Extreme Landscape Makeover *(continued)*

Smoothing the Transition between Foreground and Background

Our original image had a nice contrast between the dark spruce trees in the foreground and the bright lower mountain slopes in the background — a contrast we should take pains to preserve. So we have to smooth the transition between foreground and background; our best tack is to combine the two background layers so we can treat them as one element. Rather than merge them, we're going to create a group so we preserve (and can later edit) each layer.

❶ In the Layers palette, click the Mtn_Sky_1 layer to select it, and then ⌘/Ctrl + click the Mtn_Sky_1 copy layer.

The idea here is to select both layers.

❷ Choose Layer⇨Group Layers to combine both layers into one group, and then name the group Mtn_Sky.

The Folder icon you see in the Layers palette lets you know that you've got a group now.

❸ With the Mtn_Sky layer group selected, choose Layer⇨ Layer Mask⇨Reveal All.

Doing so adds a Layer Mask to the Mtn_Sky group.

❹ Select the Gradient tool from the Toolbox.

As usual, selecting the tool calls up the tool's Options bar.

❺ In the Gradient tool's Options bar, select a white-to-black linear gradient, choose Normal from the Mode drop-down menu, and set the Opacity to 100%.

6 **With the Mtn_Sky group layer mask selected, click and drag the Gradient tool down the image.**

I'd go from near the middle of the mountains or tops of the spruce trees down to near the bottom of the visible portion of the spruce trees — a distance of about 1.5 inches.

This gradient will appear on the Layer Mask, allowing the lighter mountain bottoms from the original image to show through — thereby creating more contrast between the trees and the mountain.

To bump the contrast up even more, darken the trees a bit in the foreground.

7 **Back in the Layers palette, click on the Foreground layer, then choose Layer⇨Layer Mask⇨Reveal All.**

Doing so adds a layer mask to the Foreground layer.

8 **Select the Gradient tool from the Toolbox.**

Again, selecting the tool calls up the tool's Options bar.

9 **In the Gradient tool's Options bar, select a white-to-black linear gradient, choose Normal from the Mode drop-down menu, and set the Opacity to 100%.**

10 **With the Foreground layer mask selected, click and drag the Gradient tool up across your image.**

Start just below the bottom of the visible portions of the spruce trees and drag up to near the tops of the spruce trees — a distance of about 1.5 to 2 inches.

This gradient appears on the Layer Mask, allowing the darker trees from the original image to show through.

Extreme Landscape Makeover *(continued)*

Cloning Some Lupine into the Foreground

To be honest, the very front of the foreground is a bit sparse. You could simply crop out this area, but that would change the whole vertical geometry of the image (let's not). But directly cloning from (and on) the same Foreground layer would result in problematic differences in lighting.

What to do? One solution I like is to first clone your flowers (or birds, or bushes, or whatever) from the Foreground layer onto a blank transparent layer, and then use a Layer Mask to blend the edges of whatever you've cloned. Here's how I'd do it . . .

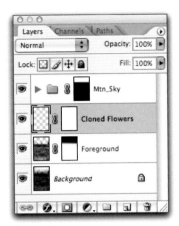

① Choose Layer⇨New⇨Layer.

Name your new layer Cloned Flowers.

② With the Cloned Flowers layer selected in the Layers palette, choose Layer⇨Layer Mask⇨Reveal All.

Doing so adds a Layer Mask to the Cloned Flowers layer.

③ In the Layers palette, click the Foreground layer thumbnail to select it (but *don't* click its Layer Mask thumbnail).

④ Select the Rubber Stamp tool from the Toolbox.

As you'd expect, doing so brings up the tool's Options bar.

⑤ In the Options bar, choose a 20-pixel-wide brush with 50% hardness, set both the Opacity and Flow to 100%, choose Normal from the Mode drop-down menu, and check the Aligned check box.

The stamp should be just a bit larger than the flower you're cloning.

⑥ Press Opt/Alt and click the top of the flower you want to clone.

The idea here is to establish this point as the start of the clone.

⑦ Now click the Cloned Flowers layer thumbnail to select it (*not* its Layer Mask thumbnail).

⑧ Using the Spacebar+⌘/Ctrl, zoom in on the area where you want to put the cloned flower, then click and drag to clone and place the flower.

⑨ Back in the Layers palette, click the Cloned Flowers layer mask.

⑩ Select the Brush tool from the Toolbox.

The tool's Options bar appears on-screen.

⑪ In the tool's Options bar, select a 15–20-pixel-wide brush with 50% hardness, set the Opacity to 50% and the Flow to 100%, and then choose Normal from the Mode drop-down menu.

⑫ Press the D key to assign the default colors.

You'll want black (the default) for the Foreground color.

⑬ Drag the Brush tool around the edges of the cloned flower to blend it in with the surrounding environment.

Adjust the width, opacity, and hardness to suit the requirements. (A pressure-sensitive cordless Wacom Pen and tablet give you a big advantage in this type of editing.)

Extreme Landscape Makeover *(continued)*

Note that your edits will show up on the Layer Mask as gray areas on the white background.

With a little practice, you'll be quickly and convincingly blending the cloned flowers into the sparse foreground areas. But here's another trick you can use: If you flip your cloned flowers horizontally, they won't look as much like clones; the human eye won't easily detect the old switcheroo.

⓮ Select the Marquee tool from the Toolbox and then use its Options bar to configure it with a 0-pixel Feather.

Note: You could use the Lasso tool here as well, but the Marquee is a quick, convenient way to select the flower.

⓯ With the Cloned Flowers layer thumbnail selected in the Layers palette, drag the Marquee tool over the flower you want to flip.

⓰ Choose Edit⇨Transform⇨ Flip Horizontal.

That's it. Your flower's been flipped.

⓱ Repeat Steps 3–16 for as many flowers as you want to clone.

Nobody said creating a virtual-flower meadow would be easy.

Adding Some YUKON Type with an Image Color

Just so our audience knows exactly what part of the world they're dealing with, add an attractive heading.

❶ Select the Eyedropper tool from the Toolbox.

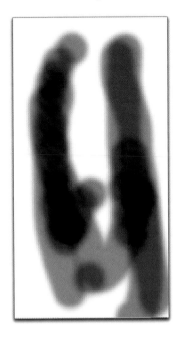

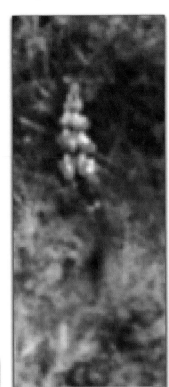

② **Using the Eyedropper tool, sample the lavender of the lupine flowers to make it the foreground color for the type.**

The idea here is to pick a color already present in the image.

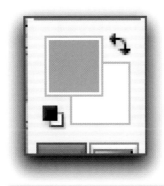

③ **Select the Horizontal Type tool from the Toolbox.**

As you'd expect, the tool's Options bar appears on-screen.

④ **Using the tool's Options bar, set the type to Gills Sans Ultra Bold Condensed at 60 pts with a Smooth Anti-Alias.**

⑤ **Using the Horizontal Type tool, click in the top center of the image, type YUKON, and then press Enter to apply the type.**

Note that the YUKON type is placed on its own layer in the Layers palette.

⑥ **Double-click the right side of the YUKON Type layer in the Layers palette.**

Doing so calls up the Layer Style dialog box.

Note: Be sure to click to the right of the layer name — you want to call up the Layer Style dialog box, not rename the layer.

⑦ **Click to select the Drop Shadow, Bevel and Emboss, and Contour check boxes; then click OK to apply the Layer Style to the YUKON type.**

You can always return later to fine-tune these Layer Style settings to your liking.

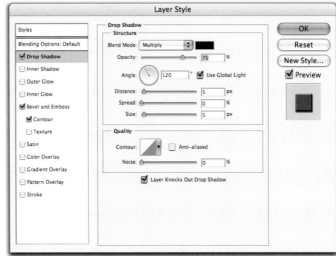

Extreme Landscape Makeover *(continued)*

⑧ With the YUKON Type layer selected in the Layers palette, click the Opacity field in the upper-right corner of the palette and select 70%.

The idea here is to make sure that the background shows through the type.

⑨ With the YUKON Type layer selected, first choose Window⇨ Character to call up the Character Palette, and then set the Tracking to 100.

This ensures that the type is spread out enough to make it fit and be easily legible.

Note: If the YUKON type characters are actually selected, be sure to press the Enter key to deselect the type before continuing.

⑩ With the Type layer selected, use the Move tool to click and drag the YUKON type to fine-tune its placement at the top of the page.

Neatness counts.

⑪ Compare your finished image with the original.

Extreme Collage Makeover

Sometimes a couple of ho-hum images can be combined together to make a dramatic collage. This makeover combines a rather typical lighthouse image with an interesting (but otherwise not spectacular) dune-grass image to make a very interesting collage. Note first that these two images, while not shot in the same location, are related environmentally; they both occupy coastal habitats, so they naturally belong together.

Any effective collage or montage starts with selecting good image components that generally fit together in terms of content, color, brightness, and contrast. Rarely does the finished image exactly match the one I have in my mind to start; it evolves.

❶ Open the Lighthouse and Dune Grass images.

Both images are available for download from the Web site associated with this book.

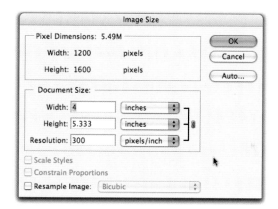

❷ Using the Image⇨Duplicate command, make copies of both images.

Always work on a copy. Always.

❸ Choose Image⇨Image Size for both images.

Extreme Collage Makeover *(continued)*

Doing so calls up the Image Size dialog box. Note that both images are 1200 pixels by 1600 pixels, with 300ppi resolution.

④ Place the Lighthouse and Dune Grass images side by side, select the Move tool, and press and hold the Shift key as you click and drag the Dune Grass image over on top of the Lighthouse image; release the Shift key when your drag is complete.

Using the Shift key here during the move centers the Dune Grass image on top of the Lighthouse image.

Note: The Dune Grass image will be brought in as a separate layer.

⑤ In the Layers palette, double-click each layer and then rename them (respectively) Lighthouse and Dune Grass.

⑥ Still in the Layers palette, click the Lighthouse layer to select it, then click the Eye icon to the left of the Dune Grass layer to hide it.

We'll work with each layer individually.

⑦ With the Lighthouse layer selected, choose Image⇨ Adjustments⇨Levels.

Doing so calls up the Levels dialog box.

Note the long flat area at the highlight end of the histogram.

⑧ Move the highlight sliders on the Red, Green, and Blue channels to the left until they are just beneath the start of the significant image data (the up-tic) in the histogram.

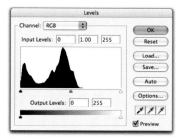

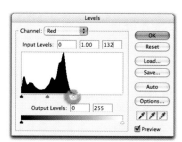

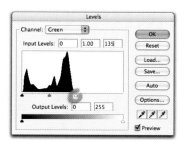

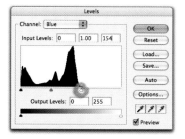

Note how the exposure of the Lighthouse image improves markedly.

What's good for the goose is good for the gander, so let's move on to the Dune Grass image.

⑨ Back in the Layers palette, click the Dune Grass layer to select it, and then click the Eye icon to the left of the Lighthouse layer to hide it.

⑩ Apply the same type of individual, channel-based tone compression to the Dune Grass layer that you used for the Lighthouse layer.

You'll see a noticeable improvement here as well.

⑪ Click the Dune Grass layer to make it active, and then choose Select⇨Color Range.

The Color Range dialog box makes an appearance.

⑫ Using the Color Range dialog box's Eyedropper tool, click the sky area in the Dune Grass layer.

The idea here is to create a mask of the sky in the Dune Grass image for later use.

⑬ In the Color Range dialog box, adjust the Fuzziness slider until enough of the sky is selected in the preview, and then click OK.

A value of 75 should work pretty well here.

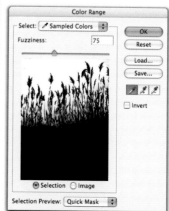

Chapter 12: Extreme Makeovers

Extreme Collage Makeover *(continued)*

14 **View the complete transparency mask by activating the QuickMask at the bottom of the Photoshop tool palette.**

You can also use the Q key to alternately show and hide the QuickMask.

Note: The QuickMask shows subtleties not apparent in the normal selection.

15 **Choose Select⇨Save Selection and then name this new (#4) Alpha channel Grass Sky Mask_1.**

16 **In the Channels palette, click your newly created channel to select it.**

Your new channel is now the active channel.

17 **Using your Spacebar and ⌘/Ctrl keys, zoom in on the edge of the mask here.**

It's pretty clear that the grass edges are a bit abrupt. Time to smooth things out with the help of a Gaussian Blur.

18 **Choose Filter Blur⇨Gaussian Blur.**

The Gaussian Blur dialog box makes an appearance.

19 **In the Gaussian Blur dialog box, set the Radius to 0.5.**

Looking better already . . .

20 **Back in the Layers palette, rename this Alpha channel Grass Sky Mask + GB_0.5.**

Yes, I really am suggesting that you carefully — dare I say anally? — label each and every layer and channel in such a way that you can remember exactly what you did to it.

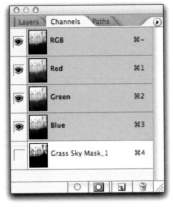

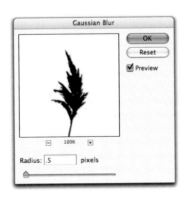

㉑ Go ahead and view the Alpha channel Grass Sky mask you just created.

Remember that the white area represents the selection that can be loaded.

Time to start putting this collage together.

㉒ In the Layers palette, click the Dune Grass layer to make it active, and then check the Eye check box next to the Lighthouse layer to toggle visibility on.

You'll want all your layers visible now.

㉓ Using the Opacity slider in the upper-right corner of the Layers palette, reduce the transparency of the Dune Grass layer to suit your liking.

Start with 50% and adjust from there.

Taz's Take: I'd try using the appearance of the top of the grasses as your visual guide here.

㉔ With the Dune Grass layer still active, Choose Layer⇨Layer Mask⇨Reveal All.

Doing so adds an opaque Layer Mask to the Dune Grass layer.

㉕ Select the Gradient tool from the Toolbox.

Doing so calls up the tool's Options bar.

㉖ In the tool's Options bar, click the Gradient Tool edit box at the far left.

The Gradient Editor dialog box appears on-screen.

Extreme Collage Makeover *(continued)*

㉗ Using the Gradient Editor dialog box, create a white-to-black (Opaque to Transparent) blend.

You can control the Opaque to Transparent transition by adjusting the grayscale values along the gradient. Here, maintain opacity for half the gradient (place a 100% white point at its midpoint).

㉘ Back in the Layers palette, click the Layer Mask icon.

Make sure that the Layer Mask (not the image portion of the Dune Grass layer) is active.

㉙ Click the top of the image and drag the Gradient tool from top to bottom.

This Layer Mask gradient blends the two images together vertically. Here the lower portion of the grass will disappear.

Taz's Take: As always, feel free to experiment with various gradients to achieve different blending effects.

Not bad for a first try, but watch what happens if we fine-tune the mask a bit. . . .

㉚ In the Layers palette, click the Dune Grass Layer Mask.

Doing so makes it the active layer.

㉛ Select either the Paintbrush or Airbrush tool from the Toolbox.

As you'd expect, this brings up the tool's Options bar.

㉜ In the Options bar, start out with a 50-pixel Brush and either choose Normal from the Mode drop-down menu for the Paintbrush or set Opacity to 50% for the Airbrush.

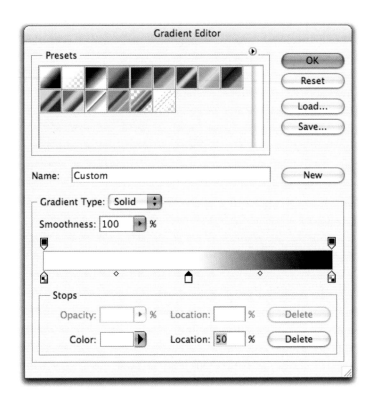

The pixel size for the tool will depend upon the resolution of the image.

33 Press D and then X to set Black as the foreground color.

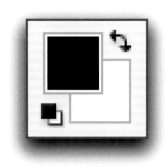

Note: If you have a Wacom pen and tablet, be sure to use the pressure-sensitive capability of the Pen tool; you can fine-tune the grayscale value (opacity) of the Layer Mask to your liking.

34 Using your tool, paint over the red-roofed house (with the Layer Mask active) to increase the transparency of the Layer Mask over the house.

This step, in turn, decreases the opacity of the Dune Grass image over the house. Your editing strokes show up on the Layer Mask.

I'd say keep painting until most of the grass is removed from the house.

35 Back in the Layers palette, click the Dune Grass layer to make it active, and then choose Layer⇨New Adjustment Layer⇨ Levels.

Name this layer Adjust Levels Grass.

36 Click OK for now to close the Levels dialog box.

Doing so adds a Levels Adjustment layer (named Adjust Levels Grass) on top of the Dune Grass layer in the Layers palette.

37 To restrict the application of this Levels Adjustment layer to just the Dune Grass layer, choose Layer⇨Create Clipping Mask.

This moves the Levels Adjustment layer to the right in the Layers palette — where it will restrict its effect to the immediate underlying area of the Dune Grass layer.

Extreme Collage Makeover *(continued)*

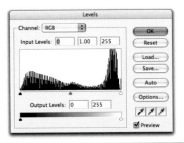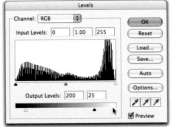

38 Double-click the Levels icon in the Levels Adjustment layer to open the Levels dialog box.

To no one's surprise, the Levels dialog box makes an appearance.

39 To reverse the tonal range of the image portion of the Dune Grass layer, you should reverse the assignment of output levels.

Doing so inverts the tonal values of the Dune Grass layer but leaves the Lighthouse layer alone so you can fine-tune these values to suit. I'd start with 200 and 25 as output values.

Note: Using the Levels dialog box here (rather than just inverting the tonal range) lets you fine-tune the image *and* adjust the input and output values together.

Now, this next bit — linking and grouping related layer groups — isn't required but it can sure simplify editing.

40 Back in the Layers palette, first select the Dune Grass layer, and then press the Shift key and click the Levels Adjustment layer (Adjust Levels Grass).

The idea here is to select both at the same time.

41 Choose Layer⇨Link Layers (or click the Link icon located at the bottom of the Layers palette).

Doing so links these two layers together. (Note the Link symbols on the right side of each linked layer.)

42 With both linked layers still selected, choose Layer⇨Group Layers.

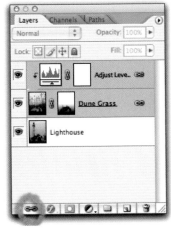

This will place both Dune Grass layers in a folder named Group 1.

43 Double-click the name of this folder and rename it Dune Grass.

44 Click the Dune Grass group to make it active.

Note that the Layer Blend Mode drop-down menu is set to Pass Through — which means the effect will be passed through this layer, unaffected by any other adjustments that may be applied to this layer.

45 Choose Darken from the Layer Blend Mode drop-down menu.

Darken mode works preferentially, allowing the darker portions of the two images to appear at the expense of the lighter portions — as readily seen here: All vestiges of grass disappear from the darker portions of the combined image.

46 For another look, choose Color Burn from the Layer Blend Mode drop-down menu.

Experiment with the various Layer Blend modes to achieve different effects.

This approach to creating a collage allows any portion of the image — background, lighthouse, dune grass, Layer Mask, and adjustment layer — to be adjusted to suit you. You could, for example, lighten the sky a bit.

47 In the Layers palette, display the contents of the Dune Grass Group folder, and then click the Dune Grass layer (*not* its Layer Mask) to select it.

48 Choose Select⇨Load Selection.

Extreme Collage Makeover *(continued)*

The Load Selection dialog box makes an appearance.

㊾ In the Load Selection dialog box, choose Grass Sky Mask+ GB.05 from the Source Channel drop-down menu, and then click OK.

Remember this mask that we made way back at the beginning of this makeover? (Check back around Step 20.)

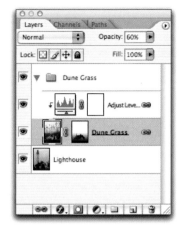

㊿ Press the Delete key to remove the dune/grass/sky — the portion of your image marked out by the mask you just loaded.

㉛ Now press ⌘/Ctrl+D to delete the selection itself.

You can now view the image without any distracting selection marks.

Taz's Take: Instead of deleting all of the dune/grass/sky from under the selection, you might try adjusting the Fill % in the upper-right corner of the Layers palette to experiment with incremental sky removal values.

Lightening the sky was fun, but why stop there? A clipping group can add a frame . . .

㉜ Back in the Layers palette, click the Lighthouse layer to select it.

Make the Dune Grass group invisible as well (click the Eye icon to the left of the Dune Grass folder).

㉝ Using your Spacebar and ⌘/Ctrl keys, zoom in on the top of the lighthouse.

The idea is to find a shape within the image that would work as a frame.

54 **Using the Toolbox's Rectangular Marquee tool (set to a 0 Feather), draw a selection around the top of the lighthouse.**

Don't include the rounded ball at the top.

55 **Choose Layer⇨New⇨Layer via Copy to copy this selection to a new layer.**

Name this layer Lighthouse Top.

56 **In the Layer's palette, toggle off the Lighthouse layer's visibility by clicking the Eye icon to the left of the layer.**

57 **Still in the Layers palette, click and drag the Lighthouse Top layer to the bottom of the palette.**

Note: If you haven't already converted your original Background layer to a normal layer and renamed it Lighthouse, now is the time to do so. Converting the background layer to a normal layer allows you to displace it here as the lower layer.

58 **With the Lighthouse Top layer active, select the Magic Wand tool from the Toolbox.**

Doing so calls up the tool's Options bar.

59 **In the tool's Options bar, set the tolerance to 40, check the Contiguous check box, but leave the Anti-Alias check box unchecked.**

60 **Click anywhere on the sky surrounding the Lighthouse Top.**

The idea here is to select just the sky background around the top. To complete this

Extreme Collage Makeover *(continued)*

step, Shift+click at the other side of the lighthouse to select the remainder of the sky surrounding the lighthouse.

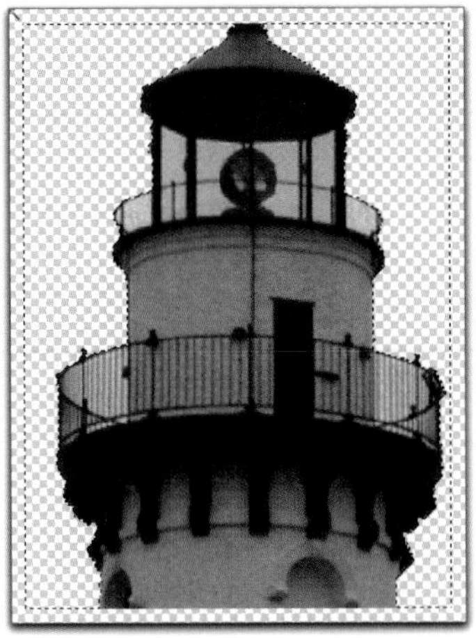

(61) Press the Delete key to delete the sky surrounding the Lighthouse top, then press ⌘/Ctrl+D to deselect the selection itself.

(62) Press the D key to set the colors to default (with Black in the foreground), and then choose Edit⇨Fill.

Doing so calls up the Fill dialog box.

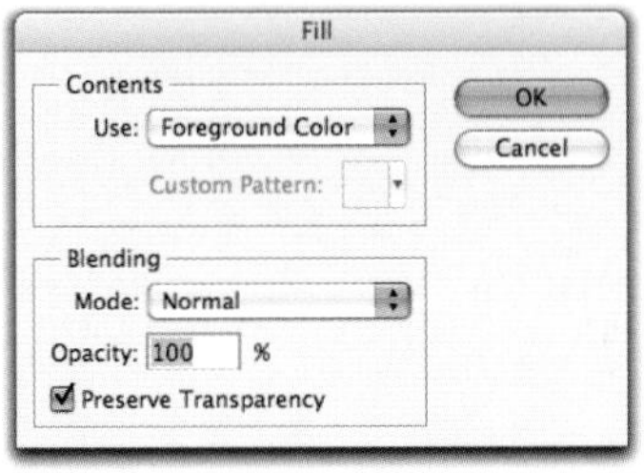

(63) In the Fill dialog box, choose Foreground Color from the Use drop-down menu, and then check the Preserve Transparency check box.

Doing so fills the shape of the Lighthouse Top with black.

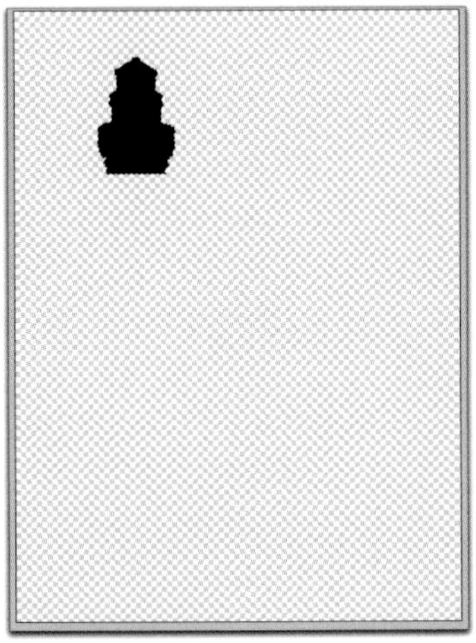

Note: If you forget to check the Preserve Transparency check box here, the whole layer fills with color. (If you make this move by mistake, press Cmd/Ctrl+Z to undo.)

(64) With the black shape selected, press ⌘/Ctrl+T.

Doing so brings up a Transform frame around your shape.

(65) Click and drag the corners of the Transform frame to enlarge the lighthouse-top shape so it fills the size of the whole image.

Feel free to stretch the Transform frame any way you like. You can also edit the shape itself by adding or subtracting pixels.

Note: Press ⌘/Ctrl and click and drag anywhere on the Transform frame's control points to skew the Transform frame.

66 Press the Enter key to apply the transformation.

Then press ⌘/Ctrl+D to remove the selection.

67 Back in the Layers palette, toggle on the visibility for both the Lighthouse and the Dune Grass folder by clicking their respective Eye icons.

68 Press the Shift key and then click both the Lighthouse and Dune Grass layers.

You want to select both of them.

69 Choose Layer⇨Smart Object⇨ Group into New Smart Object.

Doing so combines both layers into one Smart Objects layer so you can apply consistent adjustments to (or manipulate) the entire Smart Object, or edit individual components if you choose.

Note: You can edit the individual layers within this Smart Objects layer at any time (just double-click the Smart Objects layer).

70 Select the Smart Objects layer and then choose Layer⇨ Create Clipping Mask.

This creates a clipping group that uses the shape of the top of the lighthouse as a frame for the rest of the image — but leaves us with an unsightly checkerboard outside the frame. Time to fix that.

71 Choose Layer⇨New.

You've got yourself a new layer. Name it Pattern (for consistency's sake).

72 Drag your newly created Pattern layer to the bottom of the layer stack in the palette.

Extreme Collage Makeover *(continued)*

You're going to fill this layer with a pattern you've chosen to use as a background.

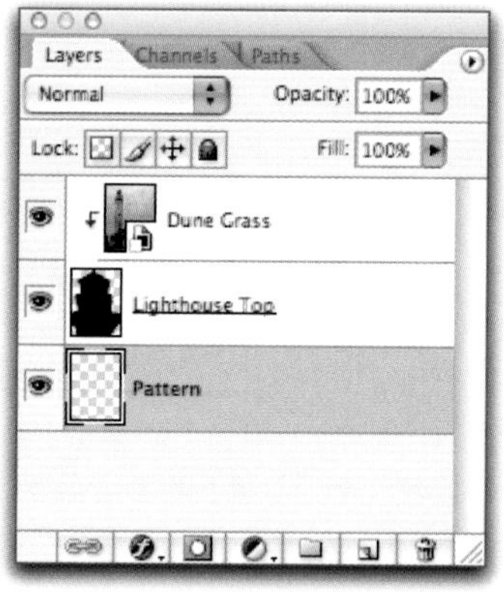

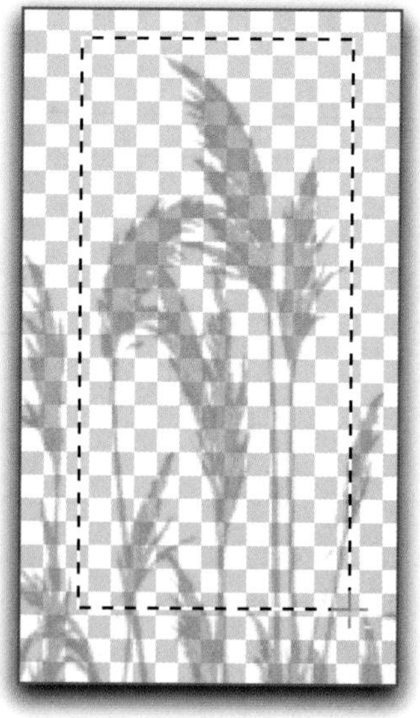

(73) Using your selection tool of choice, capture an object already present in the image.

How about clicking the Dune Grass layer and then selecting some of the grass tops from the Dune Grass layer?

(74) Choose Edit⇨Define Pattern.

Name the Pattern Grass Tops.

Then press ⌘/Ctrl+D to deselect everything.

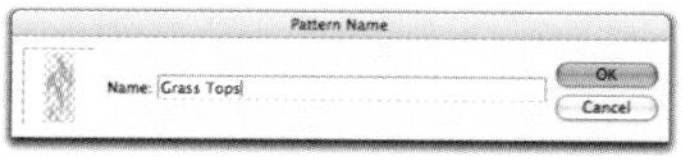

(75) With the Pattern layer selected in the Layers palette, choose Edit⇨Fill.

The Fill dialog box makes an appearance.

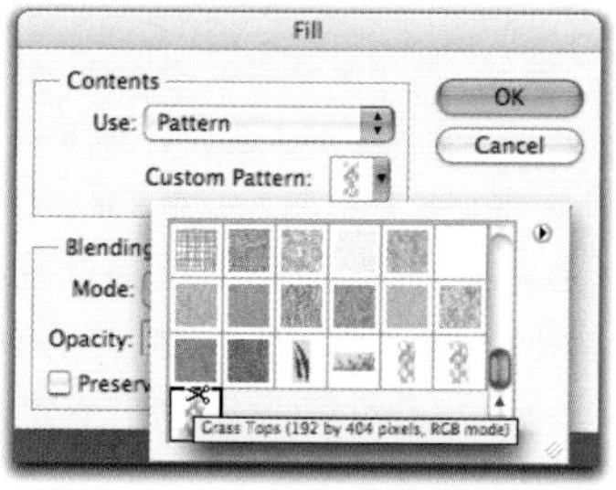

(76) In the Fill dialog box, choose Pattern from the Use drop-down menu.

(77) Still in the Fill dialog box, click the Custom Pattern drop-down menu and select the Grass Tops custom pattern you just defined.

Be sure to uncheck the Preserve Transparency check box beforehand.

(78) Click OK.

The new Pattern layer fills with your pattern and surrounds your image.

We're getting there, but the checkerboard pattern is still quite visible. More work to do.

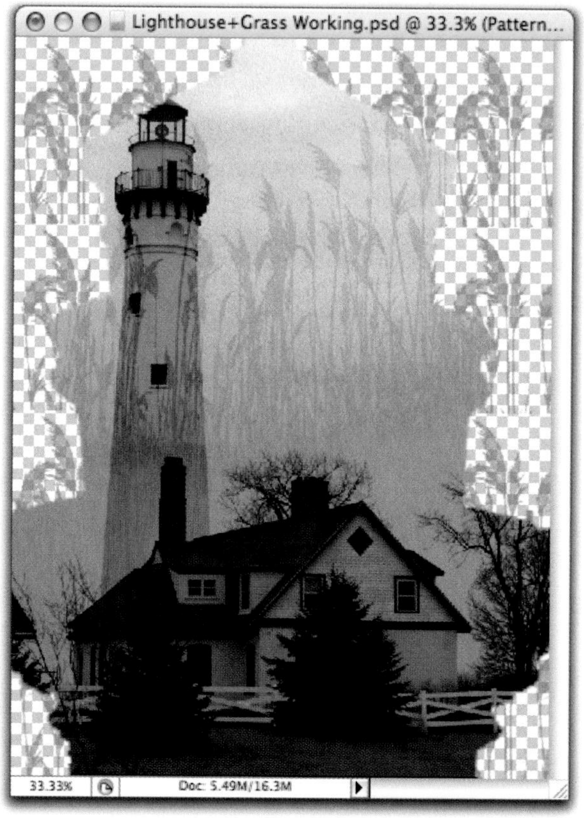

(79) Choose Layer⇨New⇨Layer.

Yet another new layer — name it Background and drag it to the bottom of the layer stack.

80 With your new Background layer active, choose Edit⇨Fill.

The Fill dialog box makes another appearance.

81 In the Fill dialog box, select White from the Use drop-down menu, and then click OK.

The new Background layer fills with white.

The Grass Tops pattern is now displayed against a white background. That's one possibility, but there are others out there.

82 With the Background layer active, choose Edit⇨Fill.

The Fill dialog box makes yet another appearance.

83 In the Fill dialog box, select Black from the Use drop-down menu, and then click OK.

The new Background layer fills with black — which means the Grass Tops pattern is now displayed against a black background.

I like this look a lot better. Now all we need is a nice typeface.

84 Back in the Layers palette, select the top (Dune Grass) layer.

Add the type here, to the topmost layer.

85 Select the Eyedropper tool from the Toolbox, and then click the blue-green grass color.

The idea here is to make this color the foreground color — and (as a result) the default Type color.

86 Select the Horizontal Type tool from the Toolbox.

Doing so calls up the tool's Options bar.

Extreme Collage Makeover *(continued)*

87 **In the tool's Options bar, set the type to Gill Sans Ultra Bold at 45-pt with Smooth Anti-Alias.**

I find this a good combination, but feel free to experiment.

88 **Using the Type tool, click the image just to the right of the top of the lighthouse, and then type the word** Seaside.

What you get is a new Type layer at the top of your Layers palette; the type itself appears in your blue-green foreground color.

89 **Back in the Layers palette, double-click the right side of the Type layer to call up the Layer Style dialog box.**

Be sure to double-click to the right of the layer name; don't click the name itself.

90 **In the Layer Style dialog box, check the Drop Shadow check box and set the shadow angle at 148°; and then set Distance, Spread, and Size all at 10.**

91 **Click OK to apply the Layer Style to the type.**

Well now, that looks pretty much done to me! Time to finish up.

92 **Make a duplicate copy of your final image, and put the fully editable version away.**

You may want to revisit this collage, so keep a version around that you can still edit.

93 **On the copy, select the Type layer and choose Layer⇨ Rasterize⇨Type.**

This converts your type to pixels, which will simplify your type layer for output.

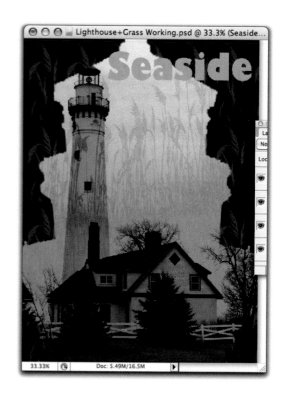

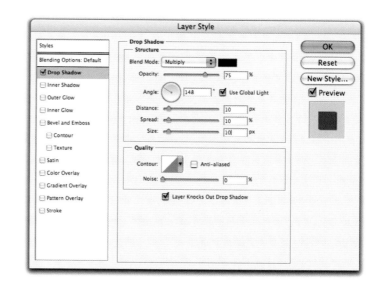

Note: This step also renders your type uneditable, but you can always return to your saved, fully editable version if you want to edit your type later.

94 Sharpen to suit.

You could apply an Unsharp Mask (Filter➪Unsharp Mask) or Smart Sharpen (Filter➪Sharpen➪Smart Sharpen) to any layer that you want to sharpen up to suit your wishes (perhaps the Lighthouse layer?).

Note: If you want to sharpen the individual layers separately, do so *before* flattening.

95 Flatten all the layers, remove the Alpha channels, and save as a TIFF file.

This can all be done through the Save As dialog box. (See Chapter 12 for more details on this process.)

So let's compare and contrast our initial images with our final Extreme Collage Seaside image.

Guest Makeover: Neil Fraser

As we were putting together this Before and After Makeover book, we thought it would be cool and fun to include an example of a makeover project from an artist who had won an award using some of the same basic tools and techniques you've picked up in this book. We took a look at the NAPP (National Association of Photoshop Professionals) Web site (at www.photoshopuser.com) to look for some category-award winners. A composition by Neil Fraser (a talented English artist) caught our eye. We asked Neil if he would share his thoughts on how he came up with such a startling makeover image. So here's Neil's account of his thoughts on the project's gestation — as well as an overview of the techniques, tools, and steps he used. Many thanks to Neil for sharing his award-winning creation with us.

The Idea (Neil Speaking . . .)

The idea for this piece came to me when I was given a design brief to come up with an advertising piece for a swimming-pool-and-spa company. Although the piece I'm presenting here did not actually appear in the final ad, I felt it did a great job of encapsulating a feeling of space and relaxation in the design — just the qualities I was trying to emphasize.

I tried several different methods to get the right look, but in the end I produced the final composite in the simplest way I could think of. And, as is often the case in Photoshop, sometimes the simplest way to do something gets the best results.

Here's how I did it . . .

❶ I first opened all three images: Woman_in_Pool.tif, Sandy_Beach.tif, and Pool.tif.

Note: The first two images I purchased from Digital Vision, the online image source. The picture of a hotel swimming pool I had taken years ago on holiday.

I used the photo of the woman in the pool as my main/base document because it was the perfect size for the advertisement.

❷ Using the Clone Stamp tool from the Toolbox — set with a soft-edged brush (with a size of about 70) — I cloned out everything on the left and right sides of the Woman in Pool image.

I Opt/Alt + clicked an area close to where I wanted to clone — I needed to make the clone as seamless as possible, so I gradually "inundated" the sides of the pool until they could no longer be seen.

❸ Using the Patch tool, I cleaned up those areas in the Woman in Pool image where the cloning was a bit too obvious.

First I drew a selection around the area I wanted to clean up with the Patch tool. Then, after making sure that the Source radio button was selected in the tool's Options bar, I simply dragged the selection over to a portion of the picture that was a good match for the selected area — and let the Patch tool do its magic.

Note: I didn't need to do the entire image because the picture of the sea was going to cover the top half of the main image anyway.

❹ Using the Crop tool, I first cropped and then dragged the Sandy Beach image over the Woman in Pool image.

I just needed the upper part of the Sandy Beach image, so I cropped out the bottom third — including the entire sandy beach!

Guest Makeover: Neil Fraser *(continued)*

Note that when I dragged the rest of the image over the girl in the pool and resized it to fit, a new layer was formed. Now all I had to do was blend the two layers together.

⑤ I added a Layer Mask to the mix by clicking the Add Layer Mask button at the bottom of the Layers palette.

Using the Layer Mask allowed me to seamlessly blend these two layers.

⑥ With Black selected as my Foreground color, I used a soft-edged brush to paint over the parts of my image (in the Layer Mask) that I wanted hidden.

The woman in my Woman in Pool image came to the foreground again.

⑦ I dragged the final image — Pool.tif — onto the composite I had already created.

At last all my pieces were in place.

⑧ Using the Transform tool (⌘/Ctrl+T), I resized the Pool.tif image to fit — and gave it the correct perspective as well.

It was looking better, but it definitely called for another Layer Mask.

⑨ I repeated Steps 5 and 6, this time using the Layer Mask to blend in the swimming pool edges.

I also used a small, hard-edged brush to paint around both the woman on the Layer Mask and the pool she was leaning on.

⑩ Back in the Layers palette, I chose Luminosity from the Layer Blending Mode drop-down menu.

Because my original goal here was to create a (relatively small) print ad, I wanted to use the Luminosity mode to exaggerate the fact that the images showed a swimming pool rather than the (expected) ocean.

If I'd wanted to be a bit subtler (say, if I was doing this for a larger fine-art print), I could have chosen Overlay from the Layer Blending Mode drop-down menu.

The image was complete.

⑪ I finished up by using the Dodge and Burn tools from the Toolbox to give the woman a touch more tone.

And there you have it — the final image as it was posted on the NAPP Web site.

Before

After

Index

Numbers

A

B

C

V

vector logos, described, 240
Vertical Ruler scale, image presentation titles, 234
Vertical Type tool
  collages, 248–249
  image presentation titles, 231–233
vignettes
  Crop tool, 149
  Elliptical Marquee tool selections, 145–146
  Eyedropper tool, 148–149
  Feather Selection dialog box, 147
  Fill dialog box, 147–148
  inverting selections, 147

W

Warp Text dialog box, photo effects, 302
weather corrections
  Curves dialog box, 155
  deleting selected pixels, 151
  Free Transform dialog box, 154
  Lasso tool selections, 152–153
  Load Selection dialog box, 152–155
  Magic Wand tool selections, 150–152
  Polygonal Lasso tool, 151
  resizing transformations, 154
  Save Selection dialog box, 151, 153
Web-bound images
  preference guidelines, 11
  print-oriented image adjustments, 43–47
width
  Crop tool selections, 48
  image adjustments, 40–47
wood-grain images, sharpening techniques, 269–273
wrinkle-removal
  Clone Stamp tool, 177–180
  Healing Brush tool, 177, 179

Z

zoom
  image/image window preferences, 9
  object view advantages, 311
  panorama adjustments, 56
  QuickMask selections, 25